Talking Cure

TALKING CURE

Mind and Method of The Tavistock Clinic

Edited by
David Taylor

Duckworth

First published in 1999 by
Gerald Duckworth & Co. Ltd.
61 Frith Street, London W1V 5TA
Tel: 0171 434 4242
Fax: 0171 434 4420
Email: enquiries@duckworth-publishers.co.uk

A catalogue record for this book is available from the British Library.

ISBN 0 7156 2924 7

Typeset by Ray Davies
Printed in Great Britain by
Biddles Limited, Guildford and King's Lynn

Contents

Acknowledgements

The reader will be struck by the way case histories (child or adult, individual or family) form the basis of so many of the chapters. The detailed study of the encounter between the patient and the clinician has been the source of all the knowledge and expertise in this book. Without the generosity and thoughtfulness of so many of our patients the book would not have been possible or if possible it would have lacked something essential. Of course, the consent of Clinic patients was carefully sought and the individual facts of the case material have been changed beyond any recognition so as to preserve the confidentiality and privacy of those involved.

The motive for the almost universal agreement given by our patients was their feeling that nothing but good could come from making the awareness of that inner life we so often cannot talk about, more widely available in the public domain. As well, and for reasons extending beyond the writing of this book, I, and all the other authors too, would like to record our debt of gratitude to all our patients for what they have taught us. It is a rare privilege for us to be able to see the important struggles of so many lives, the courage so many bring to their difficulties, as well as to glimpse those mysterious, fateful patterns with their awesome beauty which seem sometimes to govern the way the mind and the individual life unfolds.

The reader of this book will also soon notice that the writers have drawn upon the findings of many different types of scientific and artistic knowledge. Many colleagues, within and without our particular speciality, have been generous with their knowledge and with their work. Amongst them are the following:

From the Tavistock Clinic: David Armstrong, David Campbell, Barbara Dale, Maxine Dennis, Dr Andrew Elder, Mrs Vicky Franks, Dr Anthony Garelick, Dr Sebastian Kraemer, Julian Lousada, Dr Jane Milton, Sue Reid, Prof. Alan Stein and Sharon Warden.

From the Institute of Psycho-Analysis: Dr Ronald Britton, Patricia Daniel, Dr Michael Feldman, Dr John Steiner and Dr Richard Lucas (and N. Middlesex Hospital).

Mr Demetrios Economides (Dept. Obstetrics and Gynaecology, Royal Free and University College Medical School), Prof. Stephen Franks (Dept. of Reproductive Science and Medicine, Imperial College School of Medicine), Prof. M.J. Geller (Dept. of Hebrew and Jewish Studies, University College London), Prof. Kypros Nicolaides (Harris Birthright Research Centre for Fetal Medicine), Mr T.G. Teoh (Div. Paediatrics, Obstetrics and Gynaecology, St Mary's Hospital, London), and Dr Ian Wilmut (Roslin Institute).

We are grateful to Wendy Cope and Faber & Faber for permission to quote *As Sweet from Serious Concerns*. Mrs Joyce Robertson and Concord Video and Film Council generously gave permission for us to use stills from *A Two-Year-Old Goes to Hospital*.

Anton Obholzer, as Chief Executive of the Tavistock and Portman NHS Trust, has played a crucial role in looking after the organisation and enabling it to vigorously develop from its auspicious past rather than to ossify as so often happens. Nick Temple and Margot Waddell, both as colleagues and as the Tavistock Clinic Series editors, were characteristically excellent. Nick Temple (Chair of the Clinic's Professional Committee) quietly carries his many responsibilities and looks after the morale of many people including the editor's. Beth Holgate and Ines Cavill, the BBC programme makers were always supportive of the book and helpful with comments and illustrations. They impressed with their tact, professionalism and the natural respect they showed to the members of the general public who having suffered from various problems – illness and accidents – volunteered to be 'subjects' in the programmes. They always tried to find the real significance of the work they were filming and scrupulously avoided any easy sensationalism. Martin Rynja, the Duckworth editor, showed great intelligence and sensitivity in his handling of amateur writing and editing. He almost succeeded in turning it into plain English. Paula Shonuga, Eleanor Morgan, Marcos and Michelle Noble da Lima, Joseph Anderson, Alice and Myfanwy Taylor and Lynne Warne were all very generous and efficient in their secretarial and other assistance. Without their enthusiasm and flexibility the manuscript would not have made the very tight schedule. Caroline Garland has been an immensely hard-working alter ego and auxiliary editor. Without her help, taste, standards and support the book would not have been finished on time.

Picture Credits

Plate section: 1) © Wellcome Trust; 2) Courtesy Mr Demetrios Economides; 3) © Caroline Tutin in *Play: Its Role in Development and Evolution*, Penguin, 1976; 4) © The British Museum; 5) *Madonna and Child*, Luis de Morales (1500-1586), © the Prado, Madrid; 6) © The Estate of Weegee; 7) © James and Joyce Robertson, The Robertson Centre; 8) Goya, *Sueño de la mentra y la inconstancia*; 9) © The British Museum; 10) Goya, *Il Sueño de la razon produce monstruos*; 11) Anonymous; 12) Anonymous; 13) The Tavistock Clinic; 14) Courtesy © David Katznelson; 15) Courtesy Ian Wilmat, Roslin Institute; 16) Courtesy Mr Demetrios Economides; 17) © Wellcome Trust.

Figures: 1) Anonymous; 2) Anonymous; 3) Anonymous; 4) based on J.O. Forfar and G.C. Arneil *Textbook of Paediatrics* Vol. 1, 3rd ed., Churchill Livingstone 1984; 5) Roger Lewin (ed.) *Child Alive: New Insights into the Development of Young Children*, Temple Smith 1975; 6) Wilder Penfield, Theodore Rasmussen, *The Cerebral Cortex*, 1952; 7) Wilder Penfield, Theodore Rasmussen, *The Cerebral Cortex*, 1952; 8) Maurice Hall, © *Punch*; 9) Mike Turner, © *Spectator*; 10) Clive Collins, © *Punch*; 11) Anonymous; 12) *Bürgerkrieg*, 1928, © the Estate of Gerd Arntz; 13) *Ameisen*, © the Estate of George Grosz; 14) Korent, *Punch* 1981; 15) © P.J. Taylor and J. Gunn, 'Homicides by people with Mental Illness, 1999; 16) © M. Schatzman, *Soul Murder: Persecution in the Family*, Random House; 17) © Maurice Hall, *Punch*; 18) Etchings by Rembrandt.

Foreword

This book was written to accompany a BBC 2 TV series about the Tavistock Clinic, an NHS mental health institute which treats patients and trains mental health professionals. The six programmes of the series are about therapy – talking – as a way of dealing with the personal difficulties that life can entail. Accidents, personal misfortunes, illnesses, emotional conflicts as well as mental disorders are not as exceptional as we tend to assume. Realistically, they are part and parcel of an average life. At the same time, the way people react to events like these provides a view on human nature which is a subject of enduring interest to all of us.

Although the distant past is very different from the present, the character of men and women has remained unchanged over history. When we write that human nature is of enduring interest, 'enduring' does mean exactly that. The problems that preoccupy men and women have remained fundamentally the same for the last four millennia. If we look at the earliest documents in the earliest form of writing known to us, 200,000 inscribed clay tablets from Mesopotamia in the vaults of the British Museum, we get a detailed view of what the city-dwellers of Babylon (Ninevah) were concerned with four thousand years ago. They visited scribes who systematically recorded dreams in their cuneiform script and these tablets record the words actually spoken in the priests' incantations aiming to bring some relief to those suffering the anxieties of everyday life.

> You there, child, human born, now that you have come out, now that you have seen the daylight, why didn't you act this way in your mother's womb? Instead of treating your father properly, or letting your mother go out in public, you have upset your nursemaid, and you have kept the wetnurse awake. Because of your crying, the household god cannot sleep, nor does sleep overcome the household goddess.[1]

> If a man always looks at his woman's pudendum, he will have good health, and he will acquire whatever is not his. If a man is facing a woman and he is always looking at his own penis, no matter what he seeks will not be permanent in his house.

> If a man saw a bad dream during the night … He says as follows to the clod (of earth): 'O Clod, in the part of you which is pinched off, part of me is pinched off, and in the part of me (which) is pinched off (is) your pinched off piece.' He reports to the clod as many dreams as he saw. (Then he says:) '(Just as) I will throw you,

O Clod, into (running) water, and (you) will crumble (and) disintegrate – so (may) the evil of all the dream(s) which I saw disappear! May it dissolve!'[2]

Most of us can recognise at least something of our own experiences in these ancient records. Disappointments in love, impotence, rivalry, crying babies, guilt, fears, misfortunes, depression, existed in Babylon as much as they do today in any modern home, office or government. You do not have to be a modern Hamlet to want to get rid of bad dreams. Many of us have been unable to get the baby off to sleep or have suffered other more prolonged failures. The worries of the Babylonians would not be so out of place in any GP's surgery on a Monday morning.

The knowledge we have from modern psychology and psychoanalysis may be more systematised than the beliefs of the Babylonians. Today's language and conclusions are more technical and tested. Nonetheless the problems addressed are the same problems: men and women nearly always have more anxieties than there are real dangers to explain them. Our imagination shapes how we see the world. We continually need to explain and understand our experience of ourselves, of other people and of our world. It is ideas about these aspects of life which is the subject of this book. Its seventeen chapters are organised in five parts, roughly following the sequence of life as understood in psychoanalysis.

Our book is based on a set of related ideas. The first of these is the importance of emotional development over the whole lifespan, from infancy through childhood and adolescence to adult life, maturity and old age. There are key periods when change takes place with which we all struggle to some extent, though for some individuals these developmental tasks can become crises. The second idea is that human beings are fundamentally social animals. Our relationships with other people profoundly affect who and what we are, how we feel and what preoccupations we have. The third idea is that the nature of the human mind arises out of biological needs to survive, to feed, and to reproduce within a social setting.

The picture of the mind we try to give is not only of the objective, rational mind but also to show how important our emotions and passions are to the way we function. The heart does have its reasons that reason knows not of. We seek to describe our important relationships, indicating the nature of group life as it shows itself in families, at work and in society. Consequently we examine what it is to be normal, and consider the spectrum from mental distress to mental illness. Importantly, we also consider the future because the fact that modern man or woman is essentially the same kind of person as lived in ancient times means that in the future he will continue to struggle to adapt to change.

The television programmes cover some of the Tavistock Clinic's range of subjects and activities. One follows the developments of a baby's first year through the regular weekly observations of a baby by a young clinician. This method of baby observation was pioneered at the Tavistock and is now widely used as an important part of the training of child and adult psychotherapists and psychoanalysts. The trainee can learn what an infant is like and can see the continuities that exist between the infant and the adult they will later become as well as the importance of the mother-infant relationship to all later relationships.

The emotional consequences of someone having been involved in a tragic fatal accident is the subject of two of the programmes. These two are also intended to give an idea of the general method of a psychotherapeutic interview and to show how a therapist tries to clarify the meaning and cause of the accident with those concerned. Our feelings of guilt and pain may be so powerful that they have to be denied, though they continue to exert a damaging influence upon the individual's future life. Therapeutic interviews like these indicate how any major event, not just traumatic accidents, involves a reappraisal of a person's whole life. It causes self-questioning and raises fundamental issues about childhood, parents, family and character. Much of the Tavistock work in this area was recently collected in *Understanding Trauma*, a book edited by Caroline Garland (who appears as a therapist in one of the programmes).

Therapy is not only done in an individual setting. It can be offered in group and in family settings. Two of the programmes show how therapists try to help families deal with serious illness in one of its members or how family work can help a young person with emotional trouble. The first of these films shows the distressing challenge illness can pose for the family and the dilemmas each individual has to face. It shows how the family can be helped to marshal its resources and cope with the anger, guilt, grief and loss these conditions lead to. Such situations will never be easy but some of the damaging consequences the family has to face can be reduced. Some of the Tavistock family work was published in *Multiple Voices*. The sixth programme is about organisational consultancy: the subject is a school where the headmaster was concerned about what his school had to deal with. *The Unconscious at Work* by Anton Obholzer and P. Vega Roberts gives details of this type of work.

The Tavistock Clinic

The Tavistock Clinic has a long tradition of applying the psychological understanding of human relations beyond its origins in the treatment and understanding of mental distress and mental illness. It has made a special study of groups and of the social, institutional or organisational setting of everyday life. This work, which began with the idea of 'leaderless' groups as an original and effective way of selecting officers in WWII, has extended to understanding the importance of emotional and social processes in a wide variety of businesses, types of work and workplace and there is an organisation – the Tavistock Consultancy Service – to help institutions or organisations in trouble or needing to change.

The Tavistock is organised into three main departments – Child and Family, Adolescent, and Adult – whose first job is to provide consultations and therapy to the patients referred to them by schools, GPs, social workers and other professionals in the mental health field. Sometimes patients refer themselves. The Tavistock Clinic is also a clinical university which has close links with several more traditional universities. It is one of the nation's main teaching and training institutions in mental health with post-graduate students coming from all parts of the country and from abroad. It is a research institute and throughout its nearly seventy year history it has been the source of many innovative methods of work.

The Tavistock Clinic as part of the Health Service is funded by the taxpayer. Its 'business' is mental health. But because its angle on mental health is based upon a core of inter-related ideas, as described in this book, it is quite unlike conventional psychiatry with its over-emphasis upon the idea of mental diseases and its too exclusive dependence upon drugs (although drugs have an important place in treatment). The human perspective is an absolutely necessary addition and corrective to this narrow point of view.

Whilst the Tavistock may be special in some ways it is by no means unique. It is not the sole possessor or originator of its ideas. It leans heavily upon psychoanalysis, group dynamics and upon systems theory. This is one of the reasons why the BBC thought it was important to make these films. The Tavistock approach is emblematic of a broader community of knowledge about human nature.

Notes

1. 'Freud, Magic and Mesopotamia: How the Magic Works', M.J. Geller in *Folklore*, 108:1-7..
2. *Mesopotamian Conceptions of Dreams and Dream Rituals*, S. A. L. Butler, 1998.

1

Beginning of the Mind

In the Creation story of the Book of Genesis, God laboured for six days followed by a day of rest to observe his work. This myth, where God divides the light from the dark, the sea from the land, the physical from the spiritual, is a powerful pre-scientific account of the creation of the world and of man. We know now that it took several million years for man to evolve from his primate ancestors. Likewise, the belief in the *tabula rasa*, the blank slate of the new-born's mind, which originates from philosophers of earlier generations, is no longer compatible with what we know. It has given way to the idea that a new-born baby brings a mind with him. In the same way that an antelope calf staggers to its feet immediately after birth, this mind is capable of communicating as well as many other mental activities.

If the mind is not a blank slate at birth, when does our mind begin? What is going on when the baby is growing in the womb, at a level beyond the physical changes? Does the baby in the womb have a way of registering its experience? How does a mind begin to take shape before birth?

Research on the abilities of the new-born confirms that babies differentiate very early on between their mother's face and those of others, and are able to recognise their mother's voice. Babies also use their sense of vision, hearing, smell, touch and taste to link these different elements of their experience, and are able to relate them to a single source which they are able to conceive of as having several characteristics. Mothers have always thought of babies as persons. We talk to babies, albeit in a special tone of voice which is higher in tone and which we strongly emphasise rhythmically. We sing to them in ways which take for granted that this is a communication. We don't expect our words to be understood, but we do feel that our voice conveys something to the baby – being held, comfort, sympathy, an understanding of the baby's distress or delight – and that this is a response to what the baby is saying (see Plate 1).

The Mind before Birth

What happens between infants and mothers can be seen more clearly if we compare it with other circumstances such as premature birth, when things are not straightforward. In the past decades, the care of premature babies has been changed by the realisation that the incubator and other technology which very tiny or ill premature babies need to survive physically does not provide all they require to flourish. Premature babies usually spend their first weeks or even months without the continuous presence of a person who is living with them through their first encounters with the outside world, and it has been realised how important is human touch or a finger for the baby to suck on. Their mental and physical condition is improved by giving them more 'living', less artificial, textures such as a fleece and playing gentle music to counterbalance the noise of the life-support machinery.

Psychotherapists studying the development of very young babies have recently observed premature babies in neo-natal intensive care units. These observations are of a baby boy born at twenty six weeks (three and a half months early) in a hospital in Germany.

> At first the baby's condition was dominated by its unstable and precarious breathing patterns. The crises which punctuated the baby's breathing looked like earthquakes, shaking the baby's body almost to pieces. All the baby's energy seemed taken up by the struggle to sustain its bodily stability and was directed inwards. At this stage the observer found that if she did not take detailed notes she subsequently could recollect little of her regular hour-long observations.
>
> At twenty three days (twenty nine and a half weeks since conception) when the baby's nurse and the observer happened to arrive at the incubator at the same moment, the baby opened his eyes. He began to gaze at her and to search the room with his eyes whenever the process of digestion, excretion and so on shook his body. The observer thought, 'There is someone in there'.

It amazed the observer to realise that several things had occurred at around the same time. The baby seemed to be looking for something outside himself (the observer's face, a familiar shape, and a light) which he remembered and by which he seemed to feel supported when his body was disturbed from within. He seemed to be beginning to experience a boundary between what was inside him and what was outside, and others were beginning to see him as a person. Simultaneously, the observer found that she could now remember her observations in sequence, without having to make detailed notes at the time. The baby's ability to sustain a continuity of personal being seemed to let him cope more easily with breathing and digestion. These functions are more assured and automatic in a baby born in the course of a more usual pregnancy but are huge physiological strains for a premature baby.

At this point the baby seemed to have managed a 'psychological' birth, in the sense of being in emotional contact with other people and of having some resources to engage with them. The observer also recorded much-increased eye contact and tiny laughs. She felt herself to be in the presence of the first days of a 'mind' in this baby who in normal circumstances would have been in the womb for a further two and a half months. She was very interested to see that her own thoughts had run in parallel with the baby's mental presence. Observation indicates that the minds of babies are affected by the presence of an adult mind which thinks about and relates to them. The general idea is that one mind, especially the infant mind, can only come into being by finding another mind.

Research observing babies in the womb with ultrasound technology suggests that the baby in the womb may have a primitive awareness of a distinction between what is me and what is not 'me'. Studies of twins show patterns of behaviour between the siblings in the womb – for example of one recurrently hitting the other – which, to the astonishment of the researcher persisted after the babies were born. Striking continuities like this of relationship-behaviour before and after birth suggest clearly that the individuality of the person begins inside the womb. In the special case of twins, each twin may have awareness that his watery inside world is inhabited by something alongside himself. Even without the particular factor of twinship, a foetus might well be aware that the walls of the uterus and the placenta, encountered in the many movements within the womb, represent something beyond the boundary of its own body.

To help us imagine the psychological potential of the baby in the later stages of its development in the womb it is useful to be reminded of its capacities. Its movements are often purposeful and much more than a mere reflex response to outside stimulation. It is also common for the foetus to put its thumb in its mouth. It can hear and responds to the main sources of sound in the womb – the mother's voice and the pulsation of the artery going to the womb. Babies a few months after birth prefer to listen to stories, poems or nursery rhymes which their mother read to them before they were born – the rhymes seem to be recognised as familiar. Furthermore, breast-fed babies have a preference for the left breast and closeness to the mother's heart beat has been suggested as one reason for this (see Plate 2).

From time to time, we come across examples in therapy with older children which suggest that intense preoccupation with events that took place during their time in the womb is a powerful factor in their current state of mind. An Italian researcher has reported evidence of the distressed awareness of a dead twin in the womb in a very young child who had not heard about this from her parents. As the years go by, it is difficult to be sure whether these effects are caused by remembered experience before birth or by the impact after birth of the parents' mourning for the lost child. However, there is a growing consensus that experiences before birth can have profound effects which can be reinforced or modified by later events.

> Jenny was a triplet born some weeks prematurely. She spent her early weeks in an incubator. One of her brothers had died in the womb and the other a few weeks after the birth. She came to the clinic when she was twelve, after having rung Childline and failed to get through. When she told her mother about this, her mother contacted the Tavistock, feeling that her daughter needed help. Jenny also had difficulties at school and was often depressed and lacked confidence in herself. Her depression probably intensified when her parents' marriage broke down with the result that her father was mostly absent from Jenny's life. In her therapy, the theme of her two lost brothers was prominent. There was evidence of many kinds

> that Jenny's thoughts were often taken up with the dead siblings. The sadness of being in a perpetual state of mourning was often evident in her play and drawings.
>
> From the beginning Jenny emphasised to her therapist that the trouble was with threes. Fours and twos were all right, but threes never worked out. Jenny had a rather masculine style, and later on had passionate relationships with other girls. It often seemed that she felt that she had to make up for the lost lives of her brothers by taking on aspects of their identities. She almost consciously believed that her brothers had died because she had consumed an unfair share of the food inside their mother.
>
> This idea was a source of crippling guilt and it weighed more heavily as she entered adolescence. The ordinary adolescent wishes of making a life for oneself were interfered with by her feeling that she had to share things out between three. For example, she had agreed with her therapist that she would miss the session which fell on the day of her thirteenth birthday, so that she could have a party. The literalness with which she had to provide for her two lost brothers became clearer when she missed the two subsequent sessions, just as if there had to be space for a party for each of them.

At first the therapist found herself incredulous that these events should have so impressed themselves on Jenny's emotional and mental life, but she became gradually convinced that Jenny's main identity was being the surviving one of three. The problem for the therapist was how to help Jenny to claim her life for herself. While Jenny was aware of her tie to her lost siblings in many ways, she was not in touch with what she was doing to herself. It was others who had to be aware of what she was letting slip. At school, her truancy worried her teacher; at the clinic her therapist sat through sessions worrying when she did not appear. They had to ponder on where she had disappeared to, whether she was all right, and how to make contact.

Her parents' distress and grief about their lost sons may well have made it difficult for them to be emotionally available to the surviving baby. The loss of a baby is very traumatic to the mature adult mind but such events may get into the baby's mind in a particularly enduring way. Her first experiences of life had been premature and traumatising for her and unmediated by adults able to absorb or register the baby's state. Therapy provided a space in which the therapist's mind might register what Jenny's could not, and where a relationship could be built which might be strong enough to tackle her problems and her deep-rooted identification with her dead brothers.

The Mind after Birth

A mind lights up in response to meeting another mind. This idea illuminates the crucial first relationship between baby and mother. The baby approaches life from the beginning with the expectation of finding someone who will provide physical care *and* ordinary, emotional understanding.

These two aspects of infant care are integrated quite naturally when things go well: mothers (and fathers) look and smile at and talk to their tiny babies as they feed and clean and comfort and play with them. They mirror the baby's sounds and his facial expressions and give the baby the sense of being understood and sympathised with. A mother seems to feel the baby's feelings with him. She responds to the little shivers of cold or startle, the hugeness of yawns, the delight of a satisfying feed or the sometimes-painful effort of digestion and excretion.

Looking at a baby looking at his mother's face, and particularly into her eyes, offers us a moment of seeing a mind in the making. Here is a description of a nine week old baby boy, Jonah, who was already able to turn to others in the family:

> The baby's parents were sitting by the fire talking to a friend. Jonah was propped up in a soft chair with cushions supporting him, when his aunt arrived to visit. She sat on the sofa to Jonah's left. Jonah had been looking at his father who was sitting more or less directly in front of him, and he seemed very wide-awake and happy. He turned to look at his aunt and gave her a huge smile as she greeted him. They began a reciprocal exchange of smiles as his aunt talked to him while the rest of the family continued their conversation. Jonah made many little sounds, energetically waving his arms and clasping his hands together with apparent satisfaction. His 'speaking' was in harmony with his movements. To match his broad smiles, his tongue darted in and out of his mouth in a rhythmic dance. Happiness and liveliness suffused his whole body. Jonah could sustain this exchange for many minutes until his father picked him up to allow him to stretch his whole body. He held him in a quasi-walking position and they played at Jonah 'walking'. His mother said that he had had a nice feed a little while ago.

What is happening in Jonah's mind during this time? Perhaps we can surmise that Jonah felt full of goodness, a tummy full of milk, but also his mind was full of delightful things, his mother's love of him and his of her. When his aunt arrives, her greeting offers him a picture of himself as a lovely growing baby which he responds to. He then amplifies this, showing how all of his body is full of this good feeling. In the repeated bringing together of his two hands and the darting of his tongue, he is perhaps demonstrating his feeling that two can come together and make something happen. The physical and emotional link between baby's mouth and his mother's nipple comes to mind as one considers the meaning of his mouth full of rhythmic movement. It is tempting to assume that he is 'telling' his aunt about the gorgeous feed he had. The variety of cooing sounds that accompany the movements and smiles suggest that for Jonah the music of voices and mutual gazing are an intrinsic part of the whole experience. It is no surprise to learn that Jonah's mother tells him stories all the time and when father changes his nappy he talks to him about everything that is happening.

The integration of bodily experience and emotion such as Jonah's can easily fall apart, however, when a baby is under stress.

> When Polly, aged eight months, was left for the first time to be cared for by a nanny while her parents had a brief holiday, she slept for sixteen hours out of twenty four during her parents' absence. The nanny described her 'staring and staring' as if not recognising people around her and she became feverish. She could still eat but only

mechanically. Feeding no longer had any connection with feeling herself being recognised or understood. It was as if her psychological life stopped dead for a few days. It only resumed when her mother and father returned.

Even a baby of a few days may remember losing someone who has provided their very first point of contact and the beginnings of their sense of identity.

Maureen, a girl of ten, was adopted when she was a few days old. In the first year of her weekly therapy her neediness made the therapy sessions very important to her. Compared to this, the schooltime she had to miss because of the sessions didn't matter.

But after a year or so she began to indicate that now she was regretting what she had to miss at school because of coming to the clinic. She clearly felt better and this marked the beginning of thinking about ending the therapy. When the therapist and she came to speak about this the therapist was careful to emphasise that the ending would be planned well in advance and there would be plenty of time to work towards this.

The following week, when the therapist went to the waiting room to collect her, Maureen was in tears on her mother's lap. She was inconsolable and most unusually did not want to come to the therapist's room. After her mother's encouragement had had no effect on her, the therapist suggested that her mother come too. Once in the therapist's room Maureen clung tearfully to her for half an hour. Whenever her mother made any move to leave she wound herself more tightly round her mother's body. The therapist gradually formed a view of what was happening to Maureen and eventually felt she could suggest to Maureen's mother that she might leave.

Then she spoke to Maureen about her fear of the therapist, saying that she had turned into someone with whom Maureen did not feel safe, because the therapist had in the previous week spoken about leaving her. The therapist suggested that she felt to Maureen like her long-ago first Mummy, who had not been able to look after her and had given her to her mum and dad. How could a baby feel safe with a Mummy who was not going to keep her and how could Maureen feel safe with a therapist who would be saying goodbye to her when therapy ended? As the therapist spoke Maureen quietened and listened intently, looking at her instead of hiding her face in her sleeve and jumper. Maureen could *recognise* these feelings in herself rather than be completely overwhelmed by them.

The therapist's hypothesis was that Maureen had a deep memory of a primitive kind, of the loss of the mother who had given birth to her and of being handed on by her. She unconsciously believed that holding on tight was absolutely necessary to prevent a recurrence of this early catastrophe. This very early disruption of feeling safe might have played some part in one of her symptoms – bed-wetting – which seemed to express her difficulty with holding on to some of her feelings.

Few of us consciously remember anything much of our first few years of life, but we seem to have memories-in-feeling, which can erupt in disturbing ways when triggered by events resembling the original situation. Memories of this sort involve a sense of recognition without our fully knowing what we are recognising. By the following week, Maureen had forgotten the episode and could communicate quite ordinarily. However this kind of 'forgetting' would have left Maureen vulnerable to losses later in life. Therefore, working with her reaction to the parting that the end of the therapy involved was a very important part of the final phase of her treatment.

Developing the Ability to Think

Physical damage to the brain sustained through birth injury or through congenital disorders can cause permanent disability. Aside from many physical causes, sometimes minds and thinking can fail to develop in a more subtle way. There can be psychological reasons for such failure to thrive in the life of the mind and it is important to consider carefully all of the possible physical and psychological causes when exploring the need for help. Major illnesses, accidents, or physical neglect and abuse have a big emotional impact. Most children are very resilient, but sometimes the difficulties experienced by parents as they struggle with problems from their own childhood can have a big effect upon their children.

We now know that there is a frontier zone where psychology and neurology overlap because problems in early relationships can directly affect brain cell connections. Each individual's development is unique, and there will be many exceptions to what is expected. This is particularly so in respect of the baby's rate of development. This is important to remember in relation to setting standard achievements in education: it is absolutely normal for children to learn to walk, speak, read, count and think abstractly at very different rates. The slow or late developer is not necessarily the one who will finish last. Occasionally in therapy, the way a child's mind begins to function and the way a child can become aware of having a mind can be observed. These steps can occur through the first use of words or the first steps in symbolic play.

In therapy each child has a small box of individual toys and play materials for his or her own use, and is seen in the same room at a regular time. The reliability of the setting helps the child know where they are. It helps make clear that the therapy is an important time set aside for a special kind of endeavour.

> Peter was nine years old and of above average intelligence. His school and his rather elderly parents were very puzzled about his difficulties in learning to read or write. It was agreed that Peter would come to see his therapist for weekly sessions. He brought a schoolbook to one of his early sessions, a neatly written English exercise book. As his therapist tried to read the two-page story he had written, she realised that he was not able to spell a single word. At a distance, the writing looked fine. Close up, each word was a meaningless collection of letters. Yet each letter was well formed and each word looked like a word. The 'words' varied in length as they would in ordinary prose, and were in 'sentences'.
>
> Always on time and arriving willingly, Peter would then sit down at the opposite side of the table, fall silent and remain immobile and show no interest in the therapist, the room, or the toys. He seemed to get lost inside himself. For many weeks when trying to understand what was happening and to establish contact, the therapist could only use what she could glean from his physical state, posture and

> expression or from noticing the thoughts and feelings that were being stirred in her by being with him.
>
> Physically, Peter was a slightly bulky, well-grown boy but she felt that psychologically speaking, he was a small and immature being. The therapist wondered if Peter was showing her the side of himself that had not really started out on life: not yet able to move, still dependent on being picked up and carried around, shown things, fed and so on. He seemed to lack any will and direction. It seemed that she would have to have mind enough for two if they were to get anywhere. She spoke to him about this passive side of himself as being like a baby who seemed to hope that she would know how to go about things.

The therapist's hope was that Peter would recognise what she had said about him and that this would initiate a process of his getting to know himself.

But it was not to be so easy. The strange pattern of the therapy continued. Regularly, the therapist found herself having peculiar and disorienting feelings. While being perfectly wide awake, she had the sensation of drifting through time, hardly aware of her immediate surroundings.

When she reflected upon this, she was reminded of the school exercise book. Peter's story had looked like a proper story. But actually everything was jumbled. Outwardly this looked like a proper psychotherapy session but nothing made sense. These disturbing experiences of the therapist's might have been an indication that Peter was communicating in a very primitive non-verbal way. Perhaps, some feelings of unreality that Peter had were stirring up similar feelings in his therapist through subtle cues and inflections. The therapist thought that her earlier understanding of Peter's behaviour as showing an infantile passive side of him was much too sophisticated.

What she now thought was that Peter might have a primitive belief that he could get into her mind and curl up there. In this way he could become a part of her and remain unaware of any separation or distance between them. As this idea took shape in the therapist's mind she suddenly felt clear-headed and grounded. She felt she had resumed her own manner of thinking through these ideas of hers which had led her to feel solid again. She then talked to Peter about his wish to be so small that he would be like a baby not yet ready to be born, living in her mind and not yet having a mind of his own to think with. He looked at her intently as if these strange ideas made sense to him.

> When the therapist asked Peter from time to time what he was thinking about, he had replied occasionally with a sentence. Once he replied to her enquiry with, 'If I learn?' Another day he said, 'Waiting is one of my sports.'

These odd responses seemed memorable. The therapist so wanted these communications to be meaningful and yet they also resembled suspiciously the pseudo-sense of Peter's writing. She also wondered whether Peter might be coming to recognise a 'sport of waiting' that was being played with her. It was torture to spend so much time waiting for him to move or speak, or give evidence of his aliveness. After all, this largely mute person looked as if he could think and have something to say.

> Peter's increasing level of anxiety as he approached the first holiday break in the therapy made itself felt in a characteristically indirect way. The therapist having begun to feel clearer about the events of the therapy now began to feel she was not being able to keep the thread of her thoughts and the sequence in the sessions alive. Each session involved a struggle to revive a sense of potential for this silent and almost motionless boy. Already the gap from one Thursday to the next seemed too long to be able to do this. She decided to increase his sessions to twice a week, hoping that the greater frequency might hold the contact more firmly. Because the therapist felt that he might see this extra session as a confirmation that he really could live as an attachment to her, she also began to be a bit more probing with comments and questions.
>
> One day he told her he was thinking of a tree outside his much older sister's window. In line with her somewhat more active approach she asked him to describe it and when he could not find words she suggested that he might draw it, pointing out the pencil and paper provided.
>
> Peter turned out to be very good at drawing, and this led on to a long series of sessions where for the first 25 minutes, he was mainly still and silent. As usual the therapist tried to establish communication by understanding what was going on. Then, after about 25 minutes, Peter, as if on a cue, would say 'Can I draw now?' This was a strange question because it would have been clear that the therapist had wanted him to draw or speak from the beginning. Peter drew intricate comic strips showing the adventures of a boy who went into the past or the future but who had no existence in the present.

Through these drawing sessions the therapist was able to understand much more fully the way in which Peter felt imprisoned in an ideal and sufficient past. Perhaps, in his fantasy this was like the time before he was born into the difficulty of being a person in his own right in the world. In his imagination, he lived either in that past or sometimes in a fantasised future, and avoided the necessity to be himself in the here and now, and to struggle with his great difficulties in connecting with the world of others.

Gradually, Peter's drawings came to depict his first forays into the present. He became quite interested in the way his own mind was working including his ways of stopping it doing anything further. He was more in touch with everyday emotions.

Why was Peter as he was? Two ideas came to seem relevant to the therapist. Though loved, Peter had not been an expected baby. His parents had seen themselves as beyond producing babies when he was conceived, and his mother was unwell and may have been depressed for some time after his birth. Perhaps, she felt very far away to Peter. There also seemed a kind of mismatch between child and parents. They were ordinary people, but a bit lacking in imagination. By contrast, Peter had a strange but considerable intelligence and a very un-ordinary way of seeing things. He must have found it difficult to make himself understood, and felt very lonely and cut off.

Peter's comment, 'Waiting is one of my sports' was but one example of his quirky striking way of expressing himself. It was worthy of a character in a Beckett play, the therapist thought. Given its poetic spareness and demanding, dramatic originality, Beckett's work has an unlikely popular appeal. He succeeds in calling up those near wordless states of mind – 'memories in feeling' or 'anxieties-in-feeling' – that have a universal significance. Some of Peter's strange comments or drawings had a way of evoking something of the same dumb states.

How the Mind Needs Emotional Support

It is common for emotional factors to occur alongside physical causes of developmental slowness, often making them worse.

> Winston who is of Afro-Caribbean descent, was sixteen years old and in foster-care following abandonment by his mother when he was eight. He had a learning disability with an IQ below normal. However, a bigger difficulty for him was his severe depression.
>
> He had remained very attached to his mother whom he believed to be looking for him all the time. He thought that she had gone out to do something and lost him and then could never find her way back to social services to get him. In fact the last time he saw her was 8 years ago. He had some continuing contact with his father and a variety of half-siblings, aunts and uncles.
>
> Unfortunately, Winston's first therapist had to leave her job before Winston's therapy was completed and there was a gap before another therapist could be found. All this had strong echoes of the loss of his mother and confirmed his feelings that no one cared very much. When he started his sessions with the new therapist he was apathetic and gave the impression of nothing much going on in his mind. He was deep in despair much of the time and the absence of a mental life seemed connected with his feeling that he had been dropped when he went into foster-care.
>
> He became livelier in the sessions when he felt the therapist was interested in him. For example, once when he was telling the therapist about a trip with his foster mother to one of the West Indian Islands he described the fish market. The following week he was amazed when the therapist referred to the fish market because he hadn't expected that she would remember.

Two months later Winston's social worker left his post and at the same time his foster mother went away, leaving him in the care of another family member. As a result, the arrangements to bring him to the clinic broke down and Winston disappeared for many months. At the last moment his foster mother's daughter, a young mother herself, brought him to his session, quite out of the blue, saying that she was sure he needed to come to the clinic because he didn't know how to express himself, and this made him lonely. She had some feeling for him. The contrast between her lively young children and Winston was very obvious. It appeared Winston could not say he wanted to come, but if others noticed his need and exerted themselves he would acquiesce.

At this point Winston's new social worker, who had recently been appointed, thought that he might be able to make the journey to the clinic on his own. He had to leave college at the right time and get on and off the right trains but he usually arrived very late to his sessions which were taken up with talk about stations, train times, underground exits and so on.

> Winston began to be able to describe what happened to prevent his arriving on time: he would set off to the station but he would pass a shop and see just the folder he needed for college. So he would go in and buy the stationery and end up arriving half way through the session. He warmed to the theme of how he could not keep two things in his mind at the same time. He described ruefully how at home he would be asked to do something but then 'forget' it on his way to do it, his attention having been caught by something else. It seemed that in Winston's mind his own mother had got lost and he identified with her as 'someone who forgot people and got lost'. It was a way of denying the very painful reality of her abandoning him. In this way he could hold on to the conviction that one day she would come back for him.
>
> One day, after another late arrival, Winston was talking about the Jubilee and Metropolitan train lines which run in parallel at the station from which he leaves. On the platform he had been thinking about the destination of the Metropolitan trains and where they had come from. As a result he let several Jubilee line trains go by and was late, as usual.
>
> The therapist pointed out that he had been able to see both sets of lines. Knowing that there are two sets of tracks, he gets stuck, pre-occupied with only one. He was realising that getting stuck on the Metropolitan line had meant he missed half his session. In the same way his being stuck in thinking about his mother's return meant that his life was going by.
>
> Winston responded by asking the therapist quite precisely what time they would be ending. The therapist thought that this was to remind himself that she did not make up the time he misses by extending the session at the other end.
>
> In the past, noticing these consequences had depended wholly on the therapist. Now Winston was working them out for himself and the therapist felt his mind was growing. At the beginning of the next session he arrived on time but the therapist was one minute late. Winston looked hard at his watch. He had acquired his own sense of time and could make the point that he felt that other people should have one too. Subsequently, when he was ill and he had to miss a session he would telephone the therapist to explain not only that he could not come but also that he thought she would want to know otherwise she might be worried about him. Winston was now regarding his therapist as someone who might be concerned about him.

Winston needed to know that other people thought about him for a consistent and lengthy period before he could recover from his apathetic state. He had been making himself like the environment in which he lived and which he experienced as forgetful and neglectful. Because of his learning problems Winston had a particular vulnerability to feeling lost and confused but these problems were made worse by his life experiences where his parents had many problems in looking after him. His dullness of mind was a defence against the painfulness of his situation, which prevented him from having even a day-to-day sense of continuity, and he lacked a sense of the story of his life. For Winston, in the end, it was essential that other people – social worker, foster mother, therapist and others – could just about hold on to treating him as a person who had a mind and a future. The whole situation constantly invited those involved in his care to become demoralised, neglectful and careless. Belief in his person had to be asserted by others for a long time to stand any chance of pulling him out of a position where he was barely a person at all.

Just as minds may become active, so they may go quiescent, and the conditions that promote and those that impede mental (and probably brain) growth are important. It is possible that the mind's potentialities may be pushed into activity precociously by overwhelming experiences inside the womb; post-natal emotional influences can stymie mental growth. However, the human mind, whilst easily affected in these ways, has an enormous potential for new beginnings. Minds are not static in their contents or functioning. They are the dynamic elements in our relationship to ourselves – our internal world of emotional meaning and value – and to the external world of our relationships with other people, with our work, the physical environment, culture and so on. Aspects of our minds can continue to surprise us throughout life because they have this dynamic potential that is brought alive by contact with all that is 'other', the not-self that expands our consciousness. That is why new ideas and radical thinkers are so important.

2

Play

> And the streets of the city shall be full of boys and girls playing in the streets thereof. (Zechariah Viii. 5).

Introduction

Even tiny babies know how to play. The mother copies and elaborates the baby's more disorganised movements and gives them some order; the baby then copies these copies and alters them, and this in turn is further copied by the mother. Is this a game? It certainly seems to have playful qualities. Later when babies throw things out of their chairs and invite a parent to pick them up, only to repeat the action often with a smile or a gurgle, we can certainly think of this as a game.

Although playing is most intensive in childhood and adolescence it remains part of our activity throughout life. Indeed, we usually think of those who can remain playful in their adult lives as being those most full of life. The word play used in the sense of drama suggests that culturally we have made a connection between children's play and adult activities, especially art. These activities which form the fabric of human civilisation and culture and are deeply important to large sections of society can be thought of as adult derivatives of children's play. The notion of play is also associated with fun. But although pleasure and laughter are often associated with play, adult playing can also be a very committed activity. Likewise children's play can be very serious.

> A young boy whose father had been seriously injured in a fall played over and over again a game of a man falling and being rescued and taken to hospital.

This repeated game was clearly play although it had few, if any, qualities of fun. Play of this sort has the aim of dealing with a frightening event in a child's life. The repetition also indicates how much the event continues to affect the child who experienced it.

Play is also seen widely in the animal kingdom. It occurs in all mammals and something like it is seen in birds. We have only to see dogs chasing one another or running about with humans to see how intensely they play. Dolphins in the wild are observed chasing each other, or teasing older ones. One observer noticed how when he stood blowing smoke on the dry side of an observation window, the dolphin calf behind it immediately went and filled her mouth with her mother's milk and 'blew' it back at the observer.

In higher primates play has been most systematically studied. Young chimpanzees begin to play in the context of their own long relationships with their mothers. This seems to be not only connected to the direct interaction between the two of them, but also with the security she provides.

Young chimpanzees can be seen sitting with their mothers who are 'fishing' for termites. A stick is carefully selected for size, the bark is stripped from it and it is wetted with saliva. The stick is then pushed through a suitably sized hole in a termite hill; when the stick is pulled out, it is covered in termites, which are licked off and eaten with relish. Baby chimps sitting beside their mothers first play with sticks, pulling the bark off and poking them into termite holes. Very gradually this behaviour evolves into the fully-fledged activity of termite fishing (see Plate 3).

Jane Goodall, the famous primate researcher, noticed that an orphan chimpanzee who had been brought up by his siblings had never learned to 'fish' properly. Not having had a mother to provide a safe setting, had impaired his ability to learn. Primate researchers noticed that one of the advantages of playing is that it relieves essential activities from the pressure of having to succeed during a period of learning them. A modern human equivalent might be children playing computer games. Young people are completely comfortable with computers in a way that most of us whose childhood preceded computers and did not play with them will never fully achieve. Thus play helps young animals adapt to the material aspects of the world.

Another of its functions, just as important, lies in social development. In play animals learn to engage with each other, to control their aggression and to manage their relationships. For example, the play of dogs and dolphins (another very social animal) may be related to developing an ability for amicable responsiveness which is important in their adult life.

Chimpanzees, who have still more complex social structures, certainly use play in this way. They use a special expression, the 'play face', which signals to the other participants that whatever they do is 'only pretend' – so that chasing, biting and pulling at each other will lead to a reciprocal joining in the game instead of to serious aggression. In general, it seems clear that the longer the period of infancy in a given species and the more complex the adult mind, the more complex, diverse and important is the play. Humans with their extremely long period of dependency, their highly developed mental capacities, and especially their language ability, have by far the greatest and most complex repertoire of play in the animal kingdom.

Although some very interesting empirical studies have been carried out on human play, we can also develop ideas about the *meaning* of play for humans. This chapter will be concentrating on the meaning of play for the players, and its role in human development. We will consider the way play evolves as children get older, as well as the way play is a language in its own right, a way of communicating. This aspect of play is used by child analysts and psychotherapists in trying to understand what troubles children or what is affecting them adversely. For some children the very capacity to play is interfered with. How will this affect their development? Adults also have a powerful influence over children's play through the marketing and manufacture of children's toys and games, such as computers and video games. What effect does this have?

Play as Part of Our Development

Above the question was raised whether or not we could call playful the very early, and obviously enjoyable, 'to and fro' of imitation between mothers and babies. It seems there is no absolute discernible point at which play begins. Play develops within the playful interaction between the mother and baby, as well as with others who are closely involved. At first, this activity is probably initiated by the mother – orchestrated by her – and the baby is a willing participant. But gradually the baby will assume greater control and will begin to initiate the play.

The timing of this change is closely related to an important pre-condition of the baby's developing a capacity to play – namely the beginnings of an ability in the baby to have some sense of separateness from the mother. It is this gradually evolving sense of being a separate person that allows the baby to experience a world in which events can be more controlled, and to begin to develop imagination. For this to happen, it appears the baby needs to be able to tolerate small amounts of being alone.

'Peep-Boo!', one of the very earliest games, is about a disappearance and a return. It gives us an interesting and significant idea of one of the functions of play. The timing of the mother's hiding her face before allowing it to reappear, often not quite where expected, is absolutely crucial. Too brief and too predictable and the baby will quickly become bored. Too long and too unexpected will make the baby's capacity to play break down and be replaced by real anxiety about the whereabouts of the mother.

Getting it just right is an enormous pleasure. The baby's gurgles and giggles are highly infectious and groups of relatives or other on-lookers will watch delightedly. Just as the young chimpanzees rehearsed their termite-fishing, this apparently universal game has the function of allowing a central and often anxious preoccupation of coping with the absence of the mother to be rehearsed in a safe way. Peep-boo involves hiding the face only. Hide-and-seek, a pretend-disappearance – and thus a true game – where the mother hides her whole self is not 'played' by babies. From a baby's point of view, a hidden mother is not a pretend-gone mother, but a truly-gone mother. When peep-boo is done properly it gives to the baby a sense of his developing capacity to cope with the changeability of his environment.

The idea that there is a 'just right' length of time for the baby to be left with mother's vanished face amounts to a rule. All games have rules, even one this simple. This rule amounts to a structure, one which appears to control the baby's anxiety and allows fears of being abandoned, a precursor of the fear of death itself, to be made safe. Peep-boo has a number of related variants. One of them

Freud wrote about as the 'Cotton-reel game' in which his baby grandson threw away a cotton reel which was tied to his cot, and which he could then retrieve by pulling it back again on its piece of string. Freud suggested that in this game his grandson was symbolically controlling his mother – losing her and then retrieving her. Possibly there was also some aggression in the violent flinging away of the cotton reel (mother), which could then reassuringly be retrieved unscathed.

Donald Winnicott, a famous psychoanalyst who specialised in the treatment of children, developed ideas about how children gradually move on from a total dependence upon mother. From very early in life, children who have been able to develop some basic security begin to move out from a world which has been emotionally centred on the mother, her body, her voice, food, into a world which can be felt as separate from that – a world that is almost a not-mother world, but is also almost a not-me world either. Winnicott called this area 'the transitional space'.

He called it 'transitional' because developmentally it exists in between the proper external world and the baby's intense involvement with the mother. At first the baby's transitional space would be connected with physical objects that the baby experienced as possessions, such as the thumb or a blanket or perhaps a teddy – the famous 'transitional object'. It is in this transitional space that play can take place. Winnicott noted how parents have an instinctive respect for this space, treating it as somewhere which has been invented by and which belongs to the child. Although it is not treated on the same level as external reality, it is not without a status of its own.

> A little girl in a supermarket was overheard talking with her father. She was speaking animatedly about when she would be bigger. At one point she announced, 'I am really a boy and I am going to be a man when I grow up'. She said it in a serious way, though not without a hint of fun. It was clear that this was a kind of game. Her father sensitively neither contradicted her nor agreed with her, but said, 'Oh, I see!' in a friendly tone. In this way he conveyed that he knew that she was fantasising, but that he respected this and was not going to challenge it.

This notion of a bounded world, a kind of make-believe world, in which all sorts of activities can take place, a world which is spared the usual demands of reality, is one of the absolute fundamentals of human play. It is therefore a world which can allow free reign to imagination but, as well, one which can function like a laboratory, where experiments can take place which explore the possible outcomes of different actions.

One of the difficult tasks of development is to learn to cope with intense and contradictory feelings – to love and possess one moment, to hate and be rid of the next. Play can allow such contradictions. Freud's grandson could 'throw his mother away' in the form of the cotton reel, only to retrieve her the next minute.

Indeed, one of the functions of that particular activity would be to join the two wishes by making them part of a single game. In this way the little boy could have a place where such contradictions can be reconciled. We have to live with contradictions in ourselves and have to avoid becoming so inhibited by them that in order to be secure from their conflict we feel we have to restrict our imagination and our actions.

This notion that imagination can be dangerous raises the issue about the symbolism of play. To have a game in which there is *pretending* means that we must be able to make a distinction between what is done in the play and what it represents. A baby can only play peep-boo when the memory of the mother's face can be held on to long enough for its reappearance to be half expected in the baby's mind. That is one reason why the wait must not be too long (and perhaps why adults find Monty Python's World Hide and Seek Championship funny, in which the final search takes twenty years).

Some children cannot achieve this distinction between the actual and the symbolic and consequently cannot play 'let's pretend'. They cannot exercise and develop their imagination, as play is one area in which this distinction can begin to be sorted out and the tensions of irreconcilable wishes begin to be dealt with.

> Billy is eleven months old and is in his cot. On waking he begins playing with his Fisher Price activity centre. He also has two teddies in his cot, a large one and a small one. He spins the yellow and pink cylinder of the activity centre, turning towards the observer and laughing. He then concentrates on the plastic dome which, if pressed hard, will ring a bell – this is very difficult for him but he persists. He is enjoying playing and being with the observer.
>
> Then he suddenly notices the large teddy out of the corner of his eye and scowls. Teddy's presence seems to put him off in his struggle at the activity centre. He can't get back to playing. Then he grabs the teddy and pushes it through the bars of the cot onto the floor.
>
> He is overjoyed and laughing and returns to the activity centre. In his excitement he is almost hitting the toy and he finally makes the bell ring – his pleasure seems complete. However, shortly after this he hesitates and goes to the side of the cot.
>
> Billy looks on to the floor for the teddy and starts pointing at it and 'calling' for it. When teddy is restored to him again he again starts hitting it and soon pushes it out through the bars once more. Again, he rings the bell on the centre with pleasure. This sequence is repeated until he then sees the small teddy, which also gets pushed out through the bars. Now it is as though he imagines having the activity centre and the observer entirely to himself and he is lord of his domain, but his mood seems rather flat and he cannot regain his former enthusiasm.

In this sequence, which in some ways is like an elaborated version of Freud's cotton reel game, there is obviously a little drama taking place. Billy is playing a game in which he is the triumphant winner of some prize – perhaps the activity centre or the female observer? It almost has the feel of a youth at a fairground impressing his girlfriend by hitting the button which rings the bell. This triumph might well symbolise the repossession of his mother whom he had to let go after his recent weaning. But something is getting in the way, some unwelcome presence is interfering with his attempt to achieve this ultimate prize.

Is it teddy's gaze? Is he looking down on Billy, scorning his puny efforts like some superior rival, perhaps Billy's father? Whoever it is, Billy despatches him and can then enjoy his triumph ... except that there is something in his relationship with big teddy that won't leave him with a clear conscience. Teddy must be retrieved and he must give up his claims to being master of this world. But no! As soon as he renounces his position, his old ambitions resurface, and this time even the previously quiet little teddy must be exiled too – a little baby brother perhaps, who will take possession of his mother's breast which he has just relinquished? Yet the final act of this little drama is sobering. He must suffer either sadness and guilt over his defeated enemies, or the sadness of giving up his fight – the perfect state eludes him.

In following this sequence, it is possible to see that Billy throws into it features which trouble all mankind and which have been the subject of much great literature. Billy in a quite intuitive way has found the means of articulating something which preoccupies him and which he does not have the means of exploring in any other way. As he does so, the question of whether this is play or 'real life' frequently becomes blurred.

When big teddy is first identified as an intruder, is this play or is it a delusion? It hovers on the edge of both – and this is what the best play does. In this way it can resonate with real life dramas and anxieties, like the best trapeze acts where we truly fear that the acrobat will fall. Play should arouse anxiety but not too much; it should not be overwhelming. When that happens, play breaks down and it all ends in tears. Another way of putting it is to say that the capacity to symbolise, to have a play space, a transitional space, has broken down.

In addition to its material functions, important in the animal world, play in humans has an additional function: that of helping to explore the world of intense and conflicting emotions, a function of our complex minds and social structures. Play is not the only way we do this. In particular, we do it in our relationships with those who care for us and bring us up. Indeed, play cannot take place unless we are in an environment which is protective and felt to be reasonably safe. However, when these conditions are present, it provides a means of exploring different scenes and events springing from the imagination within and external life from without.

Play also functions as a means of articulating the complex internal feelings that are linked with real events, especially those that are stressful. This way of articulating something difficult seems to be as much to inform the player as the onlooker.

> A mother brought her daughter to a child guidance clinic. An important cause of the little girl's disturbance had been her mother's serious illness. The daughter had not shown any obvious distress or interest in her mother's illness but had been troubled at school. While her mother was describing her illness the little girl was playing with the dolls' house. The psychiatrist noticed that one of the dolls was lying on a table, while the little girl was pushing a sharp pencil into the side of the

doll. She did not or could not say what she was doing, but it then emerged that the mother's liver had been affected by her illness and that she had had a liver biopsy. Of course the little girl had not been present at the biopsy, nor had she been talked to about it, but she must have overheard the grown ups talking about it. This present conversation had clearly raised her anxieties and her play had expressed something she could not put into words.

Another example is of a boy whose mother was in the early stages of pregnancy, having had an earlier late miscarriage.

His mother had decided to have an amniocentesis and, because of this, the couple thought they would say nothing of the pregnancy to their four-year-old son until they had the results. Whilst waiting for these results, the parents noticed that the little boy was repeatedly pushing a little toy rabbit down his sweater and was letting it fall out between his legs. This was not a game that he usually played. It seemed inescapable that this game seemed to symbolise the birth or perhaps the miscarriage, or perhaps both, of a baby.

His parents did not interfere with this game by asking about it, but the boy seemed to have no conscious idea that he was worried about this and certainly did not ask them about any baby. Yet he seemed to be involved with the idea that a baby might be born. This is of course a common enough idea for any four-year-old child, but for it to emerge at this particular time meant that he not only had his thoughts and feelings to contend with, but also anxieties picked up from conversations (which grown ups always think that children do not notice) concerning his mother's precarious pregnancy. His play seemed to emerge under some inner pressure to express this to himself – and possibly to his parents as well.

In these two examples the children used objects at hand to set out the scene – the rabbit represented a baby, the doll represented the little girl's mother and the pencil was used to represent the needle used in the liver biopsy. Billy used the teddies to represent significant other people. Many games require an actual other person. In peep-boo it is usually an adult or an older sibling.

As children become more verbal they can use other people to allow them to enact some idea. A child may say to a parent, 'You're a tiger and you're chasing me and try to eat me but I get away!' This kind of play leads on to the possibility of children involving each other in play. This requires new capacities: one child has an idea and needs another child to co-operate.

A little girl with a curtain wrapped around her was walking in a sexy way in the garden, while her little brother at her side was pulling at the cloak. She turned to him and said, 'You're not supposed to do that, you're my boyfriend'.

She obviously had some idea of being followed and admired, as well as clearly obeyed by a pretend boyfriend. Such an experiment with her hopes for the future is made much more vivid by the presence of someone to play the admiring boyfriend. This kind of game is one of a whole range in which one child will be a baby, another a mother or father. These can be elaborated into fairy tale games with kings and queens and princes and princesses. Sometimes there is a move into games of doctors and nurses, where sexual activity between children is played out.

Sometimes these games break down when they become too real, or it becomes impossible to manage the rivalry, or the pretend aspect of sexuality. A little mother looking after her little baby is also a big sister rivalrous to her little brother, and once such feelings surface it is not long before they break out and the game ends. In *Lord of the Flies*, by William Golding, there is a vivid description of a game that loses its playful and symbolic quality. Faced with isolation, absent adults, and fearing for their very survival, the children's traditional games of tribal wars, or cowboys and Indians, break down and real murder takes place. Although this is a story written by an adult and did not really happen it can be seen as a myth about the real primitive violence which underlies all children's play and about our universal fears of what might happen if its playful quality were to break down.

Play as Therapy

The capacity of children to express themselves through play is used by psychotherapists and psychoanalysts as a language which can help them understand what may be upsetting and disturbing them. The child's play, together with the spoken language that accompanies it, is thought about by the therapist who then talks to the child about what its possible meaning might be. In that way a dialogue is opened up. Its aim is to be able to explore the nature of the child's difficulties in just the same way that an adult patient will talk about spontaneous feelings and fantasies – the 'free associations' that occur during sessions. Even little children can engage in this kind of work and can be motivated by the relief they find from it. This relief may not only come from the loss of troublesome symptoms, but also from the satisfaction of finding a way to express something which is causing distress.

The following sequence comes from an assessment of a boy of six called Freddie. Freddie was referred because he was having difficulties relating and playing with other children. He was adopted, but before his adoption he had suffered considerable physical and emotional abuse. The therapist describes an assessment session.

> Freddie was obviously anxious about seeing me, but there was something in him which wanted despite this to engage with me. He indicated that he might not like feeling controlled or trapped when he told me that the time he liked best at school was called 'choice'. Quite soon he said he wanted to draw and I showed him where the crayons and felt-tips were and he began drawing (see Figure 1). I could sense the drawing raised anxieties in him and he began very cautiously drawing the grass at the bottom of the picture in the corner furthest away from me. It looked as though it would take a very long time, which seemed to be expressing his opposing wishes, to express himself and also to keep everything hidden.
>
> Then he managed to finish the grass by contenting himself with drawing the grass on the right in a much more cursory way and getting on with the main picture.

Figure 1: The ability of children to express themselves through play can be used in a similar way as free association in an adult to help a therapist understand what may be disturbing them.

Again, starting from the side of the page furthermost from where I was sitting he drew a tree and began to gain confidence. He said he would draw the leaves of the tree and then the apples. Drawing the trunk he drew a round hole and said with a smile, 'That is for an owl'.

He proceeded with this, carefully joining the apples to the tree with stalks. Then a more mischievous but perhaps not quite so nice smile came on his face and he said, 'Oh I'm going to draw a spider – they have eight eyes, you know, and eight legs'. He drew the spider, adding that it was 'a poisonous spider'. He commented on his knowledge of spiders and then drew an ivy-like plant to the right which wound itself round and round the tree. He said, 'This is a plant that strangles trees.' In response I said I thought the tree might say something about his own wish to grow up in a good way to produce good things, but I thought he was also showing me that there were real difficulties for him such as the difficulties that he had already had – all the things that seem to have prevented him from growing up. They felt to him like the poisonous spider and the strangling plant, which could interfere with this more healthy side of him.

Freddie replied that Mummy could prevent the tree from being strangled. The picture then continued to evolve in the way so typical of young children, where it becomes a narrative which changes as it is being drawn rather than simply reaching a finished state. He drew a wolf from Peter and the Wolf, but in this drawing the gun was possessed by the wolf. Then as he drew the gun it became a lead which attached the wolf (which he now called a 'tame wolf') to the tree. Now the tree seemed to be connected more with an idea of someone else, perhaps his father. He seemed to be trying to alter the meaning of the drawing so that the obvious danger of a wolf who can have a gun, expressing his great fear that he could not trust his potent but wild self, could in the end be nothing to worry about because the wolf was tame.

There were other aspects to his assessment, suggesting that one of Freddie's main difficulties was that, because of his earlier experiences of being ill-treated, he had learned to rely on himself rather than allow others to help him. In the language of his play, his thought seemed to be, 'If you have a wolfish side of yourself, you need real help if it is to be tamed or controlled'.

As children become older and develop greater independence from adults around the ages of six or seven, their play will be less often shared with them or supervised so closely by them. A different kind of play develops which is much more rule-bound. Often, in fact, much of the interest lies in the rules. Games are still often spontaneous but children show a greater preference for playing the same games.

Parents can sometimes be quite upset that their previously bright and imaginative children seem to have lost their imagination and become more rigid. It is probably the time when computer games have their greatest hold (especially on boys), and usually these are the games which make the least demands. Whether or not this inhibits imaginative play, as opposed to simply providing more of a structure for it, probably depends upon how manageable feelings that belonged to infancy and earlier childhood have become.

John was a boy who was interested in natural history, had an encyclopaedic knowledge of insects, and was interested in the world, wanting to know what time it was in different places in the world. He was also very interested in dressing up and in being different characters. At one time when he had been given a toy Viking helmet and axe, he got his parents to take him to the library where he looked up the Viking alphabet (runes) and learned it so that he could write secret messages to his friends. At school he wrote stories which were full of imagination. But, at around the age 8 or 9 much of this stopped. Although he still read, he restricted himself to just one science fiction writer. His play was limited to computer games and War Hammer, although this was often in the company of friends. A few of his previous interests, such as natural history, continued but almost in secret. On reaching adolescence he began to be much freer again.

In the past when the street was more of a place where children could grow up safely, communal play after the age of six or seven was dominated by street games. Iona and Peter Opie collected hundreds of street games played by children of all ages, though the majority were played by children of primary school age. Many still survive, especially the 'dipping' (or 'counting out') games to see who will be 'it' or 'he' (see Plate 4).

Ip dip sky blue,
Who's it? Not you.
God's words are true, it must be you.

or

> Ippy dippy station, my operation,
> O-U-T spells out so out you must go!

Eventually, games for boys and girls diverge. Although boys still play conkers and marbles, many prefer hand-held computers. Girls play counting and bouncing ball games, hopscotch and skipping games, but have come to be more influenced by the toy industry. They will tend to follow the current craze, My Little Pony, Barbie dolls, Furbies.

This dominance of rules seems to be a way of controlling the powerful new impulses that all children have to learn to manage. Attempting to master both the environment and themselves, they are very preoccupied with this need for control. At best, it can lead to some interesting and enriching games. At worst, all the life goes out of their play, which can become very repetitive and limited.

Not surprisingly, in psychotherapy children of this age are especially concerned with the control of their impulses, which because of this concern may become less available emotionally. A nine year old called Joe, for example, divided his therapy time into neat, organised categories that left little space for any spontaneous expression of what he might be feeling.

> 4.00-4.05: talking about my problems.
> 4.05-4.35: talking about what I have been doing.
> 4.35-4.50: playing.

Clearly the five minutes set aside for his problems meant that he did not want them to become too prominent. However, with patience, understanding and careful interpretation, he was able to extend this to include 'talking about my dreams', and occasionally he could allow five minutes of playing time to be allotted to 'my feelings'.

One boy was in therapy as a younger child and continued to stay in therapy for some years. As he grew older, he dealt with his increased need for control by giving up talking entirely at the age of eight. Nonetheless, he managed to convey very clearly something of his difficulties. Figure 2 is a simple drawing of his in a comic-strip format. Children of this age enjoy this format, perhaps because the stylised form and the slightly mocking quality seems to tone down any raw emotions which might otherwise be revealed.

> While lying on the large desk in the therapist's room, Philip drew in complete silence as usual during the first fifteen minutes of the session. When he handed her the drawing he said nothing to her comment that the head that was sticking out of the post-box was at an angle very similar to his own as he lolled on the desk. The therapist suggested that it was he who was stuck inside the letterbox, and that ordinary communication could not therefore take place. In the drawing the post-box is also occupied, and indeed claimed as a nest by the mother bird who indignantly wants this person out.

Figure 2: Children naturally seem to be drawn to the comic strip format whose stylised form is good for communicating ideas, as indeed it is for adults.

A drawing by a little girl of nine (see Figure 3) also shows how at this age there is a strong wish to keep control. It is an attractive and humorous drawing done with very great care. But the spontaneous aspects of Freddie's drawing are not there, nor is the availability of unconscious material. What we see is a very careful creature, well protected against injury and the rain, who seems impervious to the traffic which is impatiently wanting to get on.

Figure 3: Fiona's drawing shows a tortoise with a mobile phone. Out of the picture, beeping and honking is the traffic. Fiona (age 9) is self-conscious that she 'does not say much'.

Fiona is conscious that she 'does not say much' and that she feels a bit guilty about it. The traffic might represent her idea of an impatient therapist and behind that her own impatience with herself. She holds herself and her world together with great care and finds it very hard to let go. This is her way of coping with an ill parent and all the tensions that this creates. She has a book of similar very carefully done drawings. Recently, on the brink of a holiday break from her therapy, she was faced with a sudden possible move from the house she had lived in all her life. This was conveyed very vividly by the book's coming to bits, partly on its own and partly because she had pulled the pages out. It was as though she was allowing her rage at the situation to emerge. Later she realised that she could paste the pages back in and was very relieved when she had done so.

Puberty ushers in another age for children. They have now in many ways stopped being children, and play in the childhood sense largely ceases or at least diminishes markedly. Instead what is visible is the use that adolescents make of the adult world that they are now moving into. Often their behaviour has an 'as if' quality to it. However, if their toys are also potentially dangerous, such as motorbikes or cars, adults worry that their use of them is unsafe – as of course happens, often with tragic results.

A classic study of bikers in the 1960s, *Growing Up on Two Wheels*, was commissioned by the Department of Transport, who had become alarmed at the rate at which young men were being killed.[1] The study showed that these young men did not treat their bikes as a means of transport but much more as fantasy objects which were equated with their wish to be powerful and potent. They spoke about their bikes in sensual, almost sexual, terms but when they came to their interviews they preferred not to bring them, 'in case they got lost'.

Their relationships to other drivers bordered on the suicidal. One of the favourite games was to sit just behind and to one side of a car, in the driver's blind spot. This not only gave them a feeling of power, but might also cause the car driver to crash into them – for which they imagined he would be held to blame. At other times the rivalry with drivers was more straightforward, though no less dangerous. It involved the excitement of cutting in front of them, or 'cutting them up' as they termed it. This expression of rivalry, particularly with male authority figures, and the violence associated with it, was enacted but in a way that was extremely risky. Often it seemed to represent a breakdown of play rather than its pursuit.

One group of 'two wheelers' were the Mods, who in a rather more obviously playful way covered their scooters with mirrors, flags and Davey Crockett hats. Like those who customised their bikes and decorated their leathers they made a more colourful expression of their identities out of their transport. For all their bravado and threats of violence, a great deal of this behaviour was play activity. Except for the more extreme cases, the play often seemed to possess that adolescent quality of being close to the edge. Where it managed to remain just the right side of the edge, it probably did help them resolve some of their rivalrous and dangerous conflicts with authority.

Our Never-Ending Transitional Space

In Baz Luhrman's 1998 film version of *Romeo and Juliet*, too, the drama, violence, love and passion are always on the verge of spilling over into real violence, taking place in large groups and containing a great deal of voyeurism and exhibitionism. Where adolescent behaviour actually leads to violence then the capacity to play – to symbolise, to exist in a transitional space – has in one or more necessary factors failed. It is surprising how often this does *not* happen. Konrad Lorenz, the father of modern ethology, concluded that what distinguishes man from other animals is that man continues to develop throughout life because he remains curious. This is true of no other animal. The old saying 'you can't teach an old dog new tricks' is not true of man. Man retains his curious nature until he dies or is too ill or infirm. Thus to investigate play in adults, we should trace the development and outcome of that curiosity so visible in children. It is expressed in the vast number of hobbies and interests pursued away from work, as well as through an interest in the arts. For others it may also gain expression in the work place. When scientists are allowed to pursue ideas for their own sake, to follow their curiosity, the outcome may well be some profoundly original discovery. Although at the time of discovery, some may be of no material value, they may later change the world. This kind of activity is both work and play, exemplifying play at its most serious.

Note

1. 'Motorcycle: Growing Up on Two Wheels', I. Menzies-Lyth in *Sexuality and Agression*, H.S. Klein Ed. (1969).

3

Are Children Innocent?

Adults have powerful longings to believe that babies are good. When we look at a newborn baby it seems natural that the idea of purity comes to mind. The beginning of a new life, as yet untouched by all that can impinge on human beings both from within and from without, evokes in us a desire to protect and idealise the baby and our own responses to the baby. This has something to do with the way in which a new baby in a family, or small children in general, can be invested with our hopes of something better emerging in the future. The new chance represented by new life – not yet spoilt in the ways that we may feel our own lives have been – is a source of hope.

In particular, the baby born within a loving sexual partnership contains the hope of the couple that their relationship is creative. Each member of the couple feels that a part of themselves is within the baby and longs to see in the developing child good aspects of their own character and talents. Such parental idealism, too, contributes to our desire to believe in childhood innocence. We tend to look at our children as if into a mirror, like Narcissus in Greek mythology, seeing the beauty and not the blemishes. These deep longings for perfection soon come into contact with all the mixed reality of life, and both parents and babies discover that negative feelings as well as love have a place in their lives together.

Another source of our rose-tinted vision lies in the way in which the birth of babies reassures us about our deeper anxieties about ourselves. A baby can make us feel that our sexual and bodily selves have done good things – the lovely baby the midwife hands to a mother is a baby who makes her feel that her womb is a good place, that the intercourse that planted the seed was a wonderful thing. We talk, perhaps glibly, of the miracle of birth, but it does indeed seem a miraculous event to those involved. This miraculous quality has been expressed in the outpouring of religious art over the whole Christian world, depicting the Annunciation and later the birth of Jesus. The baby with a halo has an echo in the response evoked by most births.

An upsurge of hopefulness is likely to be missing when the baby is born in unhappy circumstances – such as the babies abandoned in plastic bags by mothers too young or desperate to believe by themselves in their ability to be mothers – or when the baby is born ill or handicapped. The obviously imperfect baby provides less of the reassurance we yearn for and instead stirs the unconscious anxieties of its parents about what they have done to produce such a child. Out of this intense pain arises some of the confused and distorted understanding of congenital injury – the handicapped baby may be judged a sign of original sin, or evil acts in a previous life. The human impulse to locate blame and apportion guilt goes very deep and is powerfully stirred by such primal events.

How Children See Sexuality

But what are children like themselves? What if we look at them as they are, rather than seeing them as extensions of ourselves or of our prejudices and preconceptions? The idea of innocence has two specific aspects: the child seen as a pre-sexual being, and the child seen as inherently good, without hate, anger, aggression and so on.

Everyday observation does not seem to support either belief much once we allow ourselves to look. Let us first consider children's sexuality. What is sexual and what is less definably sensual is not always easy to distinguish. But it is not possible to see small children as non-sexual unless one is turning a blind eye. Small babies' states of physical excitement sometimes clearly reveal a sexual aspect, as mothers observing their baby sons' erections and their baby daughters' ecstatic wriggling become readily aware of.

There are both continuities and very important differences between this 'infantile' experience and the later manifestations of sexuality when puberty and genital development have occurred. A little later on, children's games in the pre-school and early primary school years very often involve sexual preoccupations. Playing doctors and nurses is one long-established route for investigating the genitalia of the opposite sex, intimacies which would not ordinarily be permitted. The more risqué playground and party games are similarly a safe channel and a framework for the child's excitement, pleasure and voyeurism. A child's shame and fear about his or her sexual impulses are made more manageable by the rules within which these games are played.

The nature and particular quality of children's sexual games are also influenced by the highly sexualised visual culture of television that is now part of their everyday experience. 1990s children tend to have a lot more information about sex at their disposal than had earlier generations. What children make of this exposure to the adolescent and adult preoccupations represented in the media is shaped by their child's eye view of things and their worldliness is superficial. They are less knowledgeable in reality than it can appear.

Since an awareness of children's sexual nature may seem to some to undermine ideas of innocence, it is essential to emphasise that we are nonetheless referring to something important and real when we speak about childhood innocence. That is why we are so disturbed by occasions when the actual sexual immaturity of the child is not respected. When adults involve children in their sexual activities, they cross the boundaries that need to exist between the generations. Even when it is not physically violent, this betrayal of children's need for adults to have a caring and protective role leads to a deep-seated probably life-long confusion in these children.

The best way of indicating the ordinary, healthy sexual feelings of a small child and the child's place in the family is to provide examples from real life. Here are some excerpts from an observation of a two-year-old-boy, Nicky, who is the only child of Susan and Phil. The observation is one in a series of weekly one-hour visits to his home in which the observer recorded what she had seen as part of a study of Nicky's development.

> One day Nicky greets the observer enthusiastically with a request that she make him a gun out of some shiny junk-mail his mother had just given him to play with. She rolls the paper and then folds it. Nicky complains that she had broken it and asks her to fix it. She cannot not understand what he wants her to do and, disappointed, Nicky turns to his mother, insistently demanding that she fix it. She, too, cannot not get it right. At just this moment his father Phil arrives home. Nicky turns eagerly to him and is delighted with his version of the gun.
>
> A little later, Nicky is upset about a toy house which is divided into two halves in a game he is playing with Phil. His father has split the house to make a house and a garage. Nicky objects that it is broken and that it needs to be fixed. Phil manages to convince him that it is not broken and Nicky then builds an ambitious two storey structure with lots of bricks while his father is constructing a stairway on the garage. All male toy figures are triumphantly placed on the roof of the house.

In this example, Nicky is concerned with asserting his masculinity, but anxious about damage. The women do not seem to understand the importance of the gun he wants. Only his father, the other person in possession of a penis, seems to be able to provide the proper response and reassurance. Nicky's belief is that boys and men are superior beings. But a little later when Phil has to go to work he gets anxious. Vulnerability underlies his wish to join up with his daddy.

A week later, a little girl is visiting to play. Nicky ruthlessly ignores her and monopolises the observer.

> Nicky wants to play wolf. First the observer is the wolf and Nicky the hunter. Then they are both to hide in a cardboard house Phil built for Nicky. 'The wolf is outside' explains Nicky, and he spends a long time sealing up the door with sellotape announcing with satisfaction that 'now the wolf can't come in'. After this he shows the observer a Christmas song book and wants to lean out of the window and instruct a child who has called up from the street 'not to shout'.

Nicky is clearly not pleased to share his observer's (or we might imagine, his mother's) attention with another child, whether an invited visitor or even a child in the neighbourhood. But his jealous possessiveness makes him anxious that there could be an angry wolf shut out and trying to get in. The excluded child's intrusions have become a source of anxiety: Nicky attributes his own possessiveness to other children. One is reminded of the big bad wolves of many fairy stories and the wolf who is shut out may also represent Nicky's wish to have his mother to himself and shut out his daddy at times.

Later that day, Nicky's mother is talking about his refusal to let her give away his baby toys to a friend with a new baby. Nicky surrounds himself with the toys and sings a Christmas song to the observer about baby Jesus coming down from the stars. It seems clear that his suspicions are that an important rival baby is on the way and that this is a great problem for him. On the hand, he sings a sweet hymn of welcome, as nice children might be expected to do, on the other, he is not ready to share his child-hood possessions. His identity as mummy's special little boy is not easily given up.

A year later, when Nicky's mother becomes pregnant, all these matters acquire an urgent reality. The imagined rival baby is now actually occupying Mummy's tummy. Nicky hears his mother telling the observer that they won't be able to go on holiday in the summer because the baby is due in July. In his bath he plays at swimming and talks about the family seaside holiday. Afterwards, he is very put out when mother wants to cut his nails. But later, in a very grown-up voice, he announces he is going to sit at his daddy's desk and do his homework. He draws a large sun in the middle of the paper and asks mother to draw something too. She adds a boat and Nicky colours it in, and then asks his mother to draw a house and garden. He is meticulous at keeping inside the lines.

When Phil arrives home, Nicky is very naughty and gets told off: having mummy to himself was very hard to relinquish. The following week, just before his fourth birthday, he proudly announces he is now five. To move on from being the son who occupies all the space in mother's mind (as the sun in the picture fills the page) he has to grow up very fast indeed. In his play he struggles to allow himself to explore the meaning of the idea that his mummy and daddy might want another baby. He is no longer the king of Mummy's castle; but there may be a new position for him as a big brother.

Mark, a boy of a similar age, reveals another dimension of these passionate rivalries. One day, as the observer, arrives he shows her a huge purple balloon, telling her that his mother had blown it up and tied it for him.

> Mark attaches it to a toy truck and drags the truck up to his bedroom. His mother is giving a lesson to another child elsewhere in the house and he is in his father's care. He then puts on a Postman Pat tape and dances to the music, twirling around, balloon in hand, getting gradually wilder. The balloon bounces on his head and comes close to one of the observer's legs. Squealing with delight, he becomes more and more noisy. The observer wondered how the lesson downstairs might be going! Jumping up and down, he ran to his parents' bed. Once on the bed, each jump seems to escalate his excitement. Lying on his back he kicks his legs in the air while bouncing the enormous purple balloon on his tummy.
>
> Suddenly the balloon bursts as it catches a sharp edge. Mark collapses, distraught. His father rushes to comfort him, but he is inconsolable when he realises the balloon cannot be remade and blown up again. His father suggests they could buy a new one. But Mark objects 'But Mummy blew this one!', and when Father mentions his imminent birthday, Mark wails 'No! I don't want to be four.'

This everyday picture of disillusionment shows Mark involved in a love affair with his mummy. He feels carried away by the excitement and with his wish for a sexually tinged link to his mother. While she is busy downstairs with her pupil in reality, he is absorbed in his fantasy of mother-and-Mark as the most important couple in the family. How painful that the bubble is pricked by the balloon bursting.

The way in which children perceive adult sexuality is influenced by their own concerns. As a result, children tend to regard adult relationships through the prism of their own wishes like Mark's ecstatic bouncing. Memories of the bliss of early breast-feeding – being held close, sucking a stream of warm milk, a sense of mother as belonging wholly to baby – often serve as the prototype of intimacy (see Plate 5).

Later, in the early days of school, sex is very often seen through an anal prism: the crude drawings exchanged between children, which liken sexual intercourse to toilet functions, belong very naturally to this stage of development. They represent both children's confusion and also their hostility to any awareness of adult sexuality and of its difference from what they think they know about. Children of this age see intercourse as the passing of faeces and urine between sexual partners. This can be a denigration of the obscurely apprehended relationship because children feel excluded from it. While these ideas play some part in each child's growing up – often, but not always, quite consciously – they can become too dominant; in so doing they may prevent development and leave an individual stuck in the perception of sex as ugly and dirty, with a consequent fear of sexual relationships. The sexual graffiti in uncared-for public spaces in our cities are reminders of how these degrading views of sex persist into adolescence or beyond.

When Children Are Abused

When Freud began writing about childhood sexuality at the beginning of the century, he caused shock among polite circles, where denial of the reality of children's bodily experiences and their imaginative significance had held sway. It is worthwhile thinking about this state of affairs not only as evidence of the effects of a period of extreme sexual repression, but perhaps also as safeguarding children, in some measure, from becoming the objects of adult sexual desire.

The apparent recent increase in the sexual abuse of children is probably a result of what is acknowledged and given prominence in the public domain. In an increasingly sexualised society, the recognition of the reality of children's sexual natures places on adults a duty of protection which may be very difficult to fulfil. The ways in which the childish views of sex described above may by some be confused with adult sexual practice are very obvious. It is simpler to believe that normality requires that all these confused ideas about our bodies should be denied and put beyond the pale.

But a more realistic view would give them a place in the normal life of children and would acknowledge the many ways in which such ideas may live on in our later lives. Allowing ourselves awareness of our 'perverse' selves provides a stronger position to make the essential differentiation between fantasy and enactment. The vast market for pornography and the taste for sex and violence in print and on our screens thrives instead upon denying the existence of these perverse tendencies. They are crude versions of what our dreams portray. Most of us, however, most of the time, have a capacity to keep dream, imagination and reality distinct. Our self-awareness and self-knowledge can enable us to control our impulses to harm without too much denial (see Plate 6).

Work with children and young people who have been drawn into frankly abusive sexual relationships is a disturbing experience for the professional caseworker. The urgency for legal and social policy issues to be tackled to improve the care and protection of children has rightly been a major public concern. What has been more difficult for the public to take fully into account is the impact that actual or alleged abuse and the child protection procedures now in place have on the children involved.

While we see some horrible instances of innocence assaulted, we are also often faced with complex questions about the experience of children, their sense of responsibility and their confusion. Public concern about children's safety and their need to be protected from sexual assault is intimately linked with our ideas about children's innocence. The claim that children never lie when speaking about episodes of sexual behaviour classed as sexual abuse by the listener is strongly advocated, but hard to sustain in any simple way. This claim relies on one's setting to one side the everyday knowledge that children, like adults, often lie about all sorts of things and for all sorts of different reasons.

It also over-simplifies the issue. A child may believe he is telling the truth, but in fact be telling part of the truth or describing something which is true in one way (true of the feelings the child had) but not at the level of external reality. In this vexed area we want to see children as inhabiting a pre-sexual Garden of Eden, without yet having tasted of the complexity of the tree of knowledge, and this denies aspects of the whole child. At the same time we fail to take account of the child's immaturity of mind, and in particular the real problem of differentiating clearly and reliably between what is inside the child's mind and what has an external reality, especially when strong feelings are stirred up. Arthur Miller's play *The Crucible* is a striking account of the way in which such delusional suspicion can take root.

Often in psychotherapy with children who have suffered abusive sexualised relationships we learn about their loss of innocence in painfully vivid ways. It is not usually communicated only or mainly in words, but through patterns of behaviour which become meaningful as part of a continuing, reliable therapeutic relationship which the child can trust.

> Tim, aged ten, had been adopted as a six year old. His early life was spent with his prostitute mother, who was very attached to him but at times overwhelmed by the needs of her children, of whom Tim was the first and most loved. The children spent frequent periods in temporary foster care. When Tim was two, his mother began a relationship with a new partner who turned out to be very violent. One of Tim's younger siblings died as a result of injuries sustained at home and this led to Tim's being taken into long-term care.
>
> In his therapy, Tim gradually began to express the dreadful inner state that had been hidden behind his apparently uninvolved, feelingless way of relating to other

people. His difficult behaviour at home and at school – stealing, intrusive sexualised play with other children, much lying – were what had led his adoptive parents to seek help for him. But their deeper concern was with his whole way of being which held them so powerfully at arm's length. The clinic staff who came to observe the gap between his socially charming con-man surface, particularly evident in the waiting room, and what this concealed, soon shared their disquiet.

Tim quickly made his therapist's life close to unbearable during his sessions as he attempted to force her to get to know what it felt like to live in an unpredictable world where life-threatening neglect, physical violence or abusive verbal mockery was likely to flare up at any moment. He liked to torment his therapist about the limits she needed to set on his behaviour in the interests of his safety. He wanted to lie on top of a cupboard against the wall which provided a kind of safe-haven, but which the therapist also had to watch carefully. It was only a narrow platform, high up and near the two-floors-up window. Also problematic was Tim's delight in trying to poke holes in the ceiling tiles from this position which he knew was not allowed. Once he was 'positioned' there, the therapist had to be all-eyes.

Up there, Tim began one day to enact in word and gesture relentless scenes of perverse sexual intercourse. This was a loveless world in which the most depraved language was used and the most lewd display suggested. The therapist felt sickened, assaulted and humiliated. She said that he was showing her some ugly sex and that it would be more helpful to try and talk about all these upsetting things that his mind was full of. When she tried to get Tim to come down he interpreted this as her expressing desperation to join in. The invitation to come nearer to her was heard by him as evidence that she was overcome with excitement about his enticing body and could not keep her hands to herself. Tim was, however, able to recognise what she put into words about his feelings and had become very involved in the therapy, desperate that he should have continued access to a place where he felt that he could finally dump all that was intolerable.

At this point, the therapist felt that she understood something crucial. Forced to watch Tim's performance, she found herself in the position of Tim as a little boy, so frequently exposed to his mother's activities as a prostitute. Tim had been very attached to his mother and must have felt drawn into horrified fascination about what was going on, in just the way he tried to recreate in reversal in the therapy room. What he was enacting on top of the cupboard was his picture of adult sexual relations. This was probably a mixture of things he had actually heard and seen and a small child's interpretation of intercourse in the light of his own bodily sensations.

The problem for the therapist was how to interest Tim in thinking about his preference for adopting the role of abuser/aggressor and how to introduce him, in a bearable way, to the more vulnerable and distressed side of himself which he was using his therapist to feel on his behalf. Tim was convinced that the only way to protect himself was to find a victim on whom the misery could be inflicted.

Tim had no experience of emotional pain being lessened through understanding and he needed a long time to find out that his therapist did not use interpretations to make him suffer but instead could talk to him in a way which reduced his hatred, suspicion and desperate loneliness.

The Cruel Side of Children

The view that childhood is innocent implies that destructiveness, cruelty, greed, hatred and anger are not part of a child's nature but rather are just a response to bad treatment at the hands of others. If we take Tim's story a little further, it provides an example of the anxiety aroused in children as they become aware of the nasty aspects of their own characters. This anxiety gives rise to attempts to disown or, in Tim's case, to pass on to others the discomforting emotions, which are so disturbing to the sense of inner security.

By contrast, when a child is externally supported in recognising his difficult feelings and wishes and is not rejected for having them, he may gradually be able to integrate them into his picture of himself and to take responsibility for himself, warts and all. If we offer children the idea that a 'good' child – the kind of child many children believe adults want – should not feel jealous, angry, spiteful, envious, greedy and so on and that in order to please these emotions must be disposed of, we are purveying dangerous nonsense which will leave the child despairing about any help with the real difficulties of life.

It is crucial that we distinguish between unacceptable actions and the feelings which lie behind them. These feelings require attention and understanding. In the later stages of work with Tim, it was possible to build on two things; firstly that he knew his therapist had (just about) survived the worst he could hand out. She was not innocent of just how horrible he could be, nor unacquainted with how hard it could be for her to go on thinking in the heat of the moment – he had seen her pushed to her limit many times. Secondly, Tim could also sometimes feel that what she said was intended to help him, not to counter-attack.

In this context, sorting out who was the aggressor became possible.

> One day Tim's session began inauspiciously with a sequence of defiant activities, which tested his therapist's nerve. She was, however, aware that he was probably upset at having arrived ten minutes late, which was very unusual, and had noted how tense he looked. He made a paper bomb and exploded it noisily, ran out of the room and messed about with the lift, and followed this with constructing a catapult which he used to threaten her. She spoke of the problem they had in finding a way for him to cope with his explosive feelings in the room today and his fear and desperation about having missed some of his time with her.
>
> Tim looked for his red felt tip pen and climbed onto the cupboard. He scrawled on the wall (this was allowed as it could be washed off). First he wrote his own name, then a list of his friends, then the therapist's name with a range of expletives. He was absorbed in this activity and his therapist talked to him about its meaning. She suggested, over time, that he wanted to show her that he felt Tim must be the boss, with his name up at the top. Perhaps he felt today, having arrived late, that it was especially important to feel in control.
>
> Later she spoke of his belief that she only thought about and remembered him if he forced her to do so, by showing his name up in big red letters. Perhaps little Tim had felt forgotten by a long-ago first Mummy and now feared that she too would leave him and disappear (the end of Tim's therapy was being considered at this time). Might the friends' names be there because they are so important now

that he is thinking about therapy ending, she wondered aloud? Might he perhaps be feeling jealous about other children who could come to this room to see her? He might want them to know that Tim was here first.

In huge letters, Tim wrote 'FUCK' and 'SHIT' and his therapist responded by wondering whether he felt worried that she might want to be rid of the little-shit aspect of Tim – that he might be able to behave so badly and make her dislike him.

Towards the end of the session, after more talk about Tim's mixed feelings about the plan to end his therapy, he climbed down and fetched a wet cloth and began to clean the wall, asking for detergent. He did a very thorough job, and before leaving asked for a drink of water and spoke in a friendly way about a plan to go ice-skating on Saturday. For the first time, he seemed an ordinary boy with a life to get on with.

This account provides an example of how a child can begin to take responsibility for his own feelings of rage and jealousy and his desire to hurt and spoil and then attempt to put things on a better basis. Tim cleared up as never before. Significantly, he also felt that his therapist now had something good to offer him – a refreshing drink of water – in contrast to his initial conviction that she would give him nothing unless he forced it out of her.

Tim deeply identified with a fundamentally abusive model of relationships, with himself now in the role of abuser, no doubt determined never again to suffer as he had as a small child. In the case material described we can see him making a new choice, of facing inner emotional pain (the pain of loss, of what he had experienced, of knowing one's own failings, of guilt for the bad treatment meted out to others) and bearing it. His childhood innocence had been shattered in terrible ways but his newly gained awareness of himself was a significant step in his emotional growth. Of course, the consequences of the damage done to him remain; working through his knowledge of these matters will probably continue to be a struggle for him throughout his life.

This example is extreme. Tim's early experiences had been very damaging to him, but the structure of his emotional life highlights what is true also in a less dramatic or overt fashion for children with more fortunate backgrounds.

Innocence and Experience

Blake's famous volume *Songs of Innocence and Experience* contains two well-known poems which capture the two poles of our experience which are fundamental to growing up. First, there is Blake's picture of childhood innocence in 'The Lamb':

> Little Lamb, who made thee?
> Dost thou know who made thee?
> Gave thee life, and bid thee feed,
> By the stream and o'er the mead;
> Gave thee such a tender voice,
> Making all the vales rejoice?
> Little Lamb, who made thee?
> …

This poem is often sung as a children's hymn. In contrast there is a parallel poem, 'The Tiger'.

Tiger! Tiger! Burning bright
In the forests of the night,
What immortal hand or eye
Could frame thy fearful symmetry?

In what distant deeps or skies
Burnt the fire of thine eyes?
On what wings dare He aspire?
What the hand dare seize the fire?

And what shoulder, and what art,
Could twist the sinews of thy heart?
And when thy heart began to beat,
What dread hand? And what dread feet?

When the stars threw down their spears,
And water'd heaven with their tears,
Did He smile His work to see?
Did He who made the Lamb make thee?

The purpose in quoting these lines is to suggest that their memorability is rooted in our split and divided, but potentially related, visions of the child – both the real child and the child in ourselves. The Lamb is the pre-Oedipal child, the Garden of Eden child, the pre-sexual vision of creation and of human nature (milky, loving, well fed, grateful). This is a 'good' child. Experiences of others and ourselves introduce something 'fearful' into this over-harmonious version of the universe. This comes from the growing awareness and acknowledgement of our own destructive and creative potential and of the fiery sexuality to be found in 'the forests of the night'. Babies can seem like lambs when at peace in their mothers' arms or asleep in a cot. But they can also seem like tigers in their cries for food, their struggles with colic, their enraged rejection of proffered comfort. Innocence has to make room for sexuality, power, violence and destructiveness in order for our knowledge of the world and ourselves to become truthful.

4

How Does Growing Up Happen?

Introduction

From the moment we come into existence as a single cell to the moment our last breath leaves us, we are in a process of constant biological change. For human beings, growing up physically takes more than a quarter of our life-span. It takes place in a predetermined way under strong genetic influences whether we like it or not.

Emotional growth, on the other hand, seems to take place – at least in humans – in a different way, with huge personal influence. Successful emotional growth leads to yet more personal development whilst hold-ups inhibit further emotional development. The broad direction of mental development is also predetermined, and yet how we mature emotionally, and where we get to is variable and difficult to sort out. The personalities of identical twins, for example, can have remarkable similarities but, equally remarkably, there will be many differences: what different *people* they become. Emotional and physical growth go hand in hand during childhood and youth, but emotional growth can continue throughout our lives whereas physical decline in some form commences surprisingly early in adult life.

Physical growth has a direct influence on the growth of the mind by increasing our neurological capacity, improving cognition, memory, intelligence and so on. It also alters the way we feel about ourselves as in all its different aspects our body is full of meaning for us. Sometimes these 'body-meanings' correspond to biological reality. But often they are more evidently a product of the imagination and of our cultural and personal myths about ourselves. Being of a certain size or strength, having features we like as well as those we dislike or sounding a certain way, all these form part of our identity, our sense of who we are.

The changes that take place in the course of physical development can give substance to the ideas we have about who we will become. For most children, the experience of puberty is a good one. A girl's first awareness of her breasts developing can be pleasurable because it is a sign that she really is becoming a woman when before she may have felt this to be an unrealisable dream. Yet when anxieties predominate, the body will become the home of more disturbing ideas.

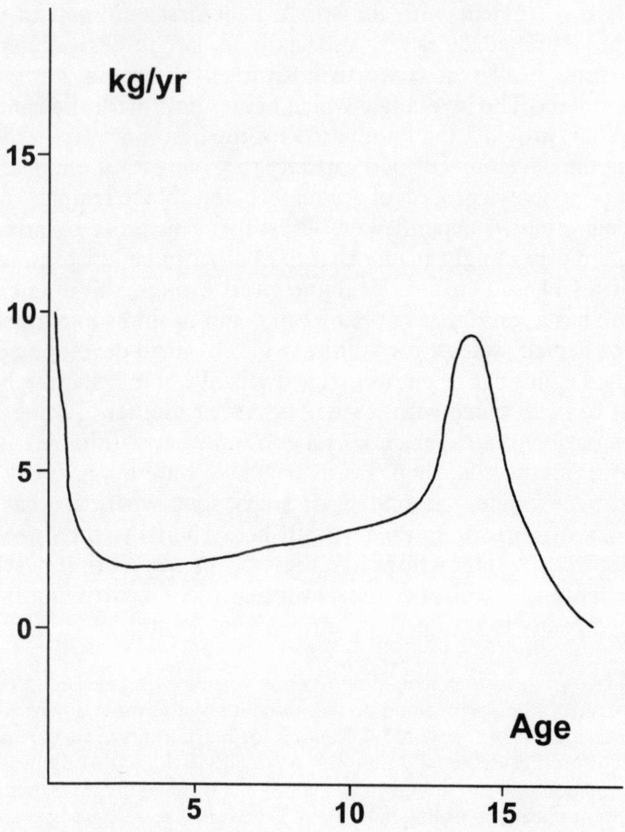

Figure 4: This weight-velocity curve shows the rate of weight gain over the first 16 years for boys. The graph for girls shows a similar growth spurt in adolescence. This evolutionary step allows more time for the young to learn in group settings.

> One patient described how when he had first noticed pubic hair on himself he was terrified and almost broke down with the pressure that something quite terrible was happening to him. He felt it was turning him into something which he could only see as hateful and disgusting, even though he did not know what it was that had disturbed him so much.

Clearly, for this adolescent something very worrying was lodged in the idea of being a sexually potent man. He believed that as long as he could remain a child, he could be free of this unwanted and intrusive image of himself. He could tell himself that this monstrous disturbance, whatever it was, was not part of him but was lodged in men. This is an extreme example, but all children experience some uneasiness about the physical changes of growing up.

The baby's involvement with the world is at first confined to the intense attachment to the immediate family, especially to the mother and her surroundings. It is as though all that is worth knowing or wanting is in and around mothers and fathers. The love-affair which babies have with their mothers, and those close to her, provides the foundation for the first moves towards the wider world and for the development of a capacity to cope with it and learn about it.

Growing up involves a process of gradually being able to manage for ourselves what in the beginning we depended on others for. This process starts very early: for example, a mother might realise that her baby can be left for a few minutes when she settles her down for the night, even though she might get a little distressed. She has a sense that her baby can begin to find some inner resources to take care of herself, at least for a short while. In small developments like this we can see the beginnings of emotional growth. We think that the baby within herself is able to be in touch with some of what her mother is doing. She is able to find a memory or past experience of a good mother within her.

If the baby cannot settle, then this manageable state might break down and be succeeded by a fragile, persecuted, or angry state where she has lost touch with a memory of a caring mother within her. The baby then needs her real mother to restore her. Interactions like these occur tens of times each day. The child's competence gradually increases, eventually leading to a more stable inner world with a capacity to take care of and manage feelings of vulnerability.

> A little girl of two years was struggling to cope with her first extended separation from her parents. She spent much of the morning of the third day clutching her teddy and staring out of the window, looking for her parents in the street outside. She became more miserable, and then felt physically sick, and so she was relieved with the suggestion that she should go to bed. As she climbed the stairs, pulling teddy after her, she was heard consoling him: 'Poor Teddy; he's so sick; poor, poor Teddy.'

The little girl was treating her teddy as that miserable sad part of herself. At the same time of great stress for her, she could also find within herself a mother for Teddy who could be kind and sympathetic in the absence of her own mother. She had some inner resources to help her manage. And eventually, as an adult, she will be able to use these fully to take care of herself and her own baby (see Plate 7).

An important part of growing up is a process of acquiring and developing abilities together with a gradual relinquishment of dependency. In a supportive environment, the process of physical growth leading to greater physical and mental competence underpins these psychological developments. The baby's intense involvement with the mother and her world will extend to the wider, less accommodating, world. There will be relationships with new people, relatives, other children, teachers, school, and through playing and learning an engagement with things, with toys and the physical world generally.

It is always a two-way pull. One is to reach out, on and up (a developmental thrust) and another is to wish to retreat to the safety of dependency. This to and fro of development repeats, in essence, the situation of the small baby's collapse and appeal for the mother when things become too much. In therapy it is an important milestone.

> Jed, a boy of ten, had been taken into care at two and a half years old having been neglected and physically abused. He had had several changes of placement, a failed adoption, and was now in long-term foster-care. He had been soiling and was failing to learn at school where they felt close to giving up on him. Despite all this adversity in his life, he was eventually able to make a good relationship with his psychotherapist. After difficult and demanding emotional work in his therapy he was beginning to settle down.
>
> A favourite game of his was to make a house under his therapist's chair and by using a blanket and a small table he could add a kind of tent. In this quite central game he appeared to convey that through his relationship to his therapist he was looking for a lost mother. Jed could imagine himself to be very close to her and even back inside her.
>
> He became very upset at the time of his therapist's holiday because he could not imagine where his therapist would be. It was as though this represented all the losses that he had suffered. His therapist reported that 'There was a sense of terrible pain in the room, as if it was too much to bear'.
>
> After some minutes Jed seemed to recover, filled a hand-basin with water and put his head in it, wetting his face with the water, and saying, 'This is lovely. I want to get right inside it and be in the water'. He took some water in a container to the window, saying 'I think the grass needs a drink.' He poured some water onto the grass outside, saying to his therapist, 'Look, come to the window! The grass needs water! Come and see!' His therapist went to the window, and Jed pointed to the daisies in the grass, saying 'they need water'. He looked at the birds and the dogs he could see outside.

This was a turning-point in Jed's treatment, and in his development. He had not been able to read before but he now began to read about animals and he became interested in bird-watching. He became curious about his origins, asking questions about his mother. At school, he was felt to have turned a corner and was seen to be learning and developing almost for the first time.

This example of a young boy's struggle to grow up after much early trauma does illustrate a tension which exists in all children. On the one hand there is the pull towards remaining small and dependent. Sometimes this is experienced as always longing to be cared for and looked after with no responsibilities. For others, like Jed, this regressive tug feels like being held back, pushed down or forced to remain a hopeless incontinent baby. On the other hand there is the draw to explore the world and everything in it. Indeed, this appetite for the world is linked to earlier wishes to possess and to know everything about our mothers and everything in them.

A Cuckoo's Chick

This process of giving up old satisfactions (and being freed from old tyrannies) and moving to new interests, raises the issue of who we feel ourselves to be as we develop. The little girl who could comfort her teddy was being a little mother to her sick and miserable self. Jed had found an identity as someone who could nourish the plants and help them grow. He had found in himself a love and concern for his own starving and stunted self.

These processes of identification represent the early steps in acquiring an adult identity, because growing up involves a gradual taking on and taking over of the function of the adults who looked after us. We wish to be like other people for a range of reasons. One of them is to deal with the loss and separation that we have to experience as we outgrow our need for our relationships in their original form.

Identification as a way of becoming an adult can have degrees of stability. For both Jed and the little girl, those close to them could sense their pain about not having been looked after as they wanted. They acquired their new capacities out of a real struggle in facing loss. Growing up for them was a painful task. Something like this, though less extreme, needs to take place in all children, even those who have not been confronted with Jed's difficulties. Real growing up is always painful to some extent.

However, sometimes the acquisition of adulthood is superficial and involves attempts to evade the fact that growing up necessarily involves struggling to achieve psychological separation from one's parents. Growing up in this way is more magical, or pretend-like, a misguided version of the innocent game of putting on your parents' shoes and dressing up in their clothes.

Especially in adolescence, the identity that is sought can be anti-parental. Trust is put in figures that glorify power, cruelty or imperviousness to pain and distress. This direction is often taken by children as a way of dealing with deprivation and abuse and there may also be a ready supply of disturbed adults to serve as examples. These kinds of identity which are supposed to be strong may lead to bullying, tyrannical traits or criminality. They are usually more unstable than expected by the adolescents.

The struggle to develop, to grow-up rather than just to dress-up, goes on throughout life, but in childhood it is more rapid because it is pushed and hurried along by the sheer pace of physical growth. In adolescence the process is especially vivid. An eleven or twelve-year-old child has much of the appearance of a larger version of what he or she was ten years earlier but the same child ten years on is like a different person. The similarities and the resemblances can still be seen but the differences are usually enormous. A twelve year old might be able to survive independently without parents but one twenty two year old, William Pitt the Younger, was once Chancellor of the Exchequer and two years later had become the Prime Minister.

In these few years, young people have to adapt to enormous changes in body and mind. There are the physical changes of sexual maturation, of size, shape, strength, appearance, voice and the biological capacity to have children. Alongside these there are social and psychological tasks which include becoming intimate with others outside the family, sexual relationships, becoming less dependent on parents and moving towards physically moving away from the family. In developed societies there are the challenges of exams, which can be the passport, or for many an obstacle, to the adult world. This list is incomplete but it conveys that no sphere of life is untouched by these changes. As with revolutions there is a sense of an old order that has been swept away. Many parents say that they wonder what happened to their 'nice' child who seems to have disappeared, ousted by the cuckoo's chick that is their belligerent and rejecting teenager.

The young person often feels increasing pressure to speed on towards adulthood, to 'put away childish things', as St Paul observed. This can be a healthy and a necessary part of growing up, but when whole aspects of ourselves are abandoned precipitately then the new-found independence is often precarious. Although this is a way of trying to be free of the other side of the conflict – the pull to remain a child for ever – it is fundamentally the same even if the outward shape seems to be so opposite. At this time, growing up can take the form of a kind of metamorphosis in which there is an overnight change from the juvenile to the adult form. Young people dressed up for parties can evoke ideas of beautiful moths or butterflies emerging from a chrysalis. On the other side, in the famous Kafka story a young man wakes up one morning in his bedroom to find that he has transformed into a repulsive insect; this fable ends fatally but many teenage children's bedrooms do become like the burrow of an insect and things do not turn out so bad. Perhaps Kafka, who was so full of anxieties and illness, imagined puberty in this way.

Of course, for many, these changes are not frightening. However, the dilemma is there for all adolescents. On the one hand growth forces them on to new powers and is embraced with great enthusiasm, but this does not snuff out a core of themselves that never wants to give up the early desires, the immature means of gratifying them, and that has wishes that are in conflict with this world forevermore.

Their new powers can be a threat, and cause anxiety because they can also gratify the most dangerous wishes, both sexual and violent. An angry little boy in a tantrum may feel quite murderous, but is too small and too lacking in cognitive capacity to do much about this. A six-foot fourteen year old in a rage may feel there is no-one who can stop him which gives him a sense of excitement, but also of terror. These extreme tensions, which have to be managed at such a rapid pace, are why so much adolescent behaviour seems so odd and contradictory. The mood can change so rapidly from optimism to depression.

The process of growing into this new world has something in common with mourning. In mourning, all the different aspects of the lost person are encountered and experienced. This experience causes suffering and results in feelings of loss. Gradually, the loss is faced and the pain becomes less, and gives way to a different kind of inner relationship to the lost person, which often leaves the mourner feeling stronger and supported by the lost person's good qualities, which they themselves have acquired through their relationship with that person. The new world with its opportunities is grasped but at the same time the old world has to be let go of. Yet the process of change is so relentless that no sooner is one 'identity' found than it must be replaced by another.

Change is the constant factor, and perhaps lies behind the fascination many young people have for sports like roller-blading, BMX-biking and snow-boarding, as though there is tremendous reassurance and satisfaction in remaining stable whilst in rapid and superbly accomplished motion.

> Ahmed, a young man of eighteen, sought help because he was in a state of tremendous anxiety. He had had an attack of vertigo, but mainly he was afraid that he was going mad because he had a sudden thought that he could seriously harm his girlfriend and that all that restrained him was his own control. He had also had sexual thoughts about his mother which disturbed him in the same way. These symptoms happened as he planned and worked towards a gap year after his A-levels.
>
> Although it appeared that the prospect of leaving home was the cause of his problems, what seemed to be the main source of anxiety was his effort to re-establish his relationship with his father with whom he had almost completely lost contact after his parents had separated when he was a small boy. He remembered having been tremendously attached to his father and recollected with distress how he would wait for hours at the window when his father, due to visit him, would be late or wouldn't arrive at all. Rather than have all the pain of his father's unreliability he seemed to have decided that he did not need him, and had more or less turned his back on him.

When Ahmed was seventeen he had re-established contact and was planning to spend his gap year abroad teaching English near his father. Although he did very well in his A-levels, as the time had got closer he began to feel more and more disturbed, until in the end he had broken down and had postponed his plan.

What had quickened this breakdown was a surge of feeling about his father because he was forced to acknowledge that he had in fact missed him, and needed him very much. In this surge of confused feelings, his sense of whether he was a little boy or a young man was very unclear. As though reflecting his sense of disorientation, his original vertigo had been a sensation that the foot of his bed had lifted up and turned him upside-down. His step of becoming an adult man had been invaded by the repudiated anxieties of the little boy who had decided that he did not need a father. Gradually, and with some psychotherapeutic help, his anxieties retreated and he was able to develop a new relationship with his father and get on with his life.

Adolescence Deferred

With Ahmed a solution to a childhood problem of loss had been put off until adolescence. It is also not uncommon for aspects of adolescent development to be deferred until later in life.

> Stephen, a very able man, sought help in his 40s because he could not sustain relationships with women. He had had a very difficult relationship with his parents

as a child when he had felt very unsafe; his parents seemed to have had difficulties in coping with their large family and with their own explosive feelings. In his adolescence, he separated from them and found an adult identity by cutting himself off entirely from his background which was Jewish and joining the local Irish community. Instead of dealing with the problem of separating from his parents, as well as with the need to acquire some parental characteristics of his own, he had adopted a radically different identity from theirs which he felt freed him from their hold.

As happens with this kind of solution, he never really escaped from his childhood anxieties. They remained unresolved and continued to affect him in his relationships with women. These relationships would often end abruptly as he developed anxieties that they had cancer, or were damaged in some other way.

In the course of his treatment, many of Stephen's anxieties were about having a relationship and he met a woman whom he planned to marry. On a trip to his home town, he went with his girlfriend to one of his old haunts. In the pub they were singing the old Irish folksongs of his adolescence. Although he still liked the old songs he felt extremely sad because he realised that he had behaved falsely by creating an illusory identity for himself as a young Irishman. He had borrowed roots.

When Stephen had come to the point where the developmental thrust of adolescence was pulling him towards independence, he had not been able to deal with this by gradually working through the separation from his parents and his own childhood. Instead he had cut himself off further, and in joining a quite different world of Irish freedom fighters in their struggle to free themselves from the British, he provided for himself some security. It was a temporary platform and he was able to go to university and qualify as a lawyer. Real maturity remained elusive and it was necessary for him to get help to complete the task of adolescence, by re-establishing a connection in his mind with his 'frightened-little-boy self' and of struggling with anxiety and with his parents. Then he could begin more truly to feel he could have his own identity as a man, a father and a husband.

The adolescent stage of growing up is characterised by fluctuating feelings of confidence and independence alternating rapidly with fears of overwhelming need. At such times, turning to parents can feel like undermining an emerging sense of independence. The use of friends or the wider peer-groups provides an alternative and these friendships can be permitted to have very infantile features: being very close with no secrets, 'living in each other's pockets', endless telephone conversations that go on and on. All these features recapture something of the hard-to-relinquish needy relationship with the parents. A common feature, though, is a shared sense of rather looking down on adults. In these ways feelings of inferiority which might be too undermining can be warded off.

Friendship and Gangs

Wider social groups can provide a temporary alternative world. From an adult perspective some of these seem to be supportive and benign, whilst others are gang-like and aim to reinforce feelings of strength, power and hardness. They are a collective way of warding off individual feelings of vulnerability, helplessness or despair. Often different purposes are mixed together. For example, the Green Movement attracts large numbers of young people (not only, of course) and mostly this is a healthy sign of wanting to take care of the earth (mother) with a bit of contempt towards the neglectful and polluting adults; a way of easing the burden of guilt towards parents from the past and in the present.

But some, the militant eco-warriors and animal-rights activists, are committing the very destruction that they are complaining about. Their activities are no more than a justification for their own destructive sides, rather than a means of finding a way of managing their own adult destructive feelings. Nevertheless, despite the discomfort for adults, these groups provide a stepping-stone from which young people can 'come back' into society, having matured enough meanwhile not to need their support so much. Other groups, who have more extreme feelings or deprivations to ward off, may be drawn into extreme political groupings which are a cul-de-sac rather than offering a route towards healthy development.

Social groups can be used as a way of avoiding some of the more difficult issues which emerge in adolescence – for example, the fear of death. In a state of denial of anxieties about one's own fragility and mortality, some adolescents engage in dangerous collective activities in which they defy death. They ride motorbikes dangerously, or take cars 'joy-riding'. Some adolescents form allegiances to pop-groups who idealise death. The idea of death is present in some form from childhood onwards but, as with so many adolescent experiences, it assumes much greater reality. They feel more directly exposed to it and to feelings of depression with conscious fears of death.

> One thirteen year old, two years after the death of his father, found himself with a nightly fear that he would not survive until morning. His fears of his own death had become very confused with the death of his father, and had been rather forced on him by this event.

The Important Role of Parents

People need to be supported in their efforts to grow. The tiny baby trying to go to sleep is completely dependent on the mother she relied upon to rescue her if she felt overwhelmed. Her mother encouraged and supported, and even pushed her a bit towards discovering her own resources. This kind of help, when appropriate to age and capacity, is what all children *and* adolescents need. Adolescents need adults who know when to step in either supportively, or firmly, when they are out of touch with their own limitations or with the dangers that they are courting, or when they are experimenting with identifications and consequently not looking after themselves well enough. To do this the adults need to be able to withstand quite a lot of pressure.

When adolescents are wrestling with extremes of feelings that threaten to overwhelm them, they may fill those caring for them with anxiety, testing their strength and endurance. If the parents or teachers can hang on and tolerate the pressures, often this will enable the adolescent to accept responsibility for himself. However, when such emotional missiles are well aimed, they succeed in making the adults have feelings that the young person is trying to be rid of. These are often about powerlessness or feelings of inadequacy. Sometimes they are about intellectual inadequacy, so that offers of help with homework turn into battle-grounds in which the adult is made to look and feel stupid. The superiority of some adolescents, referred to earlier, can often be felt quite personally.

Emotional growth will promote yet more growth. But if earlier issues dealing with separation and growth are left untouched they will make later tasks more difficult. Thus successfully negotiating earlier developmental tasks can mean that later ones turn out to be already half-accomplished. On the other hand earlier failures always mean that there will be more to do later – for example, a boy who had never learnt to sleep in his own bed at night later broke down with a school phobia. And for social and psychological reasons, it is often those adolescents most needing help – because of earlier developmental failures – who have least access to help.

Personal Growth in Adversity

Fortunately, the capacity to grow and develop is not solely dependent on what the environment provides. Some children have a capacity to make the most out of very little, which can sometimes help them overcome considerable developmental problems. Jed, whose case was described above, is almost certainly one of these. He needed help, but his responsiveness to it, and his capacity to recover from terrible early losses.

> Another example was the case of a boy, many years ago, who was brought up by very disturbed parents. They more or less kept him prisoner and forced him to dress as a girl. He was very bright and his parents provided him with a tutor who saw his plight and realised his ability. The tutor managed to help him towards gaining a scholarship to university. Once there, he thrived, became a successful academic, married happily, and fathered two very successful sons, both of whom became distinguished in the arts. They have made a particular study of artists struggling to keep working under politically repressive regimes. Their work has clearly followed their interests, and yet in a strange way it seems to have been inspired by the situation their father had to face.

Growing up does not stop with physical maturation, but can continue all our lives. One of the more remarkable things about it is that, if we are not too blocked, we can have a second, or third, or even more chances to deal with what was left undone earlier. Adolescence is the big opportunity, but so is the time of having one's own children, as well as other periods of major life change.

Although we, like all human beings, have a tendency to repeat earlier solutions, sometimes we are capable of freeing ourselves from the past. We feel moved when we see very old people still open to learning, because we see in them something of the way that, as humans with minds, we seem able to transcend biology. Sir George Solti, even in his later years, never used an old worked-upon score when he was conducting a piece of music. He wanted each performance to be a new attempt to wrestle with the composition. In this way, he never stopped trying to engage with new experiences and to arrive at an original interpretation. It is not difficult to argue for the survival value of this or to see in it the operation of the 'selfish gene', but to do so we need to acknowledge a sophisticated view of what human beings can be and can do for one another. Solti was a man who showed us that some human beings have the capacity, and the desire, to go on growing up until the very end of their lives.

5

What Causes the Mind?

'Of course history is an art – just like all the other sciences.' It is in the sense of science as an art that most psychoanalysts and psychotherapists, like the historian author of this quip, would think of themselves as researchers. They are materialists. If asked the question, 'What causes the mind?' one of their first answers would be, 'The brain'. We think of the brain as being more fundamental than the mind. In states such as deep unconsciousness, anaesthesia or death, the brain can exist without there being a mind but there are no states – at least that we know of – where mind can exist without brain. Most of us would accept this and all the evidence points in this direction.

However, as we repeatedly learn, human beings cannot bear too much reality. Correct scientific ideas are often irrationally denied. Or scientists can over-use rationalism in a defensive way. They can promote the scientific method of investigation as the only way, ruling out other facts or bodies of knowledge which are difficult to face. Neuroscience and its advances are sometimes used to make the fact that people are *persons* redundant. Persons have passions. They experience the difficulties that personal relationships often entail. They can carry troubling thoughts, feelings and wishes in their minds. Over the course of life, from being a baby in the womb to infant, from infant to child, from child to adult these relationships and these wishes influence powerfully how the mind – and brain – develops.

This chapter seeks to do justice to two avenues of approach. In one, the brain is the physical organ that leads to the mind. Through the other, much can only be learned by travelling the way offered by the awkward, sometimes unpalatable things we know about the mind through the personality and human relationships. This view holds that without other people and other minds the brain would not develop fully. Furthermore, the mind can have a powerful effect upon itself.

The Brain as the Cause of Our Mind

It has been said that the brain is the organ that produces the mind just as the liver is the organ that produces the bile. This similarity only goes so far. Today's physiologists have a good idea of just how the liver produces bile and of how bile works. This is not so with the brain's ability to produce the mind and how the mind works. The fundamental alteration that must take place to transform nerve impulses and neurotransmitter chemicals into thoughts, feelings and dreams is entirely obscure. There is an explanatory gap of a profound sort.

However, as we shall see, much is beginning to be known about how the brain works as a physical organ. Increasingly, the functioning of different brain systems – or modules – can be understood in terms of nerve impulses, neurochemicals and nerve cell functions and connections. Subjectively experienced aspects of the mental functions of memory, seeing, thinking, wishing, intending (for instance, to move an arm) can be tracked in parallel with these brain events. They can be imaged through special forms of brain scanning. Recently, for example, a paralysed man had electrodes implanted in his brain cortex which were connected to a computer. He learnt to think about moving and the electrical potential energy developed in his cortex was used as a signal to control a cursor on the computer screen. Nonetheless, the process of what is known as *the phase transition* from brain event to conscious awareness, and back again, is something about which we have very little idea.

Until very recently we had no idea of how even to begin to have an idea about it. Throughout human history, the vital power of life processes has been regarded as belonging to the gods. The creation of life and of life forms was a divine act. Gods alone were immortal. Yet versions of these achievements, along with knowing how creation works, are now within mankind's reach; the mystery of these things is almost beginning to fall away. Yet, the nature of our own consciousness still seems as mysterious to us as did over a century ago the flickering projections of the winding magic lantern. Neuroscience now stands on the threshold of discovering how the brain produces the unconscious and the conscious mind, but we have not yet crossed that threshold. The heavy door is still closed.

The texture of the brain is commonly compared to cold porridge. To the naked eye it is relatively homogeneous. Closer examination reveals something marvellously complicated. At the back there is the cerebellum which deals with smoothing our movements and balance. As far as we know, it does not have much to do with consciousness. Inside the vault of the skull are the two cerebral hemispheres, which are folded and divided like a walnut and are larger in man than in any other mammal. The outer rind of the cortices is the grey matter. The inner substance is the white matter. Within this pith are several more or less clearly defined sub-cortical structures or nuclei. Proceeding upwards as a continuation of the spinal cord is the brain stem and then the mid-brain, which connects to the two hemispheres. Running up and down within the main trunk lines of this nervous system is the reticular formation. It has a role in turning arousal on and off. It is said to announce to the higher brain regions, 'Get ready!'

However, consciousness and arousal seem to be spread 'throughout' the two hemispheres that fill the vault of the skull (the cerebrum). There doesn't seem to be a centre or location for consciousness. Removal of an entire cerebral hemisphere does not impair global consciousness, and discrete lesions (except for one or two particular 'switch' sites) do not affect consciousness. However, *what* one can be conscious of is affected by damage to different areas of the brain. Damage to the part of the cortex dealing with vision can lead to cortical blindness or 'blindsight', where the person has no *awareness* of seeing anything but still is able to negotiate obstacles.

The Split Brain

These phenomena of seeing without seeing, or of knowing without knowing, are also found in the neurological conditions connected with having a 'split brain'. Normally, nerve impulses pass from one cerebral hemisphere to the other via a bundle of fibres called the *corpus callosum*. Sometimes, this main communication bridge is severed. This can happen intentionally, as a surgical treatment for intractable epilepsy, or accidentally through lesions caused by gunshot wounds, or through tumours; in these circumstances the left and right hemispheres are isolated from each other. The brain is split.

This condition has allowed neuroscientists to work out that the two hemispheres have relatively different specialities. In normal circumstances they are integrated by the passage of information across the *corpus callosum*, the bundle of connecting fibres. The left hemisphere in most of us is what is called dominant, because it controls the right side of the body and with it usually the most adroit and preferred hand. It is also the site of language. The functions of the right hemisphere were less immediately obvious and took longer to work out. We now know that the right hemisphere is mainly responsible – is dominant – for social and emotional functioning, for non-verbal rhythmic and tonal aspects of speech and for musical ability. It enables us to orientate ourselves in space and it processes our awareness of our bodies.

When the hemispheres are split from each other, information from the right and left visual fields is not transferred from one side of the brain to the other. Because the visual fields are also cross-wired just as are our limbs it is possible to show something to one side of the brain only.

> In one test, the picture of a nude man is shown in the left visual field – that is, to the right hemisphere of a woman who has a split brain. She says she sees nothing, but blushes and giggles. When an object is placed in the patient's left hand she is unable to say what it is. If however she is then instructed to point to it from amongst a number of objects she is able to do so with the left hand, because the non-dominant right hemisphere knows what the object is.

In another test of predictive capability someone indicates his guess as to whether a light is going to appear at the top or bottom of a computer screen by pushing a button. The experimenter manipulates the situation so that 80 per cent of the time the stimulus appears at the top, but in a random sequence. It is quickly evident that the light appears more often at the top. Human subjects try to figure out the pattern and believe deeply that they can do so. However, they tended to be correct only 68 per cent of the time. Yet rats, whose brains do not have the interpreter function which figures out patterns, press only the top button and thus end up being correct more often than human beings. In the same way, the right hemispheres of split brain patients respond more closely to what is actually there. They produce more correct responses than normal people do, or left hemispheres, which is where the 'interpreter' function usually lies.

These and many other experiments demonstrate that the right and left hemispheres operate in somewhat different ways. Yet this differentiation is not absolutely fixed. In certain circumstances hemispheric 'role-reversal' can take place. Usually however, the left is always looking for order, pattern and meaning even when there is none. If we attribute to it the characteristics of an entire person, the left hemisphere is ingenious and good at sequential causal reasoning, but it can be plausible and glib. Like Odysseus, it will produce sweet explanations even when there are none. The right hemisphere seems to accumulate information – perhaps particularly non-verbal information – in a more impartial way and it has been suggested that this has a role in the revision of beliefs, during the process of deciding if they are still true or need changing. It may be particularly good at picking up non-verbal emotional cues without there being a clear awareness of what is being registered.

The Brain Development of Babies

The basic passions of love, hate, fear, anxiety, envy, hunger, greed and jealousy are important components of motivation. We feel these emotions in certain situations or states and they impel us to action. Such emotions are 'mediated' through sub-cortical structures that operate together as a unit known as the limbic system.

The emotional events of infancy, many of them intimately connected with early feeding and playing with the suckling mother, exert a powerful influence on the way the neural connections develop between the limbic system and parts of the right hemisphere. It is likely that many consequences of this early relationship are 'wired in' at this point. Early experiences of excitement and pleasure with the mother may promote neural organisations founded on some of the activating chemical neurotransmitters. Thus inhibitory neurochemical regulation of these circuits is augmented, or initiated, by the parents smoothing, soothing or limiting the infant's emotional states. Every aspect of the various and varied qualities of relationship between the mother and child will have its cumulative effect.

This 'wiring-in' can happen because at birth and in infancy the human baby's brain is immature. Its immaturity continues for far longer than it does in other animals. Most of the cells – the neurones – are there but the myriad connections (the *synapses*) need to be made and the long wire-like main conducting fibre possessed by some cells (the axone) lacks its sheath of fatty insulation (the *myelin*). In the first eighteen months of life, maturation in the right hemisphere, where language is based, progresses on an earlier schedule than that of the left hemisphere, where emotional processing occurs. The neurological consequences of these early influences affect the adults' capacity to deal with the feelings and the relationships that are served by these areas of the brain. Difficulties in making, keeping and losing love relationships are the functions most damaged in emotional and mental disorders, and those prone to emotional disorders are especially vulnerable. Evidence from many other sources confirms the indelibility of early relationships and their importance for future stability.

At eighteen months the focus of cerebral maturation shifts to the left hemisphere and to the upper and outer parts of the frontal lobe away from the inner and midline parts. This is connected with increasing capacities for abstract reasoning, and with developing language skills. Language has a special relationship with consciousness. It leads to a (self-reflexive) consciousness that we can spell out to ourselves. Consciousness, rather than being based like a searchlight that can be switched on or off and located in a single part of the brain, seems to involve patterns of activity in different parts of the brain. It is also of various

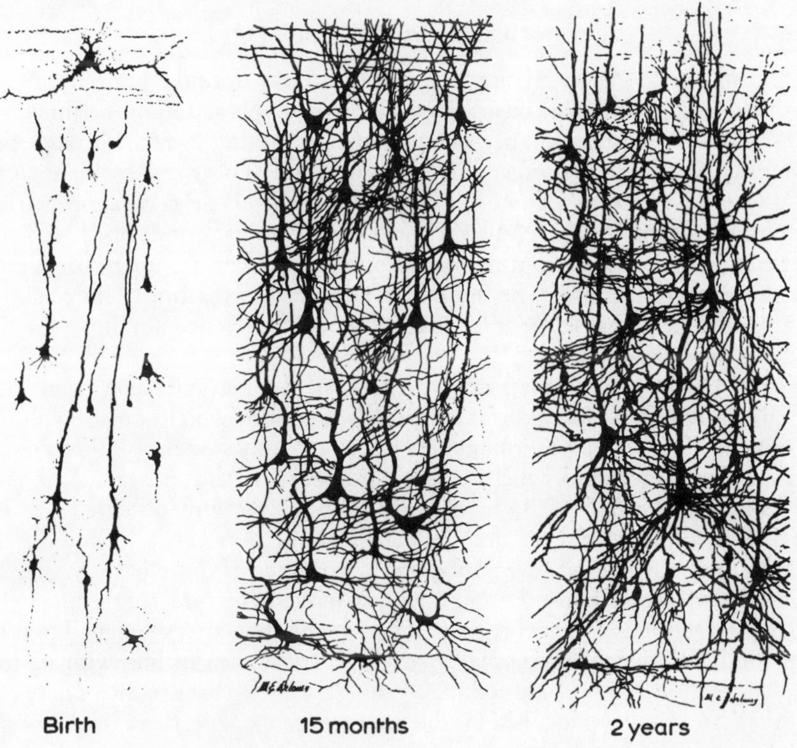

Figure 5: Although most of the cells of the human brain are present at birth, many of the interconnections only develop in the first years.

kinds. Dream consciousness differs from waking consciousness. Self-reflexive consciousness is different from a background of awareness.

Registering what is going on in our bodies, in the outside world and in our minds is an important part of the 'input' components of consciousness. Forming an intention or making a decision to act, are important 'output' components of consciousness. This last has a bearing on the age-old philosophical problems of the relationship of body to mind.

> It appears the quickest we are able to become conscious of something is about half a second after the fact. Subjectively, we consider that we decide to move our arm and then we do it. Investigations indicate that the electrical activity that precedes movement builds up in the relevant parts of the brain before we become aware of our intention. This suggests that the brain 'decides' before we do. Consciousness therefore may be a way that we can adapt what we are doing, saying or thinking. Different types of consciousness provide aural, verbal, visual, non-specific theatres, using different means of representation. They are virtual realities using different forms of symbolic medium – sound, visual images, verbal thought – applied in different manners to different kinds of input.

The Brain Experience

Yet all this knowledge still begs the questions. How does the brain do it? How does the mind work? Just consider the following explanation of the function of belief: 'By limiting the number of ways of interpreting events (through belief structures), the brain is protected from being paralysed by indecision as to how to act.' Language has to become like an off-the-road vehicle as we approach areas of enquiry where the different categories of persons, mind, body and brain intersect like a spaghetti junction. Belief structures are mental. Paralysis affects things that move. The body is paralysed, not the brain. Indecision, as far as we know paralyses people; brains do not experience anything, let alone indecision.

Figure 6 is a kind of map drawn by the neuroanatomist as a result of his investigations of the motor cortex, the part of our body which controls voluntary movements like walking or smiling. He has electrically stimulated different parts of the cortex and noted which parts of the body move as a result. The motor 'homunculus' (literally, little man) with his body parts of distorted size is an image which illustrates how the number of motor nerve cells serving different parts of the body is dependent upon the importance of those parts, rather than their physical size. Thus the face, whose movements are subtle and whose personal function is massive, has a much larger area of cortex assigned to it than does the back, which has a small, narrow cortical area in line with its much simpler postural and social function. Of course, only *we* can see this. There exists no 'real' motor homunculus in the motor cortex. All there is a complex architecture of motor nerve cells.

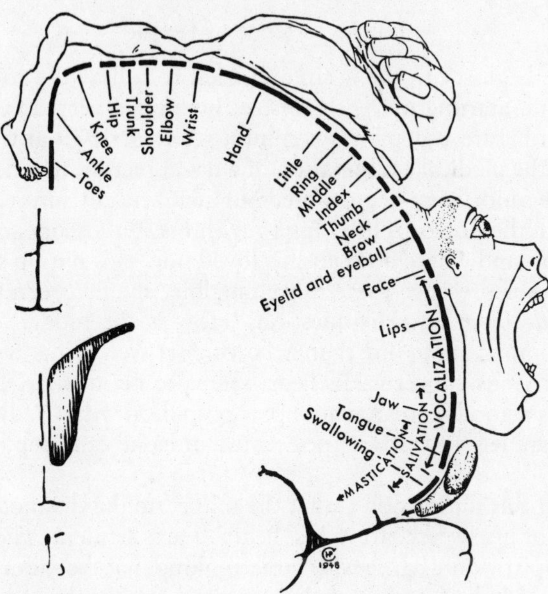

Figure 6: This is an image of a 'motor homunculus'. It shows the relative amount of cortex tissue devoted to controlling the movement of different parts of the body.

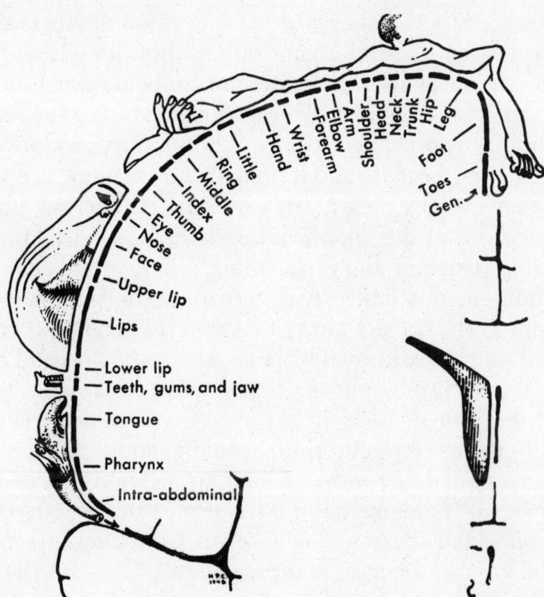

Figure 7: This is an image of a 'sensory homunculus', showing the amount of cortex devoted to the senses. It is similar but not identical to the motor homunculus.

The Experience of People

So far we have begun with the brain and tried to follow the route by which it ends up as mind. Starting out with *persons* involves a very different approach. The cartoon in Figure 8 depicts a common scene in 1939 at the beginning of World War 2: the medical examination of a naval recruit. Behind the scenes the story is that the sailor has a deep-rooted but anatomically imprecise notion that his heart, which the doctor is listening to with his stethoscope, is the seat of his loving emotions, and where he keeps his loved one – his pin-up girl (Gladys). In order to make her presence there more tangible, she has been tattooed on his chest, as an *aide memoire*. His question, 'How is she today?' shows that her health is more important to him than his own. Her well being, within him, is the object of his anxious concern. His heart seems to be in the right place, for he comes across as a good seaman whose preoccupation with Gladys indicates that in spite of the anxiety of warfare (or because of it) he can keep his mind on the right priorities.

The point of this illustration is that the sailor, unlike the motor cortex, does have a picture of his sweetheart in his 'heart'. He is sentient. The psychoanalyst or psychotherapist would agree with him, thinking that the sailor and others like him have some kind of image of their sweethearts in their minds extending deeply beyond conscious awareness. In this way, as well as in many other ways, man is an animal whose mind is comprised of meaning, symbols and representations which are built into him from the beginning of life.

Moreover it is not just as if they were projected on the surface of a computer screen. To some degree, the sailor can look within himself and envisage these images. They are active as they organise and motivate much of what he does. The sailor tends to choose women of a certain sort; he tends to experience their behaviour in familiar ways. The girl in the home port cannot be deleted from the surface of his mind because she is actually an integral, deeper part of it. In this sense 'she' may even be part of the cerebral architecture, but she is also, as are the representations of our significant early figures, wired in at the different level of personality structure and functioning.

The motor homunculus has a twin known as the sensory homunculus, an image which depicts the architecture of our senses. The two 'occupy' adjacent parts of the cerebral cortex known respectively as the *pre-* and the *post-central gyri*. Indeed, scattered throughout the virtual space of the brain there are several such images of the human body in the cerebral architecture. Psychoanalysis, which has a well-justified reputation for speaking about the unreceived traits of human nature, extended the view of human sexuality. Freud, for instance, described a number of fundamental modes of pleasure-seeking as basic motivations, and he connected these with the sensual qualities attached to different body zones – the mouth, the anus and the genitals.

This means that as neuropsychologists we should ask: how big are the genitals and how big the anal mucosal area of sensory homunculi? At different levels, these body images function as largely unacknowledged organisers of our expe-

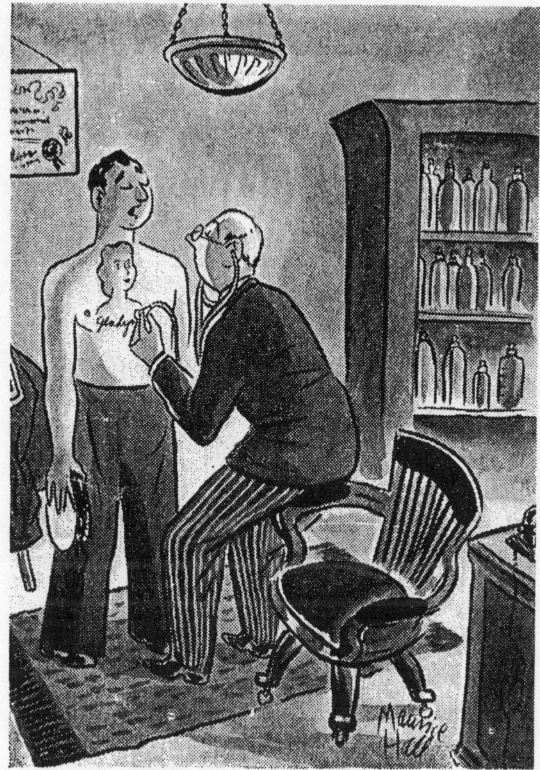

"How is she to-day, Doctor?"

Figure 8: This 1939 cartoon shows where the sailor thinks his emotions are.

rience of ourselves and of our views of other people and of our relationships. 'She' – the sailor's girl, for instance – is what we would call an internal object. What kind of state 'she' is in is really important. If her external counterpart proves to be unfaithful the sailor may get heartache and fall ill. If on the other hand she is felt to be well, loving and true the sailor will also feel well and probably fight well too. The cartoonist has managed to map all these ideas and many others in a condensed, compressed pictorial form. This is similar to the way that dreams can represent several condensed ideas with superb economy via a single image.

The Mind's Ability to Change Itself

Carefully observing what happens with and between people in therapeutic consultations, is a long-established way of investigating the impact of personal relationships and of emotionally meaningful communication upon mental functioning.

> Mr George is a thoughtful man who looks a little older than his fifty years. He is handsome but his face is lined. He has deep circles under his brown eyes. His expression carries a worn, exhausted look and his eyes are dull, reminding one of Primo Levi's description of the prisoners in Nazi concentration camps. Dividing them into 'the drowned and the saved', Levi wrote that those whose eyes remained alive still had some chance of surviving. The eyes of the 'drowned' became dull and vacant and they quickly died. The drowned had succumbed to the horror of what was happening, to the disease, starvation and the mass murder. Mr George's eyes seem to convey that he had looked on inner horrors and that his spirit seemed deeply fatigued. He seems to be closer to the drowned.
>
> As a young teenager in Canada, Mr George had a breakdown. In the run-up to this he damaged public telephones, though he has done nothing similar since. He genuinely loves learning and literature but is sometimes secretly drawn to pornography. He keeps this side of himself locked up. But in any personal situation that lacks structure he tends to get confused. For instance he concluded that a woman who happened to be ordinarily kind to him really loved him, and he wrote her unwanted letters. Mr George spoke woodenly and tended to disown any knowledge of these disturbed occasions. When the therapist doubted his puzzlement Mr George could acknowledge these disturbing impulses and sadly he described his attitude to women as 'ambivalent'. If Mr George felt close to a woman, mixed feelings of hope, love and cruelty were stirred up in him. The aim of some of those feelings was to disturb the woman's capacities: just as all those years ago with the telephones, it seemed his aim was to disrupt communications. Paradoxically, this tended to occur when he felt most isolated. At these times he longed for contact but something within him wouldn't admit to this need.

Mr George did not know what to do with this disturbed area of himself and he had no understanding of its meaning. He tried hard to suppress it by will power, turning the anger contained in his disturbance inwards, against himself and causing him to feel cold and bleak in a cold and bleak world. In this state, his mind felt to him like a barren ground, where thoughts felt like enormous weights marshalled against each other like armoured, slow-moving tanks. When he felt like this he turned to reading books on astrology. His attitude towards it ranged from belief to a more sophisticated view of astrology as a metaphor for human characteristics. He didn't want to push astrology down the therapist's throat, he said, but Saturn and Chiron were his determining planets. They epitomised hardness and coldness, he explained.

The therapist commented that in his effort to suppress his disturbed thoughts he had called upon the only mental force he had at his disposal. This was a severe effort as he was, in effect, laying himself under a siege of self-control. This led to an emotional famine. As a result he felt himself living in a bleak world with hard cold planets, rather than anything softer. These statements, which he felt were correct, visibly affected him. His previously immobile face softened and relaxed. He seemed more cheerful for a moment. He said that he also had the other good side of Saturn, which was a capacity for hard, dogged work.

Throughout his life he had applied himself in this way. This was true. For some significant moments moreover this side of himself became more available to him.

On Human Understanding and Misunderstanding

A therapist reacting effectively to another's state of mind will involve many different types of response. Understanding is not a passive or wet process, as is sometimes thought. It can lead to firmness, limits, confrontation as well as receptiveness. These different expressions of understanding are the vehicles for a therapeutic relationship but they are only refined, specialised versions of what occurs all the time in everyday life. In our daily lives we can be understood and responded to, or shut out or misunderstood. When some feeling of ours is recognised for what it is there can be enormous relief. This process of taking in everyday states of mind – satisfaction, dissatisfaction, anger, love, guilt, pain, bossiness or passivity – and responding effectively to them is what happens in the ordinary course of infantile and childhood development, when parents look after children within a framework made out of an inbuilt understanding of these feelings. People can have a tacit knowledge and a sympathy with what it is like to be a person, a parent, a child or a baby and know when to be firm and when to be more tolerant.

This kind of relationship is crucial to the child's growing mind. Through it, the child is enabled to develop its own working capacity to make use of the powerful feeling states of infancy, leading to its own capacity for intuitive understanding. In the process, the primitive but vital feelings that are characteristic of infancy are modified and eventually become the essential horsepower of the adult personality.

These working capacities come in very particular forms. They are the internalised images of parents and caregivers in their daily working mode, but they are also embellished, coloured by the feelings of the infantile imagination. Thus they may well sometimes have a fantastic aspect. This is how Mr George's parents had come to seem to him like cold planets in lonely parts of the solar system. His heavy hard feelings led to thinking which was turgid and bleak. This state could shift with the help of understanding, to a form of mental functioning that was not only more positive but also enabled him to think more freely. However, this shift tended to be temporary. There was also a side to Mr George that hated mental connections. Whenever some thoughts came together in a way that might be productive, a part of him felt inclined to destroy them. Throughout his life this problem had affected his mind very powerfully.

These facts have crucial consequences. Another person's understanding of our state of mind can produce important transformations in that state. In early development these meaningful relationships are essential to the proper development of the mind and, as we now know, of the physical make-up of the brain. When things go wrong in early relationships, the consequences include an increase in the power and crudeness of feelings, resulting in an unmodified hostility and greater destructiveness. Crudely repeated patterns of disturbed feelings and impulses possess a raw unmetabolised quality that make it very difficult for those that have them to sustain their relationships, talents, life prospects, creativity or working capacity. These disturbances result in a more precarious capacity to maintain a coherent life structure. In addition the capacity to think and reason, especially under emotional pressure, is already affected. People with difficulties like these may need more understanding and support from others throughout their lives.

The Mind's Laboratory

When physiologists are trying to discover how the body works they investigate – sometimes in a laboratory – for example, the functioning of the heart under varying conditions – at rest or at effort. For psychotherapists and psychoanalysts, intensive several-times-a-week analytic treatment is the equivalent of the physiologist's laboratory. As well it enables the patient to tolerate in himself a level of openness not usually possible in less frequent treatments.

In analytic treatments (which are 4 or 5 times a week) many surprising patterns of interaction between beliefs, illusions, the emergence of primitive feelings and the capacity to think freely can be observed, and altered. These changes can give us powerful insights into the complex and sometimes surprisingly strange way that the mind is built. Understanding these can show what type of emotions and thoughts lie at the roots of particular behaviour. This can lead us to enquire what kind of brain is necessary to produce a mind like this.

> Mr Dillon spoke of looking forward to Christmas, of decorating the tree and of seeing his sister's children enjoy themselves. The way he spoke had a carefully organised quality, in which the analyst consistently felt he was being scripted to say something already anticipated by the patient. He felt he was being presented with a trap, and sometimes felt rather like an animal approaching a strange piece of ground that might hide a camouflaged pit. Thus in contrast to the festive content of the talk, the atmosphere in the room was tense and watchful.
>
> The day before the patient had spoken of the Iraq bombing. He had been frightened that Saddam might covertly introduce germ or chemical weapons into the U.K. Was it not also surprising that in the very midst of an air raid on Baghdad, British and American journalists should be there, filming close-up with the permission of the Iraqis? This corresponded closely to the situation in the treatment, where there was also a covert surveillance and carefully controlled and manipulated watchfulness. In his everyday life the patient was always careful to look good and fearful of anything uncontrolled emerging from him.
>
> The analyst spoke of these matters; he had done so many times before. His comment was met with silence – a very long silence. Again this was not unusual. The patient stayed quiet often for 10, 20, 40 minutes, usually trying in this way to pressure the analyst to speak. When the analyst did speak, the patient regarded this as his withdrawal of the previous comment. The patient then carried on just as before, looking good but very fearful of letting anything out. Often, sometimes for good reasons, sometimes because she could find no better or more effective response, the analyst would speak and the patient's *status quo* would be preserved.
>
> On this particular occasion the analyst resisted the pressure to speak, but felt

uncomfortable doing so, and was guilty, annoyed, frustrated, and fed-up by turns. Tolerating these feelings and sticking at the task was not particularly easy. Was it all perhaps in the analyst's imagination, was she making too much of it? All the while – half an hour and more – the patient was lying perfectly motionless, indeed unnaturally so. At certain moments the analyst wondered if the patient had fallen asleep.

Gradually and intermittently through these doubts the analyst began to relate how committed the patient was to this type of controlling reaction. How, through one means or another, he was determined to hold to his way of getting by, which involved the collusion of others. He left a lot of the worry about the children to his wife. He knew that he did this, but it was as much for the principle of maintaining this state of mind as for wishing to avoid the children's troubles. He seemed to feel that he didn't have to acknowledge large parts of his life, upbringing and preoccupations and that he shouldn't have to integrate these fully in his life. The analyst realised just how far the patient would go to maintain this principle, and just how many boundaries he would ignore. This included going against many of his own values.

Then again this was followed by another wave of doubt and irritation. Eventually the analyst considered that the patient did not believe that the power of this side of him could be anything less than complete. Herein lay one of the biggest dangers to his future happiness and stability: his ignoring this side of himself also led him to ignore other important realities. Maturation and growth were permanently deferred. When in the session the analyst had lived with these thoughts for a while, some of his previous discomfort faded because he felt more sure that what he had perceived was very important for the success and safety of this patient's life. It was usually impossible to talk to Mr Dillon about these matters without appearing to be nagging him to be different. At this moment, however, a much easier emotional climate prevailed. There was less tension in the room. Mr Dillon could understand the way he was behaving.

This illustration shows how necessary it was for the analyst to struggle in order to be able, at first only gradually and fleetingly, to have a realisation about this patient's way of relating. The pressure towards speaking was to be a way round having to experience and put up with something very uncomfortable – the pressure exerted by the patient and the analyst's own reaction to this.

For the analyst, her realisation possessed that airborne quality that is characteristic of thought. This type of thought does not possess any quality of leaden physical weight but it is still substantial. It liberates the individual from the influence of external or internal coercion. To arrive at a thought of this type carries with it a characteristic satisfaction. It is not only a matter of words but of thought. As usual, Shakespeare understood: 'words without thoughts do not to Heaven go'.

Thought and Thinking

In the example, the analyst was using a carefully informed self-restraint in order to understand what was happening with Mr Dillon. The analyst resisted measures to bring an immediate relief to some uncomfortable awkward feelings and gradually a realisation arrived in her mind which concerned a very important problem of the patient's. This is a familiar occurrence in many kinds of intellectual endeavour. Experiences like these – the way that thoughts seem to come partly unbidden and partly as a result of what seems like fruitless mental work and preoccupation – have led some to adopt the idea that it is not thinking which produces thoughts but thoughts that call forth thinking.

The problem then is to deal with or cope with thoughts that can be at one and the same time amongst the most evanescent and the most enduring of human products. Some people cannot cope with certain thoughts and as a result in one way or another destroy or negate their mind. Mr Dillon believed unconsciously as well as consciously that he should always feel properly put together, and that in the final analysis he would always be able to neglect important issues in his life without there being any adverse consequences. He would always be loved and looked after whatever he didn't do. When he began to realise that matters were not as he believed he felt very disorientated. Sometimes, against his conscious wishes, he made strenuous efforts to restore the previous situation. At this time he became manipulative. When this didn't succeed he became angry and affronted.

This sequence of events – passing from unnoticed beliefs to action in order to maintain the belief when it is felt to be under threat – is universal. When the belief in question finally breaks down, feelings of great force can be released. These sequences can indicate to the analyst how the mind is organised. It is not really sensible to ask naïvely where in the brain beliefs are encoded, where thoughts occur, which neuro-system generates such powerful, primitive feelings, and how it is that all these things are so inter-related in a meaningful way? And yet at some point in the future we may be able to pose these questions in different terms, understanding the systems which 'produce' beliefs and how beliefs 'produce' brain systems.

Sometimes when fundamental beliefs break down, the force and power of the primitive, infantile feelings released are completely beyond the individual's capacity to control them. It may then be necessary for these feelings – which can include pain, anger, vulnerability, envy – to be worked through with the analyst by a protracted process of understanding the inter-personal meaning of these feelings, so that the patient can reach a new adjustment to reality.

Some personalities may have great and rather surprising difficulty in coping with certain realisations. The experiences that arise out of the intrinsic separateness and otherness of other people are nearly always difficult for the human mind. That is one reason why so many poems are concerned with the subject of loss. Poems are a way of synthesising visual images in verbal metaphors; the musical, rhythmic aspects of language are brought to bear upon experiences that are intrinsically discordant. Poems change one's state of mind. Absence and abstinence, both elements of loss, seem to be important parts of the achievement of true thought. Proust understood that memory and imagination have to be sought actively, too, by mental effort. However, we often cannot just summon up what we desire from our minds. We may fail to call up memories. The thoughts more often than not will not come. When we try to use our minds we are drawn to do anything but that. It is necessary to stick at it. Yet to make the effort is clearly an important but not sufficient part of the process.

This is a form of work, a kind of mental exercise, whose results can be compared to the results of physical exercise. Exercise and training do not cause muscles to come into being, but they do lead to muscle growth, increased power and dexterity. Using one's mind does not cause the mind, but it does lead to mental growth and development. When the mind has to struggle to understand itself, others and the nature of the world and our relation to it, it strengthens the mind. In the early months and years of childhood it is the mental and emotional functioning of the mother and father that have a powerful influence upon the child's mind and upon brain development, but if we do not use our minds, there is, as with our muscles, a corresponding waste. States of prolonged stupor, the prolonged avoidance of difficult states of mind, of painful conflicts, of the replacement of what should be in the mind by physical action, or by somatisation, will lead to an atrophy of mental capacities.

The Answer?

Posing a question is often of more interest than the answer. In Douglas Adams' *The Hitch-Hiker's Guide to the Galaxy* the super-computer was asked the answer to the world, the universe and the meaning of life. After light years of deliberation it came up with the answer, '42'. In this chapter the starting question was, 'What causes the mind?' As a result of our enquiries we know some of the ways the brain causes the mind. We also know that other human beings and their mental activities are very important in the development of our brains and our capacity to think. We know that just as we seem to be able to initiate movement by voluntary thought, we also can make our minds work, although with effort and to a limited degree. As well, in some ill-understood way, we can destroy them, especially when we are exposed to storms of more primitive emotion.

But we are not yet at the point where direct translations can be made between neuroscience and psychology. Basic questions are still undecided. Some argue that the entire idea of mind is an illusion arising out of our language and the way we think. As we understand these matters more clearly, they argue, we will no longer think along such lines. Others regard mind as an epiphenomenon which the brain happens to generate but which has no intrinsic function or efficacy. Still others consider that the brain is fundamentally different from the computers we know today and that some as yet completely unknown domain of physics is crucial to explain the phase transition from brain to mind. The kind of virtual events that seem to occur at the quantum level have been suggested as a possible candidate for the physical basis of mental events. When we begin to get answers to these questions and the biotechnology that will go with them, what will we do with this knowledge? What impact will these discoveries have upon us?

The Copernican discovery that the Earth is not the centre of the Universe was joined after two centuries by the knowledge that we were not a special creation, a seven-day wonder, but the product of mutation and Darwinian natural selection. We arose from our primate ancestors. At first this idea was considered to be blasphemous; it was a blow to our status as a special and unique creature. Now, after more than a century, we tend to feel comforted by knowing how close we are to our primate relatives. We have realised that we do not have to be the evolutionary alpha and omega of it all. It is possible that we will process this future knowledge of the origin of the mind in a similar way and that it will lead to marvellous things, but that does depend upon what it is and on the use we make of it. However, one does hope that the answer is not 42.

6

Love

There is a bawdy poem by Pushkin telling the story of Tsar Nikita, all of whose forty daughters were born without genitalia. Wishing to put this sorry state of affairs right, the Tsar sent a messenger to the local witch to ask for help. Obligingly, the witch packed up forty sets of female parts in a box, and sent the messenger off with them. He was filled with curiosity. What was in this mysterious box? He shook it but there was no noise. He sniffed at it – and detected a deeply familiar and irresistible smell. Overcome, he opened the box – and to his dismay out flew the forty little female parts, up into the trees like so many birds. He sat gloomily down by the side of the road, aware of what would befall him if he returned to the Tsar empty-handed. He was in despair until an old peasant woman came down the road and asked him what the trouble was. Simple, she said: all you have to do is get out your penis ... and at once the forty female parts fluttered back down to him and were easily caught.

Clearly, at one level, this tale is nonsense. Yet equally clearly it is about something entirely true. The powerful animal attraction of male for female and female for male that is capable of overriding all sorts of more rational processes – such as caution, prudence, duty, everything we might think of as 'better judgement' – is immediately recognisable, not just generically in man, but in ourselves. Thus 'Tsar Nikita' is, perhaps unusually, not a love story but a story about the importance of sex and sexuality, and the irresistible attraction of each sex for the other. The point is made so wittily about the attraction's being between male and female parts, rather than whole individuals, that we know it is a fable about sexual passion rather than love. Love is something that takes place between two people, not two sets of genitalia. In fact we tend to refer to individuals who are interested only in the conquest of another's genitalia as animals – and it is one of the great strengths and charms of Pushkin's poem that he can write about man's animal nature without its being brutish or crude. (Perhaps our own Chaucer is one of the very few English poets who can do the same.)

We are in fact *embodied persons*. It is not accurate simply to say that we 'have' bodies. It is more that we are our bodies, and they are us, with all the animality that that implies: bodies whose shape, structure and potential derive from our genetic inheritance, and equally drives, impulses and reflexes that arise from our physiology, our neuroanatomy – our biology. Much behaviour that we see in higher mammalian orders, particularly in the higher primates, exists equally in ourselves: sex, rivalry, territoriality, hierarchical structures. At the level of the basic emotions, even those that are less overt and obvious, there may not be that much difference between us and our primate cousins.

The embodiment of our person – both the duality and the connectedness of body and mind – is seen vividly in the arena of sexual behaviour. And it is here that Pushkin's story is seen to be emotionally as well as literally fanciful, for we know that, unlike most of the rest of the animal kingdom, sexual behaviour in humans is rarely that simple or straightforward, uncomplicatedly concerned with the irresistible and delightful union of sexual parts.

With the development of mind in human evolution emerged a feature of our behaviour that affects everything we perceive or do or feel: the powerful in-built drive to attribute meaning. The act of sex is no exception. The briefest of sexual acts is charged with fantasy, meaning and significance. Freud pointed out that in every act of sexual intercourse there are in fact more than two people in the bed, since the coupling will include some version of an imagined act involving aspects of both parental couples. It is the complex and varied meanings we attribute to sexual feelings and the sexual act that allows for the fullest expression of that range of emotions we categorise as 'love'.

Sex, Love and Hate

And not only love. The act of sex is just as capable of being used as a vehicle for hatred.

> A young woman who had mixed and mistrustful feelings about men had managed to sustain a relationship with a man. They had had a child together and gradually she became increasingly attached to and fond of him. However, during sex she found herself overwhelmed with feelings of anger towards him. Sex seemed to have become the place in which she could experience and know about her hostility towards men, particularly towards one on whom she was dependent, even if its expression was muted. She said, 'It's not I can't do it – my body works, but I'm just full of anger. My mind's full of hate'.

In this example, we can see how the act of sex stirs up primitive feelings of rage as well as love, and acts as a vehicle for their expression. In most acts of sex there is a degree of ambivalence. The sexual act lends itself to the expression of fantasy, both conscious and unconscious, much of which can get itself enacted – either lovingly through tenderness and mutual pleasure, or through violence, perversion, sadism and masochism, which are no less to do with hatred and hostility because they also happen to be linked up with sexual release.

Hamlet is a play about ambivalence, and (amongst much else) about a son's feelings about his parents' sexuality. Hamlet is appalled by his mother's remarriage to her dead husband's brother within a month of the father's funeral. He has enormous difficulty in reconciling the animal lusts he can picture so vividly in his mother with his intensely idealising and romantic feelings for her. He is tormented by having to recognise the reality of her sexual feelings. He adores his mother and he hates her. His tender feelings for the innocent girl Ophelia become contaminated with this enforced recognition of the power of sex: she too is a woman and if she marries 'Be thou as chaste as ice, as pure as snow, thou shalt not escape calumny. Get thee to a nunnery. Go, farewell!' In fact, the recognition and the toleration of ambivalence towards the loved person is one of the hallmarks of a real love; real that is as opposed to a childlike dependence on, or a wish for exclusive possession of or control of that person. Hamlet loved his mother with the ferocious imperiousness of an only son. This did not make for an uneventful adolescence and a settled domesticity. Instead we have a piece of sublime writing about love, hate and human nature.

Hamlet's passionate feelings were but one kind of love. In the following clinical extract from a once-weekly therapy group in which the members came from several different cultures, two young women were talking about their own views of love. They were listened to intently by the others present.

> Nicola had had a damaged and deprived childhood, which had included her being passed from pillar to post, but since she had become a member of her culture's religious community she had found some of the stability and encouragement and status so missing during her childhood. Hesitantly, she told the group that a few weeks earlier a young man within the community had approached her, telling her he had been noticing her for a while, and would like to ask her permission to court her. She felt quite stirred by his request. It seemed to offer her something she had never felt would be possible – a tender and mutually caring relationship with a man, and the possibility of family life. She told the group that after much thought she had decided to say yes, and that over the next months they would try to get to know each other better until they could make a joint decision about marriage. He had been pleased with her answer, and had at once told his family the good news. She broke into a smile at this point with a mixture of modesty and great radiance. Yet for Rose, a fiery and outspoken Welsh girl, there seemed to be something missing. 'You don't say you love him! Don't you desire him sexually? Does he make you long to make love with him?' She ran her hands through her long hair almost impatiently, as though the cautious, measured procedure that Nicola was describing left her unbearably frustrated. Where was the passion that was, for her, the essence of love?

Two further kinds of love – the first is mingled with hope, consisting of something that might grow between two people as they gradually come to know and trust each other; the second is concerned with love as an elemental force of nature, overpowering the individual – and even the individual's judgement – with its imperatives. To some extent these views reflect the natures as well as the culture and experience of the young women concerned. As well, they reflect something of love itself, not least its immense variety of form. For Nicola, love could exist independently of sex, although she acknowledged she would like to have children one day. For Rose, love and sex were inextricable, and sex was for her a primary way of expressing love. This exchange also shows the capacity of love itself to stir us to our roots, to grip us with its intensity, to prize it far above other experiences. Love can be animal or vegetable, tropical or temperate, deciduous or evergreen, carnivorous or vegetarian. Each is a metaphor for a version of love, but just as all are part of the natural world, so does all love derive from some similarity of emotional process. The enquiry as to what that might be is the focus of this chapter.

Falling in Love for the First Time

The inability to love, or to find lasting love, is what drives many people into therapy. Although the original Don Giovanni, with his dazzling catalogue of 2,064 conquests from every country in Europe, never felt himself to be in need of a consultation with a psychoanalyst, there are many compulsive seducers who are puzzled and even made unhappy by their inability to love – to want, or to be able, to stay with or to love any of their conquests. No sooner have they been achieved than the urgent need for closeness is replaced by an equally frantic fear of being trapped. Don Giovanni, 'far from going to hell at the conclusion of the opera ... is in it from the start.'

In order to examine those internal processes (and those external factors) that result in the ability to love; to wonder about the difference between *falling in love*, and *loving*; to see the way in which love can be replaced by hate; to look at what happens when a loved person goes away, or dies, we need to return to the first experiences of love. To re-evoke the memory of a first love is to conjure up a special state of mind – tender, amused, wistful, longing, dreamy. That first love is felt to have been both ecstatic and also impossible. How could such a feeling ever have survived reality, and the exigencies of everyday living? And in fact, as the cool statistics bear out, although some first loves evolve into long-lasting relationships, that intense, all-absorbing and deeply romantic love is not *on its own* a sufficient base on which to build something as valuable, honest, trusting, tolerant and durable as a life-long partnership or marriage.

Yet we continue to prize that state of Being in Love and seek it out as though it were the peak of human experience, the best that life can offer. In fact, it is sometimes felt to be synonymous with life itself: lovers say they have never before felt so fully alive. The state of being in love has an ineffable – unutterable or inexpressible – quality, and yet paradoxically we never stop trying to express the inexpressible, whether in words, or music or in paint on canvas.

Moreover, that instantly recognisable and highly prized state of mind is apparently universal, and independent of culture: it is in other words essentially *human*. Its roots are as biological as those of sex, part of the biological endowment of the human animal. Amazons, Eskimos, Europeans, Asians and Africans all know about being 'in love' and variously lay a hand over the heart and sigh or smile or joke or gnash their teeth according to experience. Bronislaw Malinowski, in his anthropological study of the Trobriand Islanders published in 1929, writes, 'Love is a passion to the Melanesian as to the European, and torments mind and body to a greater or lesser extent; it leads to many an impasse, scandal, or tragedy; more rarely, it illuminates life and makes the heart expand and overflow with joy'.

Yet that first experience of falling in love, no less extraordinary for being universal, has had crucial precursors in every human animal. A year of observation of a mother with a new infant has become part of any good training in psychoanalysis, or psychoanalytic psychotherapy. The trainee is usually someone already qualified in psychiatry, psychology or social work. The trainee visits the family's home once a week, during the course of the family's ordinary daily life, and watches and remembers and writes up (after each observation is over) what he or she has observed. If the circumstances are favourable, and things are going well between mother and baby, the trainee will see day by day and week by week a relationship which includes the most profound and formative elements of human experience.

Mother and baby gaze at each other, drink each other in, murmur to each other, light up at the sight of each others' raptly attentive faces. The baby appears to experience nothing less than a state of bliss when full of milk and held in the mother's arms close to her body, a state in which both the physical and the emotional needs seem met by someone who gets as much pleasure and deep satisfaction from giving to the baby as the baby does in receiving. This, for the baby, is the first falling in love. Although infants come into the world with some pre-natal experience, they also have a need for a mother, or caretaker, who can be central for them in the first months and years of childhood, without making too much of a religion of it. This experience contributes significantly to the conviction in later life that there is someone out there who is 'right' for you, someone special with whom it will be rewarding and mutually satisfying to build a life together.

Moreover, this experience of being loved and cared for by a good and consistent parent or caretaker forms the basis for, and the steady centre of the baby's rapidly developing personality. And if the baby's attempts to centre itself around the mother, or to make the mother better when she seems exhausted or depressed cannot be responded to by the mother, then there will be difficulties later on when that baby becomes a child, and then an adult. In other words, in order to be able to love it is a great help to have been loved. The individual's early experiences as a baby are active and alive within his or her own adult life. To achieve a relationship in which the emotional and spiritual experience of love can be joined with its physical expression is both the outcome of good early experience, and also in turn the cause of it in others.

The Roots of Love in Infancy and Childhood

These buried links, usually far beyond the reach of conscious memory, can sometimes be seen when the young man first catches sight of the girl with whom he falls in love. 'Falling' of course suggests there is something helpless about the experience, that it is beyond conscious control. The girl at whom the young man gazes so raptly may be at about the same age his mother was when she first held her infant son's gaze. And it is striking how often a boy will choose a girl with hair or eyes the colour his mother's were, or a smile or a wit or a temper that resembles hers. One might equally expect a girl to choose a boy resembling her young father, and often this is palpably the case.

Equally often it becomes apparent that women, quite as much as men, also long for some aspects of the care that mothers give their young babies. Advertising makes this explicit: pamper yourself, they exhort – which translates as *mother yourself* or *baby yourself*: 'treat yourself with the care a mother gives her baby'. And young women who choose a 'baby doll' way of dressing and behaving may be quite as much in need of maternal care as male sexual attention. Often the first is hidden behind or even inside the second, sometimes not very successfully. Marilyn Monroe's own tragic childhood may have contributed to her powerful capacity to get certain kinds of men to mother her before her terrible neediness drove them away. The kind of hostility such women are capable of evoking from other women may not only be a product of adult sexual rivalry – there may also be an unconscious evocation of the hostility and even rivalry that existed in the original mother which led to the kind of deprivation enacted by the child-woman.

Some kinds of homosexual love too include elements of the mother-infant relationship. The man may seek for someone who resembles himself when younger, and then offer the kind of love or care he felt his mother gave him as a boy. Freud writes of Leonardo da Vinci's pupils that, 'He treated them with kindness and consideration, looked after them, and when they were ill nursed them himself, just as his own mother might have tended him.' Since it is then a version of the self that is loved, this is a kind of love with strong narcissistic (self-referential) elements to it. In 'As Sweet' Wendy Cope writes wittily of this state of affairs between a man and a woman:

It's all because we're so alike -
Twin souls, we two.
We smile at the expression, yes,
And know it's true.

I told the shrink. He gave our love
A different name.
But he can call it what he likes –
It's still the same.

I long to see you, hear your voice,
My narcissistic object-choice.

Subsequent loves tend to have about them (though there's no guarantee) less of the irrational, the delusional, the helpless sense of 'falling in' to something, but there is still a continuity of the most significant elements of that first love between mother and baby, and it appears to remain a strong determinant of all later love choices.

Early love is the source of not only the most constructive but also the most destructive elements in any close love relationship. As the watchful trainee quickly learns, the infant not only experiences sublime love for his mother, but is also shaken by storms of primitive rage and hatred. It is not of course hatred in the same sense that adults have such feelings. In part it may be an expression of the baby's constitution – of an impulse to push against the world he finds himself in, to pit himself against *the way things are*, against reality. It may also be a recognition of and a response to that reality, both internal and external: the breast is not there when it is wanted or there is a stomach ache which cannot be assuaged.

These things can feel to the baby like suddenly having a very depriving mother, or a cruel attacking one, who must be fought or protested to violently. In order not to be overwhelmed with uncertainty, mistrust and confusion – which would make it very hard to evolve a mind which could sort, categorise and make clear assessments – the baby has to make sense of these powerful contradictory feelings of love and hate for the same crucially important figure. To do this the baby separates out these two kinds of feeling from each other, and correspondingly creates in his or her own mind two entirely different kinds of figure towards whom these feelings are directed. So far as the baby is concerned, there is not just one mother, there are two – one a good loving figure towards whom the baby can feel tenderness and gratitude; the other a cruel and depriving figure for whom the baby feels rage and hatred.

Around the time of weaning, changes can be seen in the way the baby relates to the mother. There seems to be some not very clearly formulated recognition that these two sets of feelings, love and hate, are in fact felt for the same person. The baby becomes a rather more troubled small creature, and when things go well, becomes more aware of his or her own effect upon the mother. Babies can even be seen (during the kind of observations described above) to exercise restraint, to inhibit the full expression of their own wishes out of concern for the mother's own state. These kinds of changes are an essential basis for the adult's own eventual capacity to remain in touch with the state and the needs of the partner, and eventually to hold back the uninhibited expression of his or own wishes out of consideration for the other.

Idealisation

All this raises an obvious question. If this profound relationship between mother and baby contains within it both love and hate, and since this primary experience with the mother is so significant in influencing not only the ability to fall in love at all, but also later choices of love objects, why then is *falling in love* so markedly devoid of ambivalence? So wholly positive, so apparently free of negativity? Is it really just a question of finding *the* right partner, as magazines seem to suggest: a partner so right that the negativity is never, and could never be, evoked?

Reality is hard and unyielding. The ecstatic certainty about the ineffable perfection of the beloved grows out of a heady stuff, *idealisation*. The desire for the ideal is a strong psychological force. That first love between mother and baby has something genuinely ideal about it, with the mother protecting the baby from the exigencies of everyday life. Out of it grows our capacity for our later more mature relations. Yet in adults, idealisation is a process of assertion rather than of actuality. It involves the exaggeration and elevation of the good attributes of the beloved to a pitch where it becomes impossible to see anything less than the ideal – anything just ordinarily good for instance – or to acknowledge less than ideally loving feelings felt towards that person. The beloved becomes an angel, not a person. The tales of Romeo and Juliet, Tristan and Isolde, Lancelot and Guinevere, all express the great conviction and the immense seductive power of that kind of idealised love.

'. . . and bloody well stay there!'

Figure 9: Idealisation is a precarious state of affairs.

Idealisation is the adult version of one side of the baby's split feelings for its mother, carried to a pitch where the possibility of anything else, not only now but ever, is denied. Perhaps this is why older, sadder and wiser writers have likened being in love to a delusional state. Here is Shakespeare, speaking through the figure of Rosalind in 'As You Like It'.

> 'Love is merely a madness, and I tell you, deserves as well a dark house and a whip as madmen do; and the reason why they are not so punished and cured is, that the lunacy is so ordinary, that the whippers are in love too.'

And a similar thought from a woman who has experienced both love and madness.

> If falling in love were not such a common experience, and if doctors in their private lives were not also subject to it, it might already have become a text-book subject for psychiatrists to study. For it is the one universally prevalent form that delusional disturbance takes. This is not meant as a flippant or cynical comment. Falling in love is a wonderful experience. But some psychotic experiences are indescribably wonderful too.... Anyone who has tried to reason with a person who is in love can confirm that one of the most obvious features of the condition is lack of insight ... that it is highly irrational does not detract from its real and realistic purpose ... This is not the only violently irrational condition that is rightly taken for granted as a part of normal life. Parental love of all sorts, and maternal love especially, is in its first awakening highly delusional too. What we need is to understand the meaning and purpose of the delusions, and to learn how and why these should be adjusted to the realities of external life.
>
> Morag Coate, *Beyond All Reason* (1964)

This writer is raising some interesting points. The first is about the apparent irrationality of love, its delusional nature. The overriding quality of the experience is perhaps linked with her second point concerning the value and function of this necessary illusion, or its biological relevance. If the human species is to be successful in biological terms, it must reproduce itself with no fits and starts in the process. The sexual passion that usually (although not inevitably) accompanies falling in love takes care of the process of conception; the maternal passion that follows childbirth makes more likely the infant's survival. This may sound like a crude or unromantic view of the ineffable, but it is a point of view that can authorise and licence the immense pleasures of love.

Equally, there may be a biological underpinning for the way in which adolescents almost invariably manage to be *hateful*, both to their parents and in their parents' eyes for some part of their teenage years. The separation between parent and child necessary for the child to be able to grow up, and eventually to move out to create a family of his or her own, is a necessary part of life – and it is also deeply difficult for both sides, since it involves a real loss. The notorious ghastliness of adolescents may help the process of separation, since it allows for the eventual separation to be accompanied by a certain amount of relief and satisfaction, as well as of sadness for the end of the pleasures of the childhood.

The third issue raised by the writer is more problematical. When she talks of the wonderfulness of certain psychotic experiences she is almost certainly talking about *mania*. And this points to another feature of the roots of the 'in love' state, since it can carry with it some of the inexhaustible confidence, some of the joyful optimism, of a manic state. A manic defence can operate against underlying aggression, or the fear of loss, indeed against any anxiety which might diminish the 'ideal' nature of the relationship. Idealisation always indicates the feared presence of something very much less than ideal. The man who 'adores women' and 'puts them on a pedestal' may be struggling to deal with his envy and hostility towards them, and with his wish to control their behaviour and thoughts in an omnipotent way.

A young woman who worked in a gymnasium as a personal trainer had a perfect figure and a lively, bouncy manner and had no difficulty in finding boyfriends with whom she had a lot of fun. However, none of them felt quite right to her until one day she met a man whom she said 'adored' her. As evidence, he would come to the gym and watch her while she ran her classes. In fact he would never take his eyes off her. He bought her presents every day, telephoned her frequently from work, and insisted on paying every time they went out together. At first this seemed ideal. Gradually it became restricting. He did not want her to go out with her girl-friends any more, and questioned her about the conversations she had with clients in her gym. 'If he's so jealous, he must really love me', she told herself. However, she began to resort to secrecy and lies to evade his persistent and increasingly aggressive questioning and the rows that would ensue over conversations he did not like. At one point he threatened violence, and quite suddenly she recognised that his behaviour had very little to do with love, and a great deal more to do with hostility and a tyrannical control. She ended the relationship. [Pathological jealousy is always a worrying sign in a partner and may indicate a need for professional help.]

Yet the knowledge that, in spite of our better judgement, we are all susceptible to being adored without apparent ambivalence, even idealised in that joyfully optimistic way, remains a powerful weapon in a seducer's armoury:

A good-looking man who came into treatment with the complaint that his life had no meaning had reached his middle years without getting married. However, he had seduced a quite phenomenal number of women with a finely honed and repetitive technique. He would 'target' a woman, appearing to be thunderstruck with her special qualities, gazing raptly at her in a single-minded way until, overcome with the intoxicating sense of being a highly prized and needed person, she gave herself over to him in bed. Shortly after his goal had been achieved the entranced gaze was switched off, he became bored and dissatisfied, and left in search of the next ideal object. The woman was left distressed, puzzled and wounded.

There were many features in this man's history which contributed to his behaviour, which was not by any means as simple-mindedly cruel as it sounds from this account. He had been given away by his mother to her own childless sister when the baby's father had abandoned her. When the little boy was three and a half years old, his mother had returned to take him back. From then on he did not see again the aunt he had thought of as 'mother' until he was adult.

This man's powerfully seductive behaviour showed his great need for women, but it also enabled him to punish them for evoking that need. Expressing his buried fear and hatred of them, it also contained the hope for something that could, perhaps after treatment, turn out differently. The point of the example is to show the susceptibility of the human being, man or woman, to ostensibly single-minded adoration, linking with the power of that early experience at the breast. This particular seducer, and all other such experts, are addressing and flattering the narcissistic susceptibilities in the other, the longing to be loved and desired above all others, however unrealistic this may be.

The Future of Idealisation

However reality is not as bleak as these two vignettes might seem to imply. Loving or being loved is not an all-or-nothing affair. Our loved ones feel special to us, and this implies *some* degree of idealisation – of the infant, of the parent, of the child, of the lover, of the partner. It may be an integral part of lasting love, and not to be derided. A modified form of idealisation is the way we mark out a very few people in our worlds who are different for us and deeply special, whom we have invested with special properties, and for whom we will make special efforts. It can be thought of as the glow that is left after the first blaze of passionate conviction as to the absolute perfection of the loved object has given way to something more tempered by reality. It is also perhaps part of the basis of family loyalty.

The everyday reality of even a loving relationship will for most people be accompanied by an ordinary degree of ambivalence. Babies cry when one is exhausted, lovers and partners can become irritable and demanding, or they go away when one most wants them to be present, children can be maddening with their insatiability for more sweets, bigger toys, or new sports gear. To recognise that one's loved ones are not invariably ideal or loveable is the adult version of the baby's recognition that it is one and the same mother who is both loved and hated. Idealisation perhaps develops into an especial tolerance, even fondness, for the vagaries of that particular mortal, something that manages to recognise their individuality, and hence difference, and yet continues to sustain respect and affection, loyalty and allegiance.

This is a good outcome of the initial blaze of 'falling in love'. There are others which are less constructive or happy. Some couples, whether heterosexual or homosexual, may not be able to tolerate the emergence of reality and hence ambivalence into their blissful union, and experience it as an unwelcome intrusion, even a bitter loss. One or both may then seek to recapture that early experience with other partners, and the pattern may be repeated endlessly. Since one of the intoxicating features of being in love is that of being adored, as well as adoring, the more self-regarding the partners, the less each can tolerate being found less than perfect in the other's eyes. 'If you don't love me *the way I am*, then go and find someone else', is the cry, sometimes overlooking the fact that 'the way I am' at that particular moment may be a pain in the neck and not in the least loveable.

There are no simple explanations for this kind of behaviour. It can indicate neurotic injury – *how dare you think I am not marvellous?* Alternatively it can be a painful expression of dislike for one's own behaviour, an inarticulate plea for a reprieve from the partner whom one feels one has treated rather less than well.

Other couples manage to sustain a version of an ideal 'being in love' through an implicit bargain with each other: you agree that I am perfect and wholly sufficient for your needs whatever they may be and I in return will adore only you for ever: the flawed or inadequate or unreasonable or nasty people are those outside this perfect union. These are the pairs that seem to their ordinarily squabbling and more-or-less managing friends and acquaintances to be the perfect couple. A great deal of that couple's envy and rivalry *with each other*, kept at bay by the implicit and unspoken bargain, is projected into the outside world. Everyone is made to feel that their own relationships are pretty humdrum and unromantic in comparison with The Perfect Couple's set-up.

What then causes the collapse, since such arrangements tend to break down sooner or later? Usually it is that the bargain cannot be sustained. One such marriage ran into trouble because the husband could not tolerate the wife's wish to go out to work once the children were at school – he felt supplanted, inferior and lacking in value, and in his internal world it felt to him like an infidelity. He turned to a relationship with another woman for solace. Neither partner could then forgive the other, not only for the mutual 'infidelities', but also for the public betrayal of the perfect marriage. In this case what was being concealed behind the idealisation was rivalry and hostility with others and with each other. Once the idealised aspects of the relationship have broken down, the negative aspects of the split emerge, and the outcome can be fear and hatred.

The Sacred and the Profane – Mature Love

As well as the arrival of reality – and thus ambivalence – into enduring relationships, love entails mutuality. Love that is not reciprocal, however passionate the lover may be, is still not *love*. In the late Middle Ages, the tradition of courtly love consisted of a complex system of rules and prescriptions that determined the behaviour of both the lover and his adored lady, who was almost always married to someone else, since marriage at that time was largely a commercial and political, rather than a romantic arrangement. The role of the lover was to respect, adore and serve his chosen lady, worshipping her in an almost religious way. The relics of this way of carrying on can occasionally be seen in some of our current attitudes and practices – perhaps in the romantic idealisation of love itself, although we are less inhibited about bringing sexual feeling into our notion of passionate love. Interestingly, at the same time that courtly love flourished in France and England, so also was prostitution tolerated and licensed, bringing a healthy revenue into the Church and the Universities. This polarity perhaps represented one version of the split between sacred and profane love: an idealised adoring of a 'good' woman ('nice girls don't') contrasted with the lusty physicality able to be felt for a denigrated woman, who was 'bad' because she too could experience desire. Bringing together affection and sexual desire is a major developmental task for the adolescent.

If falling in love, and the subsequent relationships can be so problematical if not tempered in time with reality, what can we say about love itself? One thing that becomes clearer over time is that the experience of love changes with development and maturity – the sixteen year old, the thirty year old, and the fifty year old can all experience love and the choice of partner is still driven by powerful unconscious factors. Even late in life, the finding of someone to love is also a re-finding, containing elements of that first and most fundamental love between baby and mother. But the nature of that love will, if all goes well, change and deepen with maturity – be less instantaneous in its dawning, but more durable and trustworthy in its expression.

One of the most necessary and significant features of a mature love is also one of the most difficult to achieve. The passionate possessiveness of the adolescent, the total losing of the self in the beloved so that there is felt to be no separation between the two of them, cannot survive reality. The hard thing to realise, over the course of time, is that the beloved is not the same as oneself. The loved one is perhaps very different indeed in some respects and is probably not going to change either to any marked degree. The shift that has to be made if love is to become love as opposed to an idealised 'in love', or the expression of possessiveness, or of control, or domination, is that the beloved has to be recognised as other, not as identical with the self.

It is only when the separateness of the other can be recognised and tolerated, and his or her Otherness can begin to be known and enjoyed that one can begin to comprehend the achievement that is love. Just as the tiny baby has had to struggle with this painful fact of life, so does the adult. For the infant, the mother who goes away, even just out of the room, is eventually recognised to be the same mother who is adored for her tender understanding, her bountiful breast. Her going away and her coming back are ultimately outside the sphere of the baby's control, and the baby has to recognise that the love and the hate are felt for the same person.

Even adults, rational and self-possessed, find it hard when their special, highly invested figures go away, however briefly. We are used to it, we know it is inevitable in adult life, we deny its significance, we find a multitude of ways to convince ourselves of the benefit of having 'time to oneself', but we do better if we can also let ourselves know how hard it is to let that other go without protest or reaction. And this is not to deny the real value of time for oneself, which is not merely regenerative but also necessary. It is more that that is not the whole story.

Figure 10: 'It's all right darling ... he's not hurt. I frightened him a little that is all.' It can be hard to realise that the beloved may not have the same priorities.

Losing and Finding

Love, a commitment to another person – a commitment to putting the other's well-being ahead of one's own personal happiness – also involves the risk of deep pain if that loved person is then lost. The separation from someone who is loved, or their loss through death, is one of the most difficult, demanding and hard to manage of the normal experiences we all have to deal with. Mourning involves a full recognition of the value and significance of that lost person, grief for that loss, and then recovery from that grief to take up the rest of one's life once more.

Yet grief can be denied, because of an unconscious fear of how overwhelming it may be; or it can become embedded in a stuck and melancholic state, in which the lost person is idealised and the self is denigrated as worthless. An entrenched melancholia may sometimes respond to professional help, but it may also be hard to shift – for that shift may involve recognising an ambivalence that was felt for the lost loved person and this may be too painful to be tolerated. However, the process of mourning (which can continue on and off for many years – it is never straightforwardly simply *over*) can mean that the lost person is eventually remembered in a relatively uncomplicated way with love and gratitude, so that the survivor can take up the rest of his or her life with curiosity, eagerness and vigour, untroubled by ghosts.

Both love and loss are enormously stimulating to creativity. Just as love has inspired much of our greatest poetry, so also has the loss of love, or the loss of the loved one. These experiences touch us to our depths and open up wells of feeling not usually accessible in ordinary day-to-day living. The impulse to put words to such internal discoveries is the impulse to link up with others, to reconnect, and thus of the force that makes us want to go on being alive even though someone felt to be crucial to life has died or gone away.

> The stars are not wanted now: put out every one;
> pack up the moon and dismantle the sun;
> Pour away the ocean and sweep up the wood.
> For nothing now can ever come to any good.

It is a despair that is communicated, however lyrically, but it is communicated *to* a someone, to a listener. W. H. Auden's love poems were written to men, but love is love and the feelings expressed are entirely recognisable to both sexes as being about love itself

Loss can also put one in touch with the realities not just of death but of what is important in life. It is only when faced with the possible loss of the man whose love she had come to take for granted that Bathsheba Everdene, heroine of Thomas Hardy's *Far From the Madding Crowd*, can bring herself to acknowledge her deep feeling for him. Up to that point she had had a childhood flirtation with him, relied upon him, liked him, trusted him – but tossed her head at his dogged devotion to her, turning instead to the dangerous and glamorous Sergeant Troy, for whom she is no more than another conquest. When Gabriel, eventually despairing of having more than crumbs from Bathsheba's table, tells her he will not be renewing his contract as her farm manager, she is devastated. She acknowledges her need for him, both practical and emotional. This kind of feeling is very different from '*It's all because we're so alike …*' Appreciation of the ways in which the other *differs* from oneself leads, as Hardy goes on to describe, to that deepest form of love, that which arises out of knowledge of each other and perhaps consists in that very same deep knowledge.

> They spoke very little of their mutual feelings; pretty phrases and warm expression being probably unnecessary between such tried friends. Theirs was that substantial affection which arises (if any arises at all) when the two who are thrown together begin first by knowing the rougher sides of each other's character, and not the best till further on, the romance growing up in the interstices of a mass of hard prosaic reality. This good-fellowship – *camaraderie* – usually occurring through similarity of pursuits, is unfortunately seldom super-added to love between the sexes,

because men and women associate, not in their labours, but in their pleasures merely. Where, however, happy circumstance permits its development, the compounded feeling proves itself to be the only love which is as strong as death – that love which many waters cannot quench, nor the floods drown, beside which the passion usually called by the name is evanescent as the stream.

Thomas Hardy, *Far From the Madding Crowd* (1874)

7

Dreaming

How do we know we are dreaming? We usually don't, at any rate not until we wake up. Dreams in which one says to oneself 'This is only a dream' are relatively rare. How we know that we are awake is a harder question. We believe that we are awake and not dreaming, but we cannot prove it. Bertrand Russell, the philosopher, wrote dryly, 'It is obviously possible that what we call waking life may be only an unusual and persistent nightmare'. Young children may know that 'dreams' are the name for the life that takes place when they are in bed with their eyes closed, but they can be confused about the reality of these events.

> A small boy awoke crying, frightened by a nightmare in which he was being pursued by a crocodile. His mother came to his bedside to comfort him, but he remained inconsolable. She said to him, 'Tell me about the crocodile, what did he look like?' With a fresh burst of tears at her obtuseness, he said, 'Well, *you* should know what he was like, *you* were there too!'

Once awake, most adults can recognise the physical laws of space and time that govern waking life. These Newtonian laws do not hold good in dreams, where strange alterations in space-time excite no comment. Most of the time we think that we keep these two worlds apart. Yet a powerful dream can affect one's mood throughout the day. Getting out of bed on the wrong side, unreasonably picking a quarrel, or alternatively being surprisingly buoyant, in a good mood, can sometimes be linked to the events of a forgotten dream (see Plate 8).

Dreaming has a necessary psychological function and every one dreams at regular intervals throughout sleep. Dreams, whether remembered or not, represent and work over issues that are important to us. As a result we can process experience in a new way. This kind of dreaming is therefore a kind of thinking whose value, like that of a prophet in his own land, is often disregarded. Although most dreams are quickly forgotten, there are states of mind when there can be open confusion, short or longer-term, between mental experiences when asleep and those when awake. 'Did this really happen or was it only a dream?' 'It felt like a bad dream, only I couldn't wake up.' These are commonplace, yet in certain kinds of mental illness the sufferer may be unable to distinguish between internal and external reality, between actual life and dream or hallucination, feeling as confused as the child described above did.

Ancient Dreams

The imagery of dreams may often be extraordinary, even bizarre. They have always fascinated man. Here is one of the world's best-known and earliest recorded dreams, dating from 1400 years B.C. The Pharaoh is speaking to Joseph, whom he has released from prison, because the Pharaoh had heard of Joseph's reputation as an interpreter of dreams.

> In my dream, behold, I stood upon the bank of the river; and behold, there came up out of the river seven kine, fatfleshed and well-favoured; and they fed in a meadow: and behold, seven other kine came up after them, poor and very ill-favoured and lean-fleshed, such as I never saw in all the land of Egypt for badness: and the lean and the ill-favoured kine did eat up the first seven fat kine ... and I saw in my dream, and, behold, seven ears came up in one stalk, full and good: and behold, seven ears, withered, thin and blasted with the east wind, sprung up after them: and the thin ears devoured the seven good ears: and I told this unto the magicians; but there was none that could declare it to me.

Joseph's view was that the repetition of the contents of the Pharaoh's dream was a sign that it was sent by God to warn of his intentions, and that seven years of plenty would be succeeded by seven years of famine. Regardless of any capacity for divination, Joseph's reading of the dream showed considerable common sense. The Egyptian harvest depended upon irrigation from the Nile's seasonal flooding. Apart from this, harvests, especially in Joseph's homeland, were unpredictable and possible famine should be prepared for.

In this story from the book of Genesis, it is clear from the interpretation that the dream was regarded as having been sent by an agency *external* to the dreamer which required a person with special powers to understand it. This view of dreams was widespread in the Ancient World, and it remains alive today in certain pre-scientific societies: 'good' dreams are sent by God, or the Gods, and 'bad' dreams by demons (see Plate 9). When the dream is felt to arise from outside the sleeper, it is thought to have an oracular function, to serve as a prophecy, a statement or a warning of what is to come, or as advice as to the best way to proceed if properly interpreted. Individuals or groups might even ask the Gods for a message, and then 'incubate' a dream which would be interpreted as bearing the Gods' response. For both the ancient Egyptians and the Greeks incubation involved special preparation and rituals, lying down to sleep on special beds, or on the skin of a ritually slaughtered animal, in order to be in the right state for dream-messages to arrive.

Aristotle, 1100 years later, and yet still three hundred years before Christ, had a different view: he saw the origin of the dream as internal to the dreamer, a product of the dreamer's own mind. Dreams of sickness, he believed, lay in the dreamer's unconscious knowledge of the state of his own body and its functioning, and in a recognition of its changes, even before they reached the level of symptoms. He thought too that individuals might unconsciously act to bring about the dream they had had and then regard the dream as having been prophetic. This is a view closer to that held by Freud at the end of the 19th Century A.D.: the dream originates in the dreamer's own mind and is a product of his current wishes and preoccupations, both conscious and, more significantly, unconscious.

Over the last four decades, starting with the discovery of paradoxical, or rapid eye movement sleep, research into dreaming has become increasingly physiological and less interested in the meaning of dreams. Recordings of brain electrical activity in sleeping volunteers who spent their nights in 'sleep laboratories' revealed a lot of the neural basis of dreaming. For a while this led to researchers regarding dreams as merely random, noise, a kind of waste-product of the brain. More recently, it has become clear that this view is wrong. The content of dreams does seem to be ordered and patterned. Woken dreamers report dreams on successive nights that show thematic consistency and development. Thus, though Freud's view of dreams as fuelled solely by psychological defences against unacceptable wishes is no longer adequate as a complete explanation of dreams, his view of dream activity as meaningful is increasingly supported by studies of brain function.

This research would have delighted Freud, since his own early work was as a brain scientist. He felt that his recognition that dreams had significance, and that their significance for the individual could be understood, was the most important of his discoveries. The unravelling of the meaning of dreams, and the understanding of the mechanisms by which the dream came to take up its particular shape, he called 'the royal road to the unconscious' – the key to understanding crucial features of the unconscious mind at work.

Dreams in Therapy

In psychotherapy, dreams have a privileged status because they can give both patient and therapists access to the various unconscious thoughts and impulses active in the patient's mind and which play such a part in shaping his or her behaviour. So they connect the patient to the therapist, just as they connect the patient to his own unconscious. Moreover patients feel dreams to be especially valuable because they are experienced as spontaneous, occurring independently of conscious intervention or inclination.

Here is a dream from a young woman in analytic treatment, showing some features of this 'royal road to the unconscious'. She had been preoccupied for some weeks with the unhappy separation and divorce of a couple who were friends of hers and her husband's. In part, the concern over the friends' divorce was linked to her longstanding anxiety over whether people meant what they said and said what they meant. In the background it had always been an issue for her that her analyst, for example, might become suddenly disenchanted and want to have a different patient in treatment. In part, divorce itself was anathema to her religious views.

> She dreamed she was in a formal garden, one in which the flower-beds and lawns were laid out in an intricate pattern and separated from each other by little low box hedges. She could see over these hedges just what was in each section of the garden. In one was a beautiful and delicately wrought little carriage, with much gold work on it; in another, quite separated from the first by these little low hedges, was a horse. As she described the horse, she went on to say how it seemed to become enormous as she was looking at it, quite frighteningly big; she couldn't imagine how it could ever be harnessed up to that delicate carriage.

When a patient tells a dream, it is rare to be able to understand it immediately. Both the patient and the analyst have to work to achieve that understanding, work that sometimes involves a reconstruction of the mental processes that have gone into making the dream in the first place. Eventually, one arrives at the point of origin of the dream: a *dream thought* that was too disturbing to be allowed into consciousness in the first place, and which had to be disguised, worked over, elaborated and constructed into a dream. Amongst other things, Freud thought of the finished dream as a fantasy: it represents a wished-for solution to an unconscious conflict.

As the young woman began to talk about her dream, she recalled the song with the words in it 'Love and marriage, love and marriage – they go together like a horse and carriage.' Yet the horse and the carriage in the dream were clearly not together, even though visible to each other. Visibly, in the case of her friends, the connection between love and marriage had broken down, and were now separate, as was the couple. Also there was the question of the discrepancy between the terrifyingly big horse and the delicate little carriage, and how they were to fit together. Here another level of the dream became apparent, for this young woman, who loved her own husband dearly, nevertheless had come to realise she found sexual intercourse with him a very difficult matter, and sometimes downright terrifying. At times, her husband would appear to her like a huge rearing stallion and she would become overwhelmed with the idea of how she and he were going to fit together at all without damage to her own body. None of this she had really been able to articulate to him. Moreover within the context of her analysis, the patient would sometimes complain that the analyst went too fast, too deep, too quickly for her, and that she felt shoved around by the interpretations, often not ready for them and so not really wanting to take them inside herself where they might help her to form a new conception of herself.

So this dream begins to look as though it was an expression of her fear of, or reluctance for, a full-blooded intercourse – whether sexual, analytic or inter-personal – and of her narcissistically vulnerable sense of her own body's fragility. Intercourse might mess up the beautiful garden or damage the little carriage, both of which were ways of representing her view of her own body. On the other hand, there is also her fear of the consequences if she rejects that intercourse

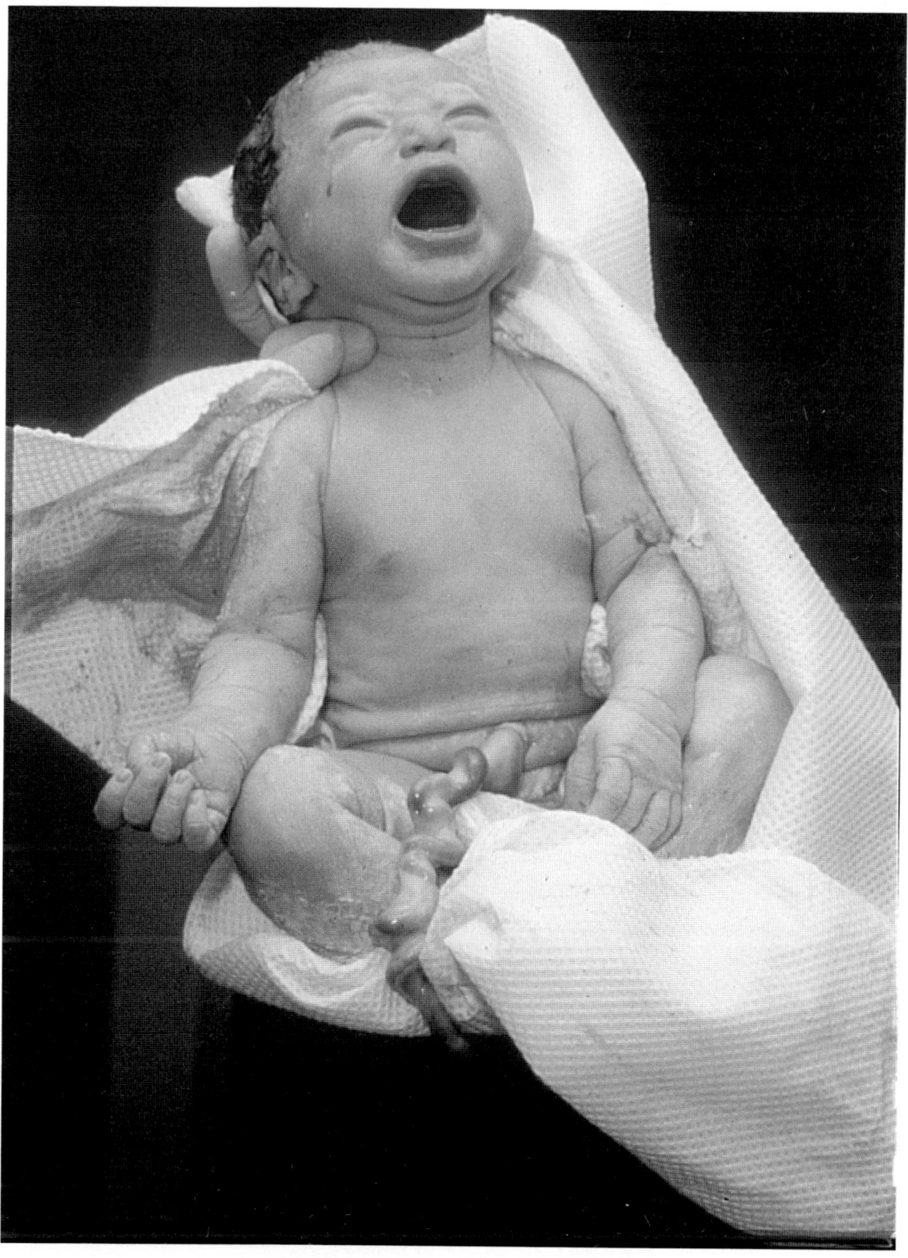

1. A cry is an essential part of respiration — and of surviving in the first minutes in the world. New born babies are also quite ready to use their minds as well as their lungs.

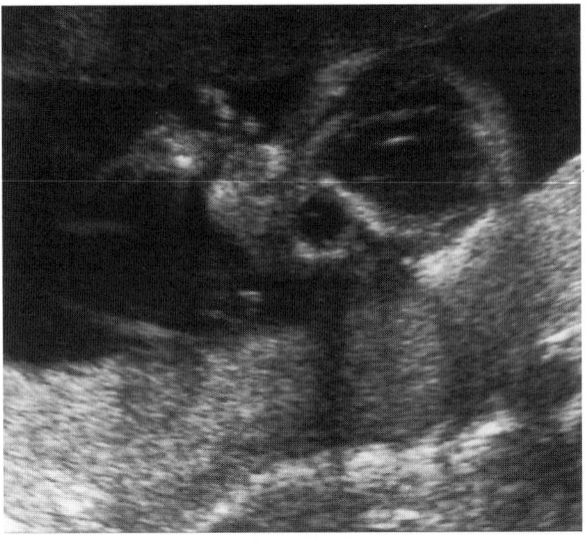

2. This high-resolution ultrasound scan shows the face of a baby in the womb in profile. In the top left corner the hand is very near the baby's face. It is possible to see the baby's eye and follow its movements.

3. A chimp fishing for termites. Like humans from different cultures, different groups have different ways of 'fishing'.

4. This mirror case from the British Museum shows Aphrodite and Pan playing fivestones. The Opies observed it still being played outside the museum in the 1950s, but it may now be dying out.

5. Even in relation to the earliest of relationships, a yearning for innocence has to contend with the healthy physicality of many of our desires.

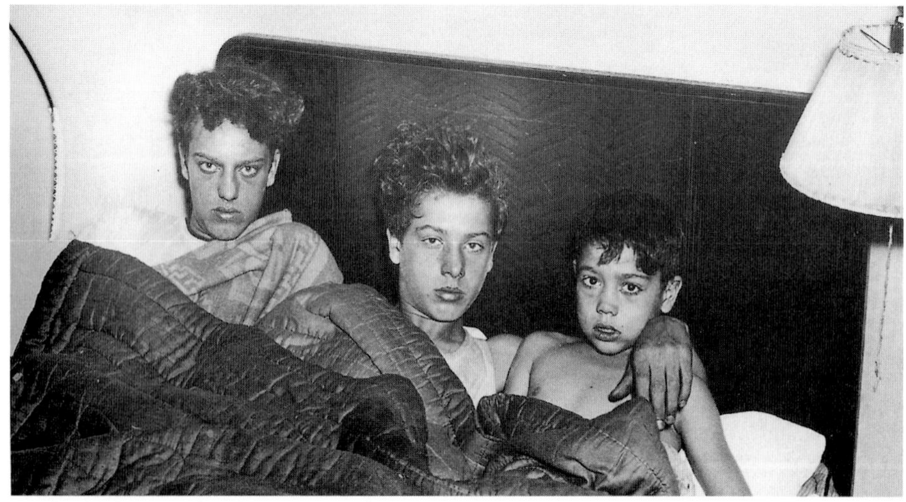

6. This disturbing photograph of three anonymous boys whose expressions are marked by experience was taken in the 1940s in the USA.

a. Laura at home and generally happy.

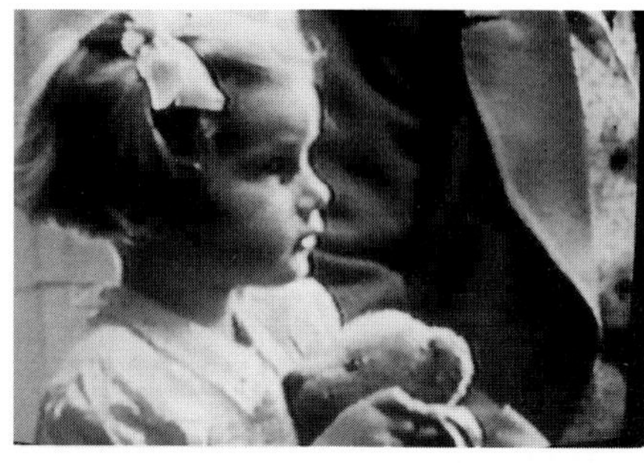

b. Laura, coping well, and her mother seeing a nurse in the hospital.

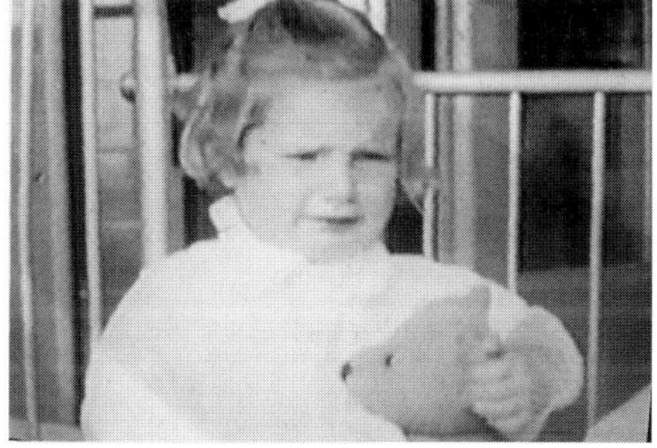

c. After some days, Laura is now more fragile.

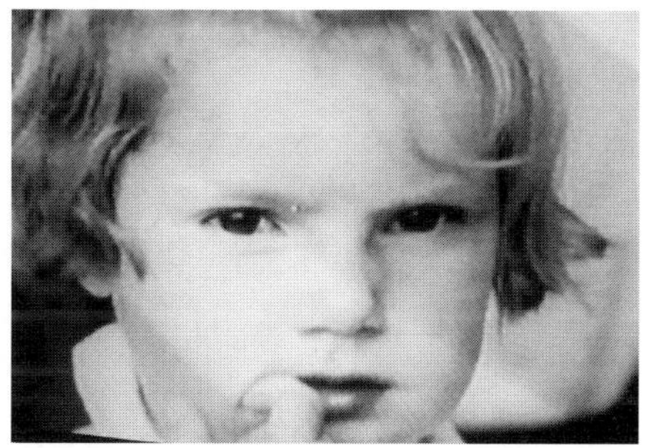

d. She has now developed a withdrawn look not previously seen.

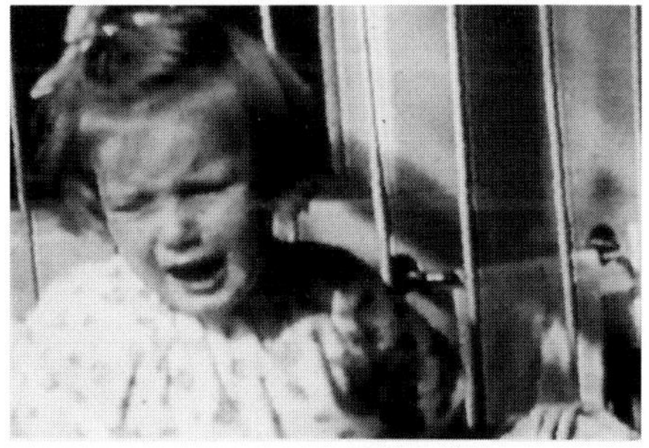

e. Laura has been told that she is going home. As she waits for her mother, all her self-control gives way and she cries unrestrainedly.

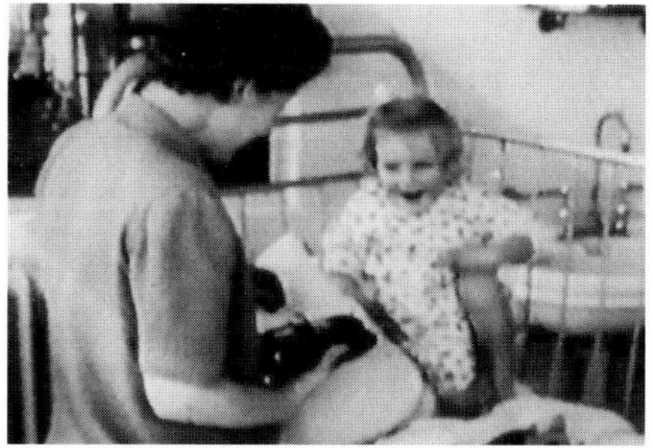

. f. When her mother arrives to take her home, Laura didn't believe her. Only when she saw her shoes was she convinced.

7. Learning to cope with brief separations from our parents and loved ones is a necessary part of growing up and adjusting often takes a while. Some 'brief separations' can cause particular problems. Until the mid 1950s there was a widespread belief that children in hospital became contented after a brief period of fretting. Visits by parents were strictly controlled as children would be upset again. The films of James and Joyce Robertson from the Clinic recorded the effects of brief hospitalisation and separation from parents on young children. These moving, understated films won many prizes. These stills are from 'A Two-Year-Old Goes to Hospital' made by them in the 1950s, showing the characteristic separation reaction in Laura, a well-adjusted little girl, during 8 days of hospitalisation when her mother had visited regularly but briefly. As a consequence of this and other films, national policy was changed and parents were encouraged to stay with children and visit them freely.

8. Goya: The Sleep of Reason Brings forth Monsters. 'It is obviously possible that what we call waking life may be only an unusual and persistent nightmare', Bertrand Russell.

9. This clay tablet is from the Mesopotamian dream 'book' from Ninevah (Babylon) in about 700 BC. The inscriptions are in the form 'if a man dreams he is in the air: then . . .' There are thousands of such dream fragments recorded.

10. Goya depicts the fear that people are deceitful, inconstant and two-faced. Sometimes fears like these are too disturbing to be allowed into waking consciousness, and can only be dreamed

11. A formal group of boarding school boys with designated roles for each player.

12. A more various group structure: a Sunday football team.

13. Freud statue outside the Tavistock Clinic, near where he lived after leaving Nazi-Germany.

14. As we grow older our identity changes and develops so that we begin to *feel* like the members of an older generation. It depends on the individual person what is done with that feeling.

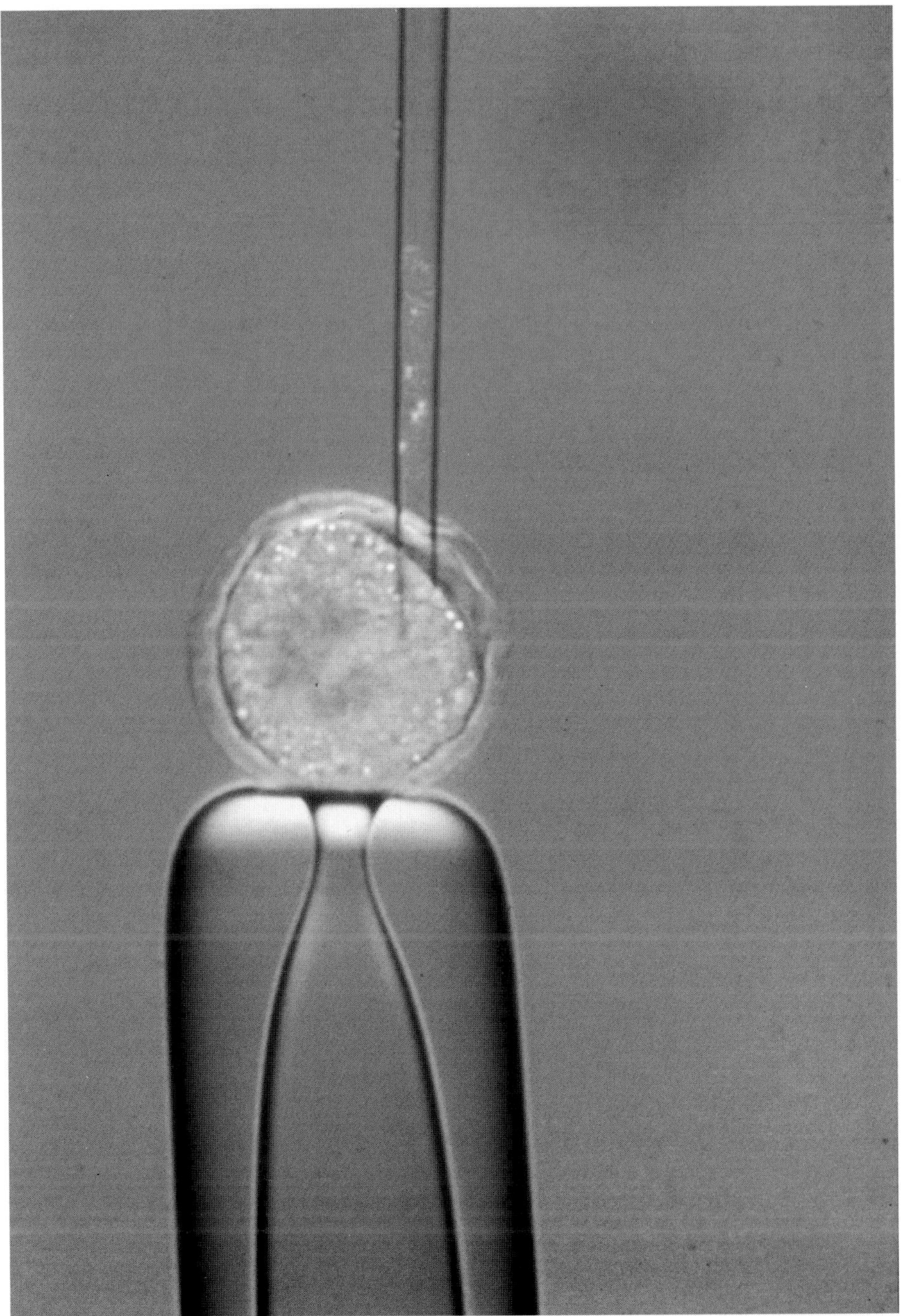

15. One of the techniques used in the type of cloning which produced Dolly the sheep. A micropipette has been used to penetrate the wall of an egg. The jelly-like substance (cytoplasm) surrounding the nucleus is being drawn off.

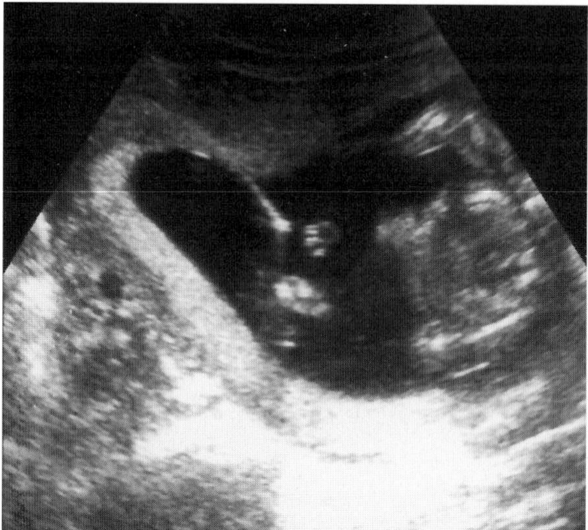

16. An ultra-sound scan showing the amniocentesis needle (the white line in the left corner) positioned carefully in the amniotic fluid (the dark area) and lying on top of the baby in the womb.

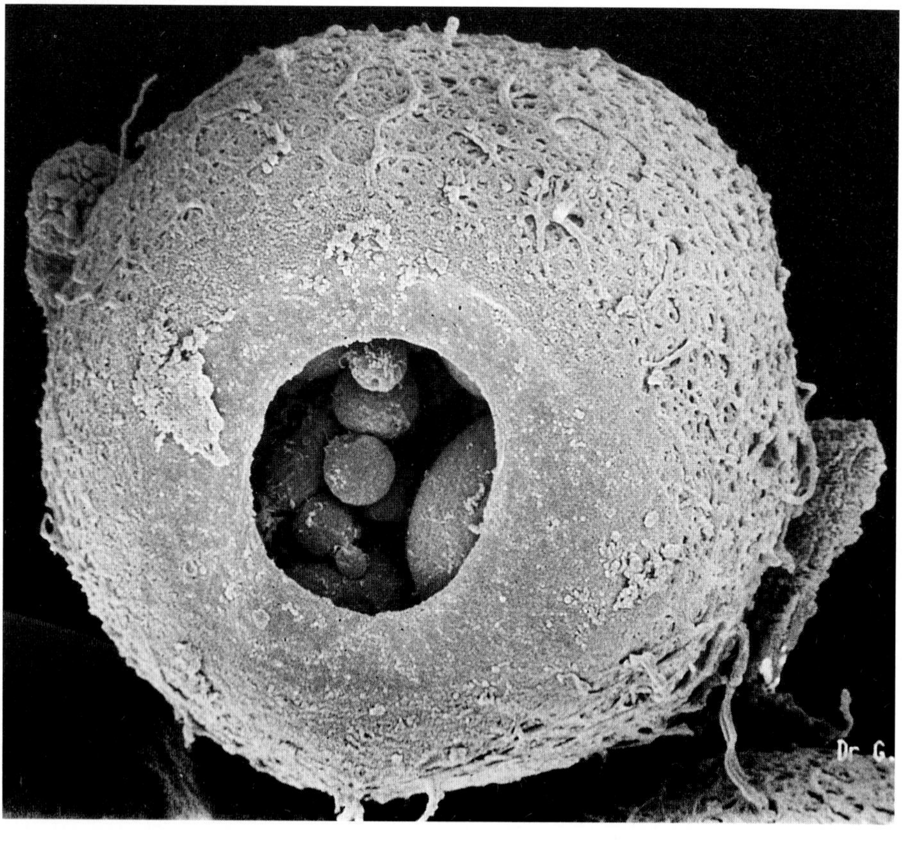

17. A three-day human embryo which was fertilised *in vitro*. An acidic solution was used to create a porthole in the wall of the embryo. A single cell is then sucked out to test that the embryo is genetically normal. Subsequently the embryo is planted in the mother's womb. This test can be used where there is a very high risk of genetic disorders.

with those figures who are important to her, whom she loves. At this point, the original conflict begins to come into view. The dream-thought, in an expanded form, might be expressed like this:

> I want love and marriage to go together like a horse and carriage, but I don't want to come together with my husband (or indeed analyst) in the way he (or she) wishes it. It frightens and sometimes disgusts me. Yet if I back away from this huge alarming horse (an image of the husband or analyst), will he/she then want to leave me and the separation be permanent, be a divorce, which is even worse? Perhaps I can put them together in a way in which the togetherness is effectively negated, hedged in, and the beautiful garden is left intact.

It is possible to see in this dream some of the unconscious mechanisms through which the *dream-work* is carried out – the mental work by which the original 'thought' is expressed in the finished dream, and which then has to be understood in the treatment.

First there is the *use of the day's events* (Freud in 1900 in 'The Interpretation of Dreams' called it 'the day residue') as the convenient vehicle for the expression of the unconscious conflict. In this case the rupture in the friends' marriage provides a way of representing the feared but also wished-for separation of love/sex and marriage in her own life. Then there is *condensation*: the use of one external situation to represent many internal predicaments. Here, the horse and carriage represent at least three kinds of relationship disturbing to the patient – that with her friends, that with her husband, and that with her analyst. There is also a kind of *representation* that is quite indirect, as well as imaginative: the kind of intercourse that is felt to be disruptive to something delicate and beautifully arranged has to be carefully controlled, or boxed in (the little box hedges), so that the young woman's quite fragile sense of her own physical integrity can be preserved uninterrupted by violent intrusions.

Whether or not the detail of the interpretation of this dream is accurate in all respects, and even though another analyst might have handled it differently, what is clear is that the dream provided a vivid way of expressing some urgent issues in this patient's life, which led to a greater understanding of the depth of her anxiety and reluctance about the most significant relationships in her life – and of some of the reasons that underlay those feelings. And it also provided analyst and patient with a symbolic medium which could be translated into language that made sense to the patient and made it possible to talk about these difficulties.

What Do Dreams Say about the Dreamer

Although the theory of dreams used here is very different from that underpinning Joseph's understanding of the Pharaoh's dream, both then and now the interpreter uses his understanding of the context of the dream in a commonsense way. The understanding of the patient's history and character, preoccupations, ways of behaving, ways of relating, are all put together when interpreting this glimpse of the dreamer's imagination at work, in order to get a deeper insight into the dreamer's engagement with his or her life and experience. In many ways one is interpreting dreamers rather than dreams.

In this 'horse and carriage dream', the content was very important. In other patients or in other dreams, the way in which the dream is told, or the use to which it is put in a psychotherapy session, may be more significant than the detail of the content. Here is a dream from a lawyer who had been emotionally involved with a colleague in the office, something that had been deeply upsetting to his wife. He had let the colleague know that he was to be giving a prestigious public lecture in a few month' time, and she had congratulated him, saying of course she'd be there. This would, he knew at once, upset his wife and make her angry. He was filled with anxiety about the predicament he had got himself into.

> He dreamed that he was making love with his wife in a room in a foreign city. Out of the corner of his eye he saw through a window that two houses away there was a fire. His wife complained that he was hurting her, making her sore. Suddenly the fire was much bigger, much closer, erupting into the room with them. He fled together with his wife and they found themselves in a public courtyard – and he was struggling to pull on his underpants which was all he'd been able to save. Then he was looking for some way to get them both back home. There seemed to be an English taxi-cab there, a Black Cab, but he somehow failed to catch the driver's eye, or to stop it or to take it.

He and his wife were in fact going abroad together shortly, so at the most immediate level, the narrative could be read as a symbolic account of his situation. Out of the corner of his eye, and at two removes, he could still see the fire – the potential that the one-time feeling for the colleague still had to cause a blazing row. His wife complained that he has hurt her, made her sore/angry. Suddenly the fire was in the lecture room with them – he tried to get out of the situation but felt he had been caught with his pants down. He longed to feel at home with his wife again, safe and sound, but was unable to use the English taxi to help them.

However, we cannot yet see the conflict that made it necessary to dream up that dream. In the session his wish to be special came into view. He wanted to be the favourite with both women and was unable to resist displaying his achievements to the colleague. But if he were then to say to her 'don't come to the lecture', effectively acknowledging that his wife's feelings were more important to him than hers, he feared she would turn away from him. He wriggled around in the session, unwilling to deal with the realities of the situation. He found strings of reasons for saying nothing further to the colleague and just hoping for the best.

The analyst felt that this linked this to something provocative in him, something that was drawn to fire-raising, that actually set up the situation in the first place. The lawyer agreed but he still felt himself to be helpless in the face of the dilemma, sighing in a pointedly hopeless way. Eventually the analyst pointed out to him how the dream was being re-enacted in the session: the patient raised a burning issue, but then in quite a deliberate and even perverse way ignored the analyst, the English taxi just sitting there, by avoiding the driver's eye (what the analyst was saying), thus evading any possible help that the taxi might be able to provide in getting him back home – to feeling at home once more with his wife. Part of this unconscious manoeuvre was also to shift the feeling of helplessness and uselessness into the analyst, who was unable to feel she could be effective. She was required to feel she was making a mess of the analysis, instead of his having to feel he was making a mess of his life.

Eventually, the 'going nowhere' atmosphere in the session was relieved as the patient became able to talk about his resentment of the fact he has to pay the analyst/taxi-driver for his session even if he doesn't make use of the analyst's words. Why should he pay if the analysis is useless? He was eventually able to see the way in which he set out to render the analyst ineffectual by 'failing to catch the driver's eye'; or, since he was the author of the dream, ignoring what she said and by prevaricating instead … refusing the ride even part way home.

With this dream, the most useful bit of work was done over elucidating its function in the session itself. This allowed the apparently minor detail of the taxi's being a Black Cab to become visible, since the meter ticking away visibly (perhaps the clock in the consulting room recording every minute that had to be paid for) meant that both analyst and patient could get to grips with the patient's resentment that he could not make the analyst do her work for love alone, rather than for love-and-money, and that in his mind she therefore could not be made to join the retinue of women whom he wished to control and manage simply through their desire for him.

The fact that dreams are a product of the dreamer cannot be emphasised too strongly. It puts dreams into the category of 'mental product', and like other mental productions, they will bear some common stamp or feature particular to that individual – his thoughts, ideas, memories, day-dreams, hallucinations, fantasies, relationships will all be linked in some significant way. Like a fingerprint, recognisably a mark made by a human hand, they will nevertheless be unique to that individual: not simply unique, but also revealing about that particular patient's mental structures or internal world.

In the first patient's dream, the formality and beauty of the garden and the carriage says something about her wish to have a body that is perfect in its own right, just so, not in need of gardeners or horses or husbands or analysts. This linked back to her early childhood, when a series of operations over a number of years had made her feel that she did not have a perfect body; that it had to be cut about and damaged by interfering figures (surgeons, parents) who seemed to feel they owned her body, in that they could say what should and would be next done to it without reference to her feelings or wishes. Thus the little scene she dreamed is marked by the absence of physical interaction, of connectedness. It seems to say 'you can look but you can't touch'; and much more work was necessary before this young woman could begin to think of intimate physical (as opposed to intellectual) connectedness with another as being productive and enjoyable – in fact, *vital*, necessary for life itself.

The Helpfulness of Dreams

This feature of dreams and other mental products, their uniqueness to the dreamer and their capacity for representing in capsule form a significant feature of internal life, can be helpful to the psychiatrist or therapist who is seeing a patient for the first time. They may ask 'Do you have any special early memories?' or 'Do you ever dream? Can you tell me a dream?' and the answer can often tell the interviewer something important about the state of the patient's internal world, not just at that point but in general (see Plate 10). Potential patients coming for a first meeting with an assessor or therapist will often have dreamed in the preceding days something relevant to that particular meeting. Here is one such dream, from a highly anxious young man. The consultant asked him if he ever dreamed.

> Yes, as a matter of fact I did have a dream the night before last that I remembered, I don't know why. I was in a huge department store and I seemed to be lost. I knew I was meant to be meeting someone there – I think it was my uncle, whom I haven't actually seen since I was a child – but I didn't know where he was. Then I found my younger brother, only it seemed to be him when he was a baby, and he was ill, crying and crying as though he had a stomach-ache or something horribly wrong with him, and I didn't know how to comfort him or make him feel better. I don't know where our mother was. No-one around in the shop seemed to notice and I couldn't make anyone hear me even though I was trying to call out. They seemed to disappear. I think it was night-time.

Some features of this dream seem clear at once. The dreamer feels he is lost and in the dark. He is in an unfamiliar building where he doesn't know how to find the person he is supposed to be meeting – perhaps the therapist in the Tavistock, which is also a large building divided into Departments. He hopes the therapist will be benign, perhaps avuncular. The consultant wondered if the absence of the mother referred to the fact that the patient was sent to a boarding school where the best you could hope for was a kindly male teacher.

Perhaps in the context of the assessment the most interesting feature of this dream was the young man represented the ill, frightened, unheard child-like aspect of himself in the person of his little brother. This allowed the consultant to know that, although there is a competent, apparently adult version of this young man who has actually got to the right place at the right time and is able to articulate some aspects of his difficulties, there is also a frightened, infantile version of himself. This side of him is in distress, afraid there is something 'horribly wrong' with him and equally afraid that *that* him will not be heard or be able to be helped, or even that anyone will want to help. When the therapist suggested this to him, the young man flushed suddenly, on the verge of tears.

He began to talk less fluently, but from a deeper level in himself, with a great deal of feeling.

This dream shows how aspects of the self, the dreamer, can be separated off from the 'I' in the dream and represented by other figures, either known or unknown to the dreamer. These aspects or parts of the self can be thoughts or feelings that the dreamer would rather not admit to his conscious mind – in this instance the fearful childlike feelings about going to a strange building for a meeting with an unknown person. Figures, parts of figures, animals, even inanimate objects can all be used to represent an aspect, or aspects, of the self in the dream.

Part of the work of therapy is not simply to clarify the nature of these separated-off parts of the self's functioning, but also to render them less alien and more acceptable to the self. The young man feared in his dream that if the people round him were to hear what sort of state he was in, they would want to turn away from him and quietly disappear. In some way he himself wishes he could make those distressed aspects of himself simply vanish, so that he could ignore them. One aim of therapy is that, with help, he will eventually become more tolerant of – and insightful about – his own infantile needs and distress and come to treat those vulnerable aspects of himself with more kindness and knowledge. In turn, this will allow the distressed baby to grow up feeling a bit better, not forever having to be shut up or avoided as an embarrassment and nuisance. Knowing about infantile feelings is not to risk regression into a permanently infantile state once more nor is it to indulge oneself. On the contrary, knowledge of one's own complex and contradictory nature increases strength, resilience and responsibilities. It gives depth and purpose to one's actions.

Whether recollected or not, dreaming is an activity that is helpful to the emotional life of the dreamer, keeping him in touch with his own daily unconscious thoughts and conflicts. It is a sign that he is working on managing and dealing with the often surprisingly profound issues which arise on a daily basis. A dream told to a therapist and understood by therapist and patient together can be deeply relieving to the patient. There are also dreams, particularly those dreamed during a period of hard work upon a particular enterprise or problem, that apparently solve problems that the dreamer is well aware of and has been struggling with quite consciously.

A well-known example is that of the nineteenth century German chemist Kekulè, who had been trying to work out the molecular structure of one of the most important organic chemicals, benzene. At that time most organic compounds were thought to consist of strings of molecules, and this model did not explain the known chemical composition of benzene. Kekulè had a dream of a number of atoms in a ring-like formation, rather like a snake chasing and swallowing its own tail. This picture allowed him to recognise on waking that the atoms could be arranged in a hexagon and not in a straight line. This entirely new 'solution' was a product of the dreamer's own mind, but it was not a view that had been available to him until he had dreamed it. Coleridge's poem 'Kubla

Khan' came to him in a similar fashion, while sleeping. It would have been an even longer poem had not the knock on the door from the importunate person from Porlock swept it from his memory, making it vanish 'like the images on the surface of a stream.' Robert Louis Stevenson writes vividly of how the central impetus for the story of 'Dr Jekyll and Mr Hyde' came to him in a dream of a man drinking a potion from a phial. Moreover, the story itself is a vivid depiction of parts of the self in relation to each other.

Perhaps here there is after all a direct line of descent from the 'incubation' practised by the Ancient Egyptians and the Greeks. If we are interested enough either consciously or unconsciously in a personal issue or an emotional conflict, or a scientific, artistic or work problem, our minds will be more than usually working on it by night as well as by day; and if we learn to pay attention to our own thoughts and mental products, taking them seriously, we may find that we know more, can notice more, and can achieve more than we at first think. And that of course is one of the goals of psychotherapy: to know the workings of your own mind so that you can make a fuller and better use of its potential.

8

What Is a Family?

The term family has different meanings for people of different ages and cultures. Family forms are changing rapidly, and more and more children are likely to spend some of their lives in families that do not fit the norm of a two parent – two child family. At the same time, British society has changed in other ways, becoming increasingly multicultural, with diverse family patterns and cultural traditions, even though the image of the 'nuclear family' continues to dominate ideas about the family. When a National Children's Bureau survey asked children to define what a family is and what families are for, it found their definitions were about love, care, mutual respect and support, regardless of gender, ethnic background and location.

How then do these comments reflect the reality of families today? Is what these children define as a family realistic or are they holding on to dreams?

These are important questions. What is it that families share and what makes each and every family unique? This chapter highlights how details of family interaction affect relationships both inside and outside of the family. In families, we are constantly trying to understand what is happening and work out what others are thinking. Some of the 'stories' or ideas we have about one another may be shared, but others are not, and it is the tension of negotiating which story will dominate that forms the core of family life.

Due to the extent to which the family has changed in recent years, we may question the value of holding on to a model that no longer fits with the experience of all families in Britain. Many people find themselves having to balance what may feel like two contradictory models, one that is reflected in the media and society outside the family, and a second one that connects with the family at home. This is both confusing and disabling. At worst, it can mean that children are not able to ask parents for help in dealing with the problems they face, for example, about teasing or racism, or even issues such as friendships and schooling.

Stories across Generations

Brigitte is the eldest of five daughters. As a child, she and her sisters had been repeatedly sexually abused by her father. She remembers having tried to talk to her mother about what was happening. Her mother, however, did not believe her and said Brigitte was just trying to make trouble for everyone. As a result, she grew up feeling confused, frightened and angry, half hoping someone else would guess what was happening, but also afraid of what they would think about her failing to protect her sisters.

As soon as she was old enough, she left home and tried to distance herself from her family. She put all her energy into developing a career, establishing new relationships, and later in meeting Tony whom she grew to love and with whom she had a daughter, Alison. Through this, she felt she had found a way of shutting her memories of abuse and betrayal in a compartment, quite separate from her 'normal' life. She kept the story of her abuse from Tony, in the hope of avoiding contaminating their relationship. Being a good mother to Alison had a very special effect on Brigitte. It helped her to re-establish her sense of self-worth, in loving and being loved by another person.

However, the experience of being a mother reminded her of her own childhood and she began to have frightening flashbacks relating to the abuse. The flashbacks brought back her fear and loathing of her father. But what she found most shocking, was that at times she felt overwhelmed by anger towards her mother for having withdrawn and been unwilling to hear or believe her. She found herself struggling to disguise her feelings from her daughter.

When emotions ran high like this, she became afraid of hurting her daughter, and felt panicked by the need to protect both Alison and herself. At these times, she tried to distance herself, putting Alison to bed early, well before supper time. She then felt guilty for shutting her out in this way. At other times she couldn't stop herself from being suspicious about what other people might do to Alison, and dealt with this by staying too close to her and becoming intrusive. Alison became increasingly angry with her mother, heightening Brigitte's concerns that there was something to hide.

Brigitte's hopes of leaving the experience of abuse behind became more and more remote. She worried how Tony would respond if he knew and kept her fears secret from him. It became more difficult for both Tony and Alison to understand or talk about her inconsistency, and he began spending more time away from home. Sadly this increased Alison's sense of isolation, pushing her into a position of feeling unloved and worthless. So too, Alison began experiencing some of the emotions that had been so terrifying for Brigitte as a child, feelings of isolation, abandonment and not being heard in her own right.

Brigitte's story illustrates how ways of relating can be passed down across generations. Our families have a profound effect on how we see ourselves and feel we are seen by others. This not only influences our subsequent relationships within the family, but has a powerful impact on how we relate to friends and even colleagues at work.

This influence can develop in several ways. One possibility is that we try to repeat patterns of relating that were similar to what happened in our family of origin. Alternately, we may want to 'correct' the past, to avoid repeating painful childhood experiences, by doing better than our parents were able to. In Brigitte's case, this meant trying to protect her daughter from situations that could threaten her safety, trying to protect her from strangers and from her own anger and frustration as a mother. However, the very process of trying to correct the past meant that she unwittingly repeated some of the very actions she most wanted to leave behind. This can happen even where what we are trying to avoid is less dramatic, like feeling our family placed too much emphasis on food, on academic success, or on not openly celebrating our achievements.

Often, neither trying to correct nor to replicate the past actually fits with what is happening in the present, and we have to find other ways of relating, ways that draw on both past experiences and the circumstances of the present. Recognising the connection that existed between the family situation and the abuse meant that Brigitte had to face the extent to which the image she had of being a good mother did not fit with what was actually happening for her daughter. What Brigitte found most painful was facing that her very attempts to safeguard her daughter meant that Alison could not turn to her to make sense of her own experience. Although this was extremely distressing, beginning to separate her childhood experiences from Alison's was the first step in freeing this family from a pattern of relating that had been passed from generation to generation. Rather than assuming that she knew what Alison was feeling, she began to listen to what Alison was actually saying. This difficult process involved more than a shift in how Brigitte related to Alison. It meant a shift in her relationship with Tony as well.

Part of this involved thinking about how Brigitte's experience fitted with Tony's own childhood experiences. He too had hoped to escape from a pattern he had found destructive, a pattern in which his parents' intrusiveness had dominated his decisions both as a child and young adult. This helped Tony and Brigitte rethink what was happening in this family, moving away from seeing Brigitte as holding all the 'blame' towards seeing how they had both become drawn into recreating patterns from the past.

They began to discuss the effect of Brigitte's panic on Tony, and why he had distanced himself from her rather than stepping in to help her see how different Alison's life had been from hers. With Tony's support, Brigitte started to imagine how she could begin to talk about the past with her father and mother. She began to question why her parents had acted in the way in which they had, wondering whether they too had experienced abuse as children.

The Family as System

Brigitte's story highlights that what happens in families cannot be explained entirely in terms of individual motivations and beliefs, but needs to take into account the context in which the individual is operating and the moment-to-moment processes of interactions between family members in the present. Family members try to understand what one another are thinking. Some of these 'stories' may be shared, but there may be as many perspectives on any issue as there are people in the family. In this case, there was no one 'true' story that could accurately describe their family life – Alison's own position in the family was very different to that of her mother or father. It is the stories which dominate and the stories which remain hidden or suppressed that shape the dynamics of family life.

One way of thinking about the family is to view it as a system. From the

1950's onwards, several theorists developed a set of ideas that became known as cybernetics. Much of this originated in the biological sciences, where it became increasingly clear that organisms, like the human body, could not be adequately explained in terms of individual parts, or specific functions. It was more correct to see the body as a set of components that operated in a coordinated and integrated way to maintain stability. This coordination was achieved by communication between parts of the system.

From this point of view, parts of any system are regarded in terms of their interactions with other elements of that system. How we identify or describe these elements, in this case family members, is in terms of what they communicate to one another, both in words and in actions. It is these patterns of communicating that come to define how we see ourselves in relation to one another. If the pattern of interaction in our family involves our acting as protector of a more vulnerable member, this can become the way in which we are seen by others, and come to define ourselves. This does not mean that being a protector is the only definition of who we are: we may act in quite a different way with a less vulnerable family member. So, who we are changes in relation to the system we are part of.

Social relationships can be seen as patterns of interactions that were developed and maintained through feedback, a 'phenomenon' first noted in the 1950s by the anthropologist Gregory Bateson. In a feedback loop, A affects B, B affects C, and C in turn affects both B and A.

Depending on where or when in the cycle the process is examined, we can regard C as either causing or being caused by what is happening to A and B. So, Brigitte's panic can be seen as causing Tony's withdrawal, or Tony's withdrawal can be seen as causing Brigitte's panic. From this perspective, the actions we commonly regard as causes or to blame can be see as arbitrary points in a complex of interacting cycles.

These feedback loops operate at all levels of human interaction, from the personal to the political, and involve both verbal and non-verbal communication. As we are constantly interacting with one another in families, patterns of relating are readily established, and just like any other system, family members work to maintain the stability of that system.

> A mother and father argue endlessly about their seven-year-old son's disruptive behaviour. Both parents feel he is extremely demanding and takes advantage of his mother. He refuses to do what she asks and whenever she tries to reprimand him, he throws toys around the house, several times narrowly missing his mother. When his behaviour reaches such a pitch, his parents argue fiercely about him, which seems to achieve little more than increasing the son's disruptiveness.
>
> At some point in the course of each argument, the mother begins to feel that the father is being too harsh and becomes afraid of what he might do. She gives in and sides with her son against the father. The father feels furious, but backs down, and leaves the room while the mother gives in to the son. For a time there is peace, until the mother again begins to find the boy's behaviour too disruptive, asks for the father's help and the cycle starts again.

One way of understanding this interaction could be to see the boy's behaviour as the cause of the parents' arguments. Alternatives could include noticing what happened just before the son started to act in a disruptive way. For example, what do periods of quiet between mother and son mean? Does their closeness become too difficult for the father, leading to some action on his part that triggers a change in the boy's behaviour? Similarly, could the son be expressing anger on behalf of the rest of the family, or might his behaviour be one way of showing his father that his mother cannot 'cope' alone, ensuring that his mother and father remain together despite difficulties in their couple relationship?

Like any of the ideas we have about what is happening in our own families at present, these hypotheses may or may not be valid. Not all the consequences of what we do may be intentional, but once we move beyond the point of seeing problems as located in *one* person, beyond seeing one person as damaged, sick or to blame, more interactional interpretations become possible. Any statement about this child's behaviour needs to take into account not only his actions, but the behaviour of parents and the meaning of that behaviour within the family system. Finally, the explanation any of us decide to adopt within our own family may say more about our own interpretations, than about any 'one real truth'.

This is perhaps the greatest strength of a 'systemic' approach. Looking at problems as evolving from and being maintained by family dynamics is less blaming, and allows how we relate to one another in the present to change. It can free families from remaining trapped in distressing situations. If the problems we are most worried about in our families are kept going by current interactions, change *can* occur by finding a way of altering the context, the pattern of relating, that is maintaining the problem.

Family Systems and Change

The family relies on the action of all its parts to function. Altering any one part (the actions of any one member) inevitably affects the operation of the whole system. Like a thermostat, the family has the capacity to compensate for change, enabling it to resume its balance, and prevent chaos and disintegration. So for example, in a family where the pattern is to 'carry on as normal' when there are problems, members will try to deal with an ageing father's increased forgetfulness and phases of confusion by covering up for him, trying to appear unaffected and continuing to defer to him as head of the household.

But no family system is static. We are continually having to respond to changed circumstances, by adapting what we have done in the past. Some changes are unpredictable, like war, illness, family separation or immigration. Others, like life cycle changes may be more predictable, but even so, we may be taken unawares by how strongly we are affected, as the family undergoes what can feel like a 'family-dectomy', having to alter its rules or structures to fit with its changed circumstances. A point may be reached where attempts to stay the same cannot be sustained. Returning to the example above, at a certain stage, the father's confusion may begin to affect the family's finances and someone else, perhaps the mother or daughter, has to take on greater responsibility, altering the family pattern of carrying on in the face of difficulty.

Yet even transitions that are longed for can still feel very risky. How we see ourselves is very closely connected with the role we play in our family, and there is often great resistance to what feels like leaving an important aspect of ourselves behind. Often we find ourselves sticking rigidly to old ways of behaving, even if we know they no longer work. It is after all hard to give up on what we know and value, particularly at times of great stress. It is this continual tension between maintaining continuity and adapting to change that forms the life blood of the family. But, change can be all the more difficult to own when it feels as if it has been at the expense of someone else's loss.

Interaction and Communication

In trying to understand any interaction, focusing only on what is said would mean missing out on much of the emotional life of the family. We are constantly trying to work out what is happening for one another, and non-verbal communication contributes enormously to a family's strength, enabling us to understand without having to put everything into words. Any communication is open to many interpretations, as the way in which we understand what is said is based both on content and what it demonstrates about our relationship to the speaker. Tone of voice, a glance, or subtle ending of eye contact, colour how we interpret what is said, and how we feel about the person we are speaking to.

However, verbal and non-verbal messages do not necessarily match one another. For example, the words used can imply someone is not angry with us, but their eyes and tone of voice may imply the opposite. Even as adults, it can be confusing as it puts us into a double-bind as to which of these two 'languages' to respond to. For young children, it is even more of a problem, and interferes with their chances of making sense of their lives, affecting their psychological resilience. By and large, clinical experience shows that children, like Seamus below, deal with the confusion of mixed messages by 'listening' to what they see rather than what they hear.

> Marilyn, a lone parent, sought help as she was concerned about her son, Seamus, aged four. She asked to be seen alone initially and said that Seamus had been dry for a year, but had started wetting the bed again and having nightmares. She and his father had separated soon after his birth. He had moved abroad and there had been no contact for at least two years. She explained that Seamus might be worried because she had been diagnosed with malignant melanoma. After her operation, when she told him: 'Mummy is better now, the nasty sickness has been taken away by the doctors', Seamus had replied, 'But, the doctor hurt you, Mummy' (referring to her scar).
>
> Marilyn began to cry as she spoke, saying that she knew the chances of a recurrence were high and that her prognosis was poor. She was worried about what would happen to him if she died and wondered whether she should be more open

> with him. However, her mother, who had looked after Seamus during her treatment, thought telling him more at this stage would make things worse. As she had been so helpful with him, Marilyn felt perhaps she may know best. She felt de-skilled as a mother and thought that whatever she did, she would be letting him down. A second session was held which included Seamus, during which the following interaction took place.
>
> Marilyn: I just think it's hard not knowing where I stand, and I'm particularly concerned because it's a hard thing to face when a child.
>
> Seamus: You have the baby, Mummy (gives mother a toy person).
>
> Marilyn: Obviously, it's been upsetting for me too, but I have other people I get support from as well.
>
> Seamus: (speaking in a deep voice into a phone) I'm ringing the office, 'hello, it's Joe'
>
> (to his mother) Mummy, it's Joe, he wants to speak to you, Mummy, Mummy!
>
> Marilyn: Tell him I'll call back, I'm busy, I'm in a meeting now.
>
> Seamus: (drops a toy) look it died … (pause) sad, sad …
>
> (picks up a small police car and makes a siren noise, shouting) help! help!
>
> Marilyn: Who needs help, darling?
>
> Seamus: I don't know, can I, can I help?
>
> Trying to understand Seamus's experience involved asking him again who might need help, and he looked at Marilyn. The therapist asked what had happened to his mother. He drew a picture of ET, and said that ET went home and got better. He then looked at his mother, who had tears in her eyes, and said 'Mummy is very sick'.

Although Marilyn had apparently not shared her fears with Seamus, he was clearly picking up on what he was seeing and hearing in the room. He knew someone needed help, and seemed to feel responsible for trying to make things better. He may have been too young to understand the words his mother was using, but his comments indicated that rather than believing her reassurances, he believed what he saw, that his mother was tearful, did not look well, and had not returned to work. His comments and play illustrated his worries about death, and his determined efforts to engage his mother's attention. Far from feeling comforted, he understood that there was something that was so dangerous he could not be told. He found it difficult to put this into words for fear that speaking could magically make things worse.

As the session continued, it emerged that Seamus had thought his mother's distraction meant she was angry with him, and that somehow, it was his fault. The therapist asked Marilyn what she could say to help Seamus understand what was happening to her. In talking and listening to him, she began to understand that Seamus was afraid she would go away and get an even bigger scar on her neck, or maybe never come back, like his Daddy.

Hearing this enabled her to reflect on what Seamus might be feeling, and begin to face the painful prospects that might be in store for them both. There was no way of making this easy, but she was determined to remain emotionally available to her son for as long as she could. Her own mother was included in some sessions, and together they tried to help Seamus with his fear and make plans for the future.

It is difficult to know what should be shared with children. Certain concerns may need to remain with adults to ensure that children are not burdened with a responsibility they cannot fulfil. However, pretending nothing has happened when there are major worries can be extremely unhelpful: in the absence of credible information, children develop their own story, a story which may be much worse than what is being hidden. The truth enables everyone to begin to work together on the difficulties they face. Our beliefs about protecting children can involve trying to hide other worrying information, for instance about finances or the possible breakdown of a relationship. But even very young children know more than we realise and can become involved in holding on to anxiety on behalf of the rest of the family.

There is a risk that protection and secrecy can disconnect children from their own experiences, but a similar pattern may develop in response to other family members who are seen as vulnerable. Attempts to reassure or protect older as well as younger family members can mean that they too are left alone with their worries about what is happening in their lives. Well intentioned but false reassurance can isolate family members from the very people they most need to turn to for solace and support.

Negotiating Differences in Families

Family members have different views about what to eat, where to holiday, and more serious differences about what is right or wrong. The challenge to negotiate difference is central to all relationships, but how does individual responsibility and difference fit in with the patterns of mutual influence described so far? As always it is over the mundane and intimate details of daily life that struggles to negotiate are likely to take place, such as decisions about whether to stick to set meal times and how much time to spend with friends.

These issues often reflect struggles of loyalty, like how often to see or speak to parents. A family is far more than the sum of its parts, and consists of individuals whose experiences, beliefs and desires may differ from one another. Power is not always based on agreement or negotiation. Family members are not equally endowed with the attributes that determine influence in a family, and the ability to manipulate emotions, financial resources and physical strength means that one person is more easily able to dominate others. In each family, there can be enormous differences in the power each individual has, be they adult or child. Sometimes one person's views dominate because they are given that power by others: the rest of the family rely on someone else's taking responsibility for decisions. In families as in other organisations, the person who appears to have the greatest power is not always the one who seems to be in control. The hierarchy may be overruled by more covert dynamics: unwittingly parents can come to rely on a demanding child to be in charge and distract them from other difficulties in the family.

This process of negotiating power and difference continues throughout family life, and is present at the outset of a new relationship. For example, whether the decision to start a couple relationship is one's own, or arranged by others, expectations of that relationship are likely to be influenced by our culture, family of origin and other unique experiences. There may or may not be wide differences in each partner's expectations and an important task of any new relationship is to build a shared 'family culture'. Even where the differences do not seem irreconcilable, decisions about which pattern, or story, of family life will dominate can feel extremely complicated.

Experiences in the previous generation may also play a part in the way brothers and sisters deal with difference. Each child occupies a unique position in the family. For example, one may tend to be the worrier, leaving others to lead more 'happy go lucky' lives; more may be expected of the oldest child than of those who are younger; there may be different expectations of girls and boys; and children may differ in their academic ability or sporting competence. It is the meaning these differences hold for other family members, too, that determines how much they dominate the story each person has of their experience. The desire to protect our children from the vicious fighting we once knew can lead us to try to stifle more able children from achieving. Alternately, differences may be increased because parents accentuate the competition between children.

Such experiences have a powerful effect on the way we handle difference as adults, and feeling second best or being uncomfortable about being more able than brothers or sisters can stay with us. Although subsequent relationships can have a powerful healing force, as in the case of Tony and Brigitte, conflicting and contradictory internal voices can hold us back, continuing to influence our actions and feelings. So, how rivalry was dealt with in our family of origin may guide the way in which we help our own children deal with these issues.

Resilience in Family Life

Most families have to cope with upsets in their lives, and show resilience and flexibility in helping their members to respond to change. Projects like Homestart are good examples of this where volunteers work alongside families in their own homes. They illustrate that the best use of professionals may not always lie in direct work with families, but in disseminating skills so people are more able to create supportive networks themselves. Initiatives like this may require increased time and resources at the outset, but reap long term benefit.

Research has demonstrated the negative consequences for children's subsequent relationships of such trauma as illness, death, ongoing parental disharmony, acrimonious divorces, physical and sexual abuse. However, there is enormous variation in children's responses to such experiences, with some showing far greater resistance than others. This resistance or resilience does not come from individual characteristics only, but from a whole range of risk and protective factors.

Research in particular highlights the value of reducing negative and increasing positive chain reactions in limiting the effect of upsetting experiences. For example, dropping out of school, or relying on drugs as a way of escaping conflicts at home, increases the likelihood of adverse experiences. The same is true for trouble with the police. Finding a way of avoiding this escalation increases the chances of a resilient outcome. Positive relationships, whenever they occur, help to mitigate the effects of earlier trauma and deprivation.

At times of difficulty, access to a confirming relationship, whether a parent or another trusted adult, can be enormously helpful. So too, having some area of competence, such as academic success, sport or another activity can contribute to the development of a positive self-image. Being able to construct a coherent story of life, no matter how difficult, enables the child to make sense of the reality of their life and move towards a sense of psychological balance.

It has become less and less useful to hold on to one idea of family as the meaning we give to the concept of the family is far from static. Many children today grow up in families that are rarely represented positively in the media, putting a strain on how much they can turn to help over their parents for a range of issues in their lives. What remains unclear is the cost of having to balance these two value systems to children, parents and the next generation. In the meantime, while each family is different, thinking in terms of a 'family of families' allows us to focus on how family life is actually sustained. Redefining the meaning of the family should be less about the correctness of any particular family form and more about the quality of the relationships and interaction between its members in providing good experiences and offering protection against bad ones.

Figure 11: A five year old's view of her family with a new baby.

9

Groups

In this chapter we widen our perspective and consider the nature of the group: the setting in which human beings join with each other in units of varying size and complexity, each greater than the sum of its parts. These social structures – many-bodied, yet in many respects functioning like a single organism – have their own dynamics, both internal and in relation to each other, which can be studied in their own right.

Human beings are profoundly social animals, 'herd animals', as we have been called in 1916 by Wilfred Trotter, both a distinguished surgeon and also an early observer of human beings in groups. It is not only that from the first moments of life we seek out the company of others of our own species. Just as our eyes are sensitive to light in the visible spectrum, our personalities are designed to function in relation to other human beings. The very structure of the human mind is such that we define our selves and our behaviour in relation to those others. Even the hermit is part of a social system, though it is one he chooses to shun. Like biologists, psychoanalysts see the drive for relatedness to our fellows as primary, an intrinsic part of our make-up – as fundamental to our being, to our mental functioning, and to our survival as the drive for food, warmth, shelter, sex.

We are born into a social group, consisting of at least three members. Although it is easy to accept the crucial nature of the link between mothers and babies, in fact there is no such thing as a unit consisting of just a mother-and-baby. Until recent developments in reproductive medicine, there has always been a father who has been physically present, even if only very briefly, in that mother's life. Without that father, or that donated sperm, there would be no baby, and the mother would not be a mother. Most importantly, whether or not the father has an existence in the mother' life, he has an existence in her mind, for good or ill, as *the father* of that baby. Babies, moreover, come into the world with an emotional and cognitive preparedness to respond to the biological roles of mother and father, and to form ideas about two parents rather than one, whatever the specific cultural variations.

From the beginning, then, each one of us is part of a biologically and psychologically primary group of *three*, regardless of whoever else may exist in the so-called nuclear family. This *threeness* has immense consequences for our mental development. In what is still called the nuclear family, mother and father will live together, will feel attached to each other, and will cooperate together on the baby's behalf. One parent will support the other in caring for the baby.

Thus a triangle is formed, in which each member will have a relationship with both other members, and at times each member will be excluded from what goes on between the other two. Sometimes, the father will have to wait while mother is breast-feeding the baby, or the baby will have to wait when mother and father choose to be alone together. How the baby responds to the shifting and rotating nature of this triangle – now in, now out, now with the other two focusing on him as the centre of their attention, now with their turning their backs on him and focusing on each other – will influence the development of the individual's mental structure and subsequent characterological strengths and vulnerabilities.

Jealousy

We call it jealousy when we feel mental pain and upset at being left out – when desired figures turn away to others for something they seem to feel we cannot offer them ourselves. Jealousy is a universally troubling emotion. At its most severe it contains a fear of being left to die – the baby who is left too long while mother and father are occupied with each other experiences himself as having been forgotten, dropped from their minds, his existence effectively annihilated. As well, he may suffer from intense feelings of envy, deprivation and rage at their turning to each other, and these feelings in turn add forcefully to the sense of annihilation. This fear of being left to die may be a potent factor in the way in

Figure 12. The large group that forms a single society can break up into warring sub-groups, in which enmities, rivalries and hostilities are acted out. Each sub-group projects all badness out into its enemies and attacks it there. There is the clear sense in this screen-print that yet further sub-groups in society benefit in various ways from this state of affairs.

which intense jealousy can lead to murder, since the desperation about psychic survival can be felt as a question of *annihilate or be annihilated*. Crimes of passion, as they are called, are regarded with a curious sympathy by all but the law itself, since every human being alive recognises the power of the impulse. (And in France, traditionally a country giving an especial importance to love, this sympathy extends even to the Law, where *crimes passionels* receive special dispensation.)

Jealousy causes much trouble, pain and distress, but it may well also have survival value. Loud protests at being left out, whether from infant or adult, ensure one is not forgotten, treated as the runt of the litter, someone expendable. Jealousy also implies fiercely guarded bonds, or the wish to protect one's self and one's own from marauders; and this, as well as rivalry, the expression of jealousy through competition, are important components of any group's dynamic life. Rivalry, jealousy, competitiveness – all derivatives of that earliest group of three – constitute a set of patterns of bonding and relating arising from man's biological endowment, strongly influenced in their expression both by the particular culture and by individual experience. Families and kinship groups are held together by these structures and impulses, as much if not more than they are likely to be blown apart by rivalry, jealousy, and competition. This is what we mean when we say that 'blood is thicker than water'.

Social Groups

Early man valued his kinship groups. There was strength and therefore safety to be derived from an extended family with shared loyalties. Over time these kinship groupings became increasingly sophisticated in their differentiation of members' functions, since survival was more sure if tasks were divided out: some hunting, some tending the young, some managing the domestic animals, some farming. Well-functioning groups were able to value the inclusion of new members who could contribute to these functions and whose loyalty could contribute to the group's as well as to the individual's well-being.

Over the course of human evolution, which eventually became human history, groups were increasingly likely to be put together for specific functions concerned with adaptation and survival. Equally, and for obvious reasons, it became clear that some people were better suited to or good at certain tasks, while others' strengths – or indeed tastes – lay in different directions. In the developed world, social and working roles have evolved rapidly, becoming increasingly specialised. We rely upon others in our very large group, called society, to help us out, doing for us things we cannot necessarily do for ourselves. We divide ourselves up into work-groups, called trades, or jobs or professions – and, unlike the family, or kinship group where you are a member whether you like it or not, membership of these groupings are by and large voluntary and selected, and involve special training or special skills.

A young school teacher went out with her boyfriend for the evening, 'forgetting' that she had left on the stove a pan of chicken scraps and bones that she was boiling up for stock. When she got back, she found a large fire engine outside the building, smoke pouring from the doors and windows, and her flat full of firemen. The tenant in the flat below had heard the smoke alarm through the floor, and, getting no answer to her phone call, had called the fire brigade. The firemen were laconically reassuring to the school-teacher's shame-faced apologies. 'Don't worry, love, happens all the time.' One of them, recognising that she taught his daughter's infant class, teased her by promising that he wouldn't tell her Head Teacher. The boyfriend was less tolerant than the fireman because the flat smelt of burnt bones for over a month.

This potentially dangerous situation demonstrates a mutual inter-dependence between categories of people, most of whom had never met each other before, yet who rely implicitly upon each other for help – for the mutual carrying out of the roles and tasks that keep society ticking over and in one piece.

This mutual support and cooperation is not easy or simple. The field of politics is where the difficult negotiations and trade-offs take place which are necessary to maintain the coherent and cooperative functioning of the various units that make up the larger social group. Sometimes the tensions generated by the group's internal politics are dealt with by the group's agreeing upon a common enemy outside its own boundaries, meaning that cooperation within a group may be bought at the cost of conflict between that group and others – and this principle may be seen operating both within and between nations.

As we have become more self-reflective and self-studying, we have come to recognise that groups – whether small and focused, or large and complex – have their own internal dynamics which can help or hinder the carrying out of their designated task. This field of study, group dynamics, is concerned with understanding the way in which groups are formed; how the working of the group in turn affects the individual members for good or ill; and how entire groups relate to each other.

What precisely is it that we would consider to be a group, capable of generating its own internal dynamics? Is a collection of people, such as those travelling to their various places of work on the top deck of a bus, a group? Usually there is no connection between them – unless something happens on that bus to draw them together around some common task. A passenger might suddenly be taken ill, which mobilises the social or group capacities of the other passengers: someone goes to tell the driver to halt the bus; someone pulls out a mobile phone to summon medical help; others might try to make the ill person comfortable, or to reassure him that he will be looked after. That disparate collection of people will have become a working group, focused on the effective carrying out of a task.

In fact, all groups come into existence for a purpose, an endeavour, and carry out work to ensure that it is achieved. That work might be to raise a family, to put out a fire, to perform an operation in a hospital, or to man a lifeboat. Sometimes the group's purpose will not be immediately concerned with the essentials of survival, and will be more connected with religious or magical activity, or various forms of play: climbing a mountain, playing football (see Plate 11), praying within a congregation, performing a Mozart symphony, or – since man will invent an endeavour if there are none at hand – giving a party.

This work, the group's *task*, and its associated activity, is the conception, the beginning of the group. Secondly, the group must develop a structure if it is to operate effectively – beginning with a boundary, delineating *inside* from *outside*. This individual is a member of our team: he can come in. This one is not: he will have to wait outside. Thus a *territory* is marked out, which might be an actual location, consisting of the operating theatre, the committee room, the home, or the football field, the mountain; or might be psychological, having more to do with friendship, shared interests, tastes and attitudes.

Then there is the issue of *time*. Often the group that has been formed to do a particular piece of work – tending the stricken bus passenger for instance – will cease to exist once that work has ended. However, some created groups survive in a loose way until their membership is terminated by death; life membership of the cricket club for example. This is still more true of our families, where membership extends beyond the individual's lifespan both for genetic ('She's got her grandmother's eyes') and for societal reasons. Our birth certificates and our death certificates define us as members of that group. We are, for better or worse, members not only for life but also after it – and for most of the time are pleased to be so. Thus the saying that 'blood is thicker than water' also means that we turn to our families for help and look out for each other when the going gets hard.

Working groups often try to select their members based on some idea of *competence* – who would be a useful and productive member of this team? Who could take up effectively the various tasks required for this kind of work: chairman, secretary, treasurer, captain, cook? Other groups, often informal, are created around the idea of *sentience*, involving preferences, tastes, common interests, affections: whom do I like and want to spend time with (see Plate 12)? If we are lucky, competence and sentience will overlap: we may enjoy the company of our colleagues at work and carry out our joint tasks more effectively for that reason.

Troubling Emotions in Groups

However, the working life of any group has a troublesome underbelly, consisting of the long lasting emotional and psychological derivatives of that earliest grouping of three already described: mother, father and child. To be in a grouping of any kind in later life evokes – and also employs – the potential for derivatives of these early feelings to be stirred up once again, and they then begin to determine not just mood but also behaviour. Jealousy, envy, rivalry, desire for special status, and the wish to control are universal and ubiquitous. They have to be managed or harnessed one way or another if the group is to function effectively and harmoniously. Those who manage to tolerate the ins and outs of group life with equanimity are felt to be good colleagues, capable of cooperation. Often they are those who can put the task first, give it primacy, get on with the job in spite of personal wishes and feelings, likes and dislikes.

However there are many people who find groups troubling, and who find membership of a group, however small or informal, difficult, even impossible. Sometimes they may find ways of remaining in society so that they can both benefit and contribute: lighthouse-keeping, for example, might be the kind of job that could, for certain individuals, solve some internal difficulties with the larger social grouping. Others maintain themselves in a solitary or isolated state within the context of a wider sociality. Human beings are quick to respond to signals that imply avoidance or fear or hostility and to label such individuals as *loners*. Loners then tend to be avoided and a self-perpetuating cycle is set up which is unlikely to improve without intervention. We can say with some certainty that when there have been difficulties in the primary (family) group, the legacy of these difficulties will become apparent in many subsequent social settings – from the one-to-one to the group, small or large.

Group Therapy

Out of this observation has developed a powerful form of therapeutic treatment which uses the group itself as the basis for treatment of difficulties within the group. *Group therapy* takes some of its basic concepts from psychoanalysis and some from the field of group dynamics. In group therapy, the impact of the group on the patient and the patient on the group can be seen in action, because each individual's internal difficulties become manifested in the session through the actual relationships that have developed between group members in the room. Seven or eight patients meet together in a neutral setting with a group therapist. The time, the location and the membership are selected by the therapist. The *task* for the individual members is to get to know each other in increasing depth. To do this they are given the opportunity, just as in individual treatment, to say to each other whatever is uppermost in their minds, without the inhibitions imposed by ordinary social custom. The therapist's job is to help these individuals change for the better, in behaviour, feeling and attitudes. He or she does this by interpreting to the group those factors, both conscious and unconscious, that impede its progress. These factors will include both those pressures that arise from the group as a whole and those unconscious resistances that exist in the mind of every one of its members.

Here is an example, taken from an out-patient group within the Department of Psychiatry in a large teaching hospital. The group was in the second year of its life. By that time its members knew each other quite well and the group realised that there was a lot of work that still needed to be done. The group had amongst its members a working musician, a freelance journalist, an apprentice architect, a civil servant (who was a haemophiliac), a primary school teacher, a housewife, a retired naval officer and an unemployed man. The main protagonist in this episode is Ralph (the freelance journalist), in his early fifties, a heavily built man with iron-grey hair brushed forward in a fringe.

> Ralph had never been married. He was the only child, born late to relatively elderly parents, both of whom were now dead. Whatever the weather, he invariably wore blue-jeans and a heavy fisherman's navy-blue sweater. He spoke in a measured, deliberate manner and his vocabulary was liberally sprinkled with jargon acquired from his earlier therapeutic ventures – mainly in 'alternative' treatments.

Ralph was one of the most reliable and staunch members of the group. He was usually the first to arrive. He always asked whether there were messages from other members when they failed to come on time, and he would often pick up on issues of the week before to see how people were feeling about it now. He broke silences by wondering 'where everyone is', challenged others to cut out the intellectualising and to talk about their feelings; and he brought his own struggles with his writing, his chronic mild depression, and his failure to engage any woman – or man for that matter – in a long-term relationship. He was recognised and appreciated by the others to be an excellent group member. And yet – from the therapist's point of view – he had not really changed in any particular respect since he had entered the group two years earlier.

In this particular session, just after the New Year, Ralph was talking about a woman whom he had been attracted to at a party, and who was returning to the States in a few days' time. Should he or shouldn't he pursue this interest in her? The group picked this up without marked enthusiasm (it was a familiar story) and began to help him think about it, although in a slightly dutiful way. One or two members were gazing at Ralph rather absently as he responded to Lucy's (the school-teacher's) promptings.

The therapist herself felt restless, sometimes thinking of other things such as the shopping for supper, but mainly preoccupied with wondering whether the haemophiliac in the group who had begun, as he sometimes did, to bleed quietly from a nick caused by that morning's shave, would notice the trickle of blood before it reached his shirt collar, and of how impossible it would be to remove the stain once it got there. She had to resist the urge to interrupt Ralph to suggest to Jack (the civil servant) he mop himself up. No-one else seemed to have noticed, or if they had, to mind. Her thoughts about Ralph were to wonder rather flatly whether the group could do more with this depressed and somewhat cut-off character than just to go on allowing him to use the group as a sort of periodic transfusion of light and warmth, the nearest he might get to having real or intimate relations with his fellow humans.

What happened next was that Lucy, going a bit pink, said suddenly with a rather intense mixture of desperation and embarrassment, 'Oh I always seem to get into this situation with you, Ralph. I don't know what it is, but I just find I'm not really listening to you even though it was me that asked the question. I just drift off. It's an awful thing to say. I'm sorry, I suppose it's me.' She had a chronic preoccupation with not being 'an intellectual', which was how she saw the other members of the group. She looked rather miserably at the therapist, then at the floor. However, this statement of hers had thoroughly woken the group up, and everyone else looked at Ralph. Ralph changed colour, and said after a pause, 'I suppose you're telling me I'm boring.'

There was a tense but very alive silence. Ralph spoke again. 'The awful thing is I know I'm being boring. I sort of go on to automatic pilot – I find I've been talking for a couple of minutes and I don't know what the hell I've been saying.' Everyone laughed and people began to chip in with how they too had been somewhere else for the past twenty minutes. Susie told Jack his face was bleeding and someone passed him a tissue to wipe it up. With some shame, Ralph went on to say, in a way that felt very real, that he fears he actually has nothing to say, that he is empty – and that he talks a lot to cover this up from those he is with. Eventually he wept as he said he believed he had even bored his own mother. He could not remember a time when he felt she had been really able to enjoy being with him. Her heart wasn't in it, he said. Paradoxically, to the group at that moment, he had never seemed more alive and present.

After Ralph had spoken, the therapist began to feel that she had some inkling about the reasons for the paralysing situation that had existed in the group before Lucy's intervention. What was being lived out in the group setting and between the members was the nature of Ralph's internal world – the relationships that existed inside him and that he felt stuck with and dominated by. What the group members, including the therapist, had been experiencing was the nature of Ralph's chronic despair about being unable to find a way to get in touch with someone important to him (his mother), someone who was baffling him unbearably by behaving 'correctly', being present, apparently interested in what was going on while in fact *her heart was not in it*. In the place of those necessary emotional nutrients, intimacy and involvement, there was only bafflement and emotional distance.

Ralph, the therapist thought, had inside him a version of his mother who was bewildered and probably frightened by him and his infantile needs. The therapist's own experience had, she felt, given her some glimpse of the mother's nature: a woman who was unable to manage her baby's primitive and intense demands, shutting them and him out by keeping her mind elsewhere, concentrating instead on the practical routines of motherhood – keeping the clothes clean and unstained, remembering the shopping. The group had been able, through Lucy, to override the verbal detail of the particular problem being discussed, and take hold of the emotional situation: the fact that everyone was giving an imitation of being in touch with Ralph, but inside themselves had abandoned him to his ruminations. The therapist did not say all this out loud. Her aim was to leave room for the group members to think about these things for themselves, thus developing their own capacities for observation and understanding. She commented that the group might keep an eye on that tendency to drift away internally because this behaviour in them, or equally in a mother, could abandon the baby to continuing on automatic pilot. She hoped they would feel freer to speak about it when it happened in the future.

How can we understand what is happening where members successfully project their inner state on the group? This happens in all groups, but it is particularly magnified in a therapy group. One reason for this is that the group has only a single task, which is ultimately to understand its own functioning. It is inward looking – it has no wood to chop, house to build or political problems to solve. Secondly it has permission to examine its own functioning out loud, something that is implicitly proscribed in everyday social life. People can say to each other what is ordinarily unsayable, and it can be revelatory – for the sayer, and for the said to, and for the listeners. Third, and most important, is the nature of the group itself. Members become extremely sensitive to each others' states of mind. Much of the time, these states of mind are picked up on unconsciously and non-verbally and are then experienced by the receiver as though they were his or her own. Sometimes they are then acted on – one member's lofty and superior calm provokes fury in another member, who then acts irritably, expressing the rage that was being denied by the provoker. Sometimes these projections are perceived before they take hold, particularly as members get to know each other well.

In the events described above, Lucy seemed to have found unbearable the state of mind she had picked up of Ralph's early experience of being unable to feel himself in touch with a mother whose heart was in her mothering. Her burst of honesty was the expression of this, the crying out of someone who is saying *I cannot stand what is happening, what is not happening, between us!* And her saying that out loud freed the rest of the group to become aware of what was happening, as well as freeing the therapist's own thinking sufficiently for her to recognise that her preoccupation with the shirt collar and the shopping were also a response to a projection, this time of the kind of mother which Ralph carried around inside him like a dead weight.

Here we have a situation that is unique to group therapy. Different aspects of the individual member's internal world are picked up on by different group members, including the therapist. The internal world becomes visible and alive, active in the relationships lived out in the room. Lucy might not have been able to experience and communicate her response to Ralph in the way she did if the therapist had not been containing the mother's hateful incomprehension of her baby's demands, turning away from them stonily towards an obsessional defence (shopping lists, clean collars). The therapist might not have felt it safe to go on with that hatred and experience it in her boredom with her patient, had Lucy not been aware of the awfulness of such a situation, which was that of the rejected and abandoned infant in Ralph. Lucy's anguish was acted out through her protest – but it was precisely this that alleviated Ralph's sense of abandonment. Then, through Ralph's recollection of his mother, the present was able to be linked with the past as an alive experience for everyone in the room.

Shouldn't the therapist have understood all this before matters went that far? Possibly. But possibly also a measured interpretation from a very on-the-ball therapist, as Ralph paused for breath, would have lacked the freshness and the real-life quality of Lucy's protest – and Ralph's sudden fusion of self-knowledge with memory and pain, and then relief as he found a different relationship with himself and with the group. And Lucy would have been deprived of the chance to find that she had a voice of her own that was valuable to others in the group. It is one of the great benefits of group therapy that patients can be a genuine help to each other and can come to recognise it; that the therapist may not be the only person in the room with something useful to contribute. Group members can say things out of their direct experience of each other that no therapist could say, and, miraculously they are not just tolerated but used. Ralph became increasingly attentive to his tendency to go on to automatic pilot, and receptive to what it did to the others, and to their ways of listening to him. In time, as he became increasingly able to believe in his fellow group members' willingness truly to bear with him, rather than just to bear him, so also did his tendency to shut them out by boring them, filling them with his own schizoid emptiness, diminish.

This is an account of a group session in which the highly complex internal events that became manifest in the room between the members could be understood and turned to the good. In this case, it was because the therapist, the group leader, had been trained in the understanding of intra-psychic and inter-personal processes, and in when and how to intervene – if at all – when things became difficult. It is a skilled job and not easy to do well. This is just as true for other kinds of group. When the leader (school teacher, social worker, business manager, vicar, prison officer or military commander, and so on) knows intuitively something of the benefits and pitfalls inherent in group functioning – and better still can back up that intuition with knowledge and experience of group dynamics – then he or she can help the group to avoid the hazards and to harness the immense potential inherent in *putting our heads together*. Well-functioning working groups can tackle issues that may be beyond the isolated individual's grasp or skills.

Crowds, Mobs and Armies

However, not all groups are as interested in listening and learning and in understanding their own process. Large groups, those too big for every member to know all the others by face and name, differ considerably from the small therapy group described above. Many of an individual's capacities for reflection, thought, problem-solving and decision making – his identity – will be submerged in and subsumed by the large group itself.

The Apocrypha, from the Greek version of the Old Testament, tells the story of how a city of the Israelites was besieged by the Assyrian army, led by the ferocious Holofernes. When the plight of the Israelites became extreme and they were on the verge of having either to surrender or to die, Judith, a beautiful Israelite widow, was permitted by the elders of the city, Bethulia, to try one last desperate strategy. She crept from the city towards the enemy camp wearing her finest clothes and jewels, bearing gifts, and accompanied only by a maid. She was, as expected, arrested by the Assyrian guards and taken to Holofernes, where she led him to believe she wanted to betray her people. Four days later, much taken by her beauty, he decided to seduce her and ordered a feast to be prepared for the two of them that night. Judith took care to see that he drank a great deal before she allowed herself to be led to his bed. Once he had fallen into a drunken stupor, she took his sword and severed his head from his body with a mighty stroke. She then fled silently back to the besieged city with it in her bag. At dawn, the Assyrian army, finding their leader headless, panicked, collapsed and fled. It seemed as though all their capacities for thought, planning and action had been invested in Holofernes, so that the army itself was effectively beheaded by Judith's act. Holofernes in turn seemed to have behaved in a foolishly grandiose way, inflated into omnipotence and thus thoughtlessness by everyone else's attribution to him of all power and competence. Both followers and followed are at risk from the kinds of processes engendered by large groups, especially where automatic obedience to the leader is a part of the basic culture.

Amongst the descriptive names for large groups are *crowd* and *mob*. A crowd is a large group with little structure or organisation, and its behaviour is unpredictable. Mobs are more coherent, but dangerously so – unruly groups in the grip of a wish to locate and destroy an enemy, whether real or imagined. Those who make up a mob will stream past the voice of reality or reason. A mob hates thought. The primitive impulses that exist as a potential in every member (in every human being) can be tapped into and amplified by unscrupulous leaders, and the outcome can be mayhem and bloodshed. In Nazi Germany at the end of the 1930s, mob feeling had firmly located the enemy in the Jews, and, during the night of 9-10 April, 1938, now known as Kristallnacht, every window in every house or shop known to be owned by Jews was smashed in an orgy of mindless violence, whipped up by Goebbels. 7,500 Jewish businesses were gutted, 177 synagogues burned or demolished and 91 Jews were killed.

Shakespeare understood mob passions. He took part of the complex history of the Roman Empire, simplifying and dramatising it to illustrate some fundamentals of group behaviour. The conspirators assassinate the Roman emperor, Julius Caesar, fearing that public adulation had turned him into an omnipotent monster (as perhaps had happened with Holofernes). There is then a dramatic public argument in the Senate between Mark Antony, loyal to Caesar, and Brutus, leader of the conspirators, with rhetoric used as powerfully as a sword. They are fighting for the control of the Roman people, depicted as a passionate and fickle mob whose feelings are running very high, swaying this way and that, running the streets in search of an enemy to lynch. They find and murder an entirely innocent man, even though they discover he is not the one they are looking for. Mob passions render innocence irrelevant. A group in such a primitive state will find or recruit a primitive leader who will serve its purpose, and if a suitable enemy cannot be found one will be created.

Cinna: Truly, my name is Cinna.
A citizen: Tear him to pieces, he's a conspirator.
Cinna: I am Cinna the poet, I am Cinna the poet.
A citizen: Tear him for his bad verses, tear him for his bad verses.
Cinna: I am not Cinna the conspirator!
A citizen: It is no matter, his name's Cinna, pluck but his name out of his heart and turn him going.
Citizens: Tear him, tear him! Come, brands, ho! Firebrands! To Brutus', to Cassius', burn all!

Versions of this scene have been acted out many times in history. Religious fervour in medieval and early modern times led to the Inquisitions, which, as their name implies, did not wait for complaints but actively sought out those whom they considered to be heretics, witches or alchemists. The use of torture as a means of exacting confessions was given Papal backing in 1252, and Tomas de Torquemada, the Spanish Grand Inquisitor, was responsible for more than 2000 burnings at the stake. Revolutionary fervour in France in 1789, provoked by a crisis in the levels of basic subsistence, led to the Reign of Terror, which resulted in 300,000 suspects and more than 17,000 executions.

Witchhunts and Idealisation: Two Sides of the Same Coin

The McCarthy witchhunts in America in the 1950s, ostensibly in search of Communists, regarded as enemies of the State, were conducted with something of the same zeal. The punishments involved the lifelong loss of the opportunity to work. Here, it is hatred that is stoked up. Equally, its opposite, love, can be stoked up and amplified to produce *idealisation*. With similar irrationality, other groups can be in the grip of the wish to possess an ideal leader, or idea or goal or principle. Although their overt behaviour may be quite different, they have more in common with the mob fuelled by hatred than might at first be imagined. Anyone who disagrees with the sacrosanct nature of the chosen leader will be ostracised or excluded from the group. Troubled young people sometimes get caught up in sects which seem at first to offer them the unconditional love and support they crave. However, when they feel more confident and begin to think about or even show a wish to discuss some of the group's fundamental tenets, or even just want to *go home*, things change dramatically. They may be made into prisoners, and be treated as criminals.

The two kinds of group – those fuelled by hatred, who are enemy-orientated, and those fuelled by idealisation, who are deity-orientated – are similar in that the members of each have submerged their own capacities for individual thought, planning, reasoning and decision-making into a leader. In 1978 Jim Jones led his group, almost a thousand strong (a quarter of whom were children) to commit mass suicide in the jungles of Guyana, so thoroughly had the individual members surrendered their own capacities for thought and reason into their leader. The leader is felt to be the one whose words carry weight, even divine weight, and individual members obey, or bow down, or submit to that leader in a mindless way.

Nations, Peoples and Creeds

Political scientists, diplomats, and experts in international relations, all have to struggle with these issues, since similar processes can also take place on a national and international level. Equally, such processes are used or frankly exploited by Heads of State to influence the national mood. Here our precise knowledge is limited, and our capacity to bring about change even more so. Yet there are times when it looks as though entire nations and cultural groupings are behaving as if those undesireable attributes such as greed, rapaciousness, bigotry, meanness, dishonesty were all located in another identifiable group. North and South, Catholics and Protestants, blacks and whites, Nazis and Jews, Jews and Palestinians, Serbs and Albanians, Arabs and Christians – each group at times is capable of appearing to believe it had a monopoly on truth, moral rectitude and decent behaviour.

The great religious and territorial conflicts owe their bloodiness to the kinds of mental mechanisms – denial and projection – that find ready expression and a dangerous amplification in groups, and are even less manageable in large national and international groups. In small groups set up for the purposes of therapy, such as the one described above, mechanisms such as these can be observed and spoken about. Yet if we acknowledge how hard it is hard to change feeling and behaviour even in therapy, how infinitely more difficult it is to affect the behaviour of an entire national, tribal or religious group. The intentional pursuit of change for the better is a long hard enterprise in both individual and group. It is all the more significant that there have been recent changes in the courts of justice leading to decisions that no-one, not even a Head of State, may have immunity from prosecution for abuses of fundamental human rights.

Knowing as much as we do about the effects of the individual on the group and the group on the individual, both for good and for ill, it is curious that we do not take these sorts of factors more readily into account. Education, politics, social services, hospitals, the police, the penal system, factories, religious groups, youth movements, business ventures could all make valuable use of a deepened understanding of groups: both the theory, and even more so, the practice. We need not ignore our own knowledge in the way we appear to. Perhaps that too is a group process. It touches on the most fundamental of human conflicts, existing within each individual and within each group: the conflict between constructiveness and destructiveness, between the wish for life and its obverse, that which psychoanalysts call *the death instinct*. Here, we are not facing something as simple as a choice. It is instead a conflict, which is lifelong and inextinguishable, and its significance cannot be underestimated.

10

Work

> The fact is that after I felt sure of myself as a welder I felt sure of myself and everything, even the way I walked.
> Primo Levi.

This quotation from the novel *The Wrench* by Primo Levi expresses the way in which our self-esteem is intimately related to our experience of work. Why should this be so? Because we get a large part of our sense of who we are, our worth and particularly our sense of our effectiveness through work. Work provides a structure to our lives, a way of being present in the here-and-now of things, rather than being bogged down in our internal worlds of memories from the past and dreams of the future.

Yet the world of work no less than that of the family, the nursery or the school engages people only if it engages with their emotional life. People go to work for money, but not only for money. All the evidence suggests that money alone, and tinkering with arrangements over pay such as bonuses, (unless this is a very significant proportion of take-home pay) has little impact on the way people perform. Other issues are at stake. People work well in organisations where there is some degree of alignment between what they value and are committed to, what they will work to achieve, and the values and commitments of the organisation.

Without this deeper engagement there is all too often an endless dance of attempts to manipulate behaviour on both sides, management and worker. The world of work is a place where a broad range of emotions may be experienced. While the emotions are similar to and have their roots in our private lives, a different set of issues regarding loyalty, loves, dislikes, hatreds, jealousy, desires and ideals comes into being in the workplace. They need to be understood in a different frame – that of the organisation, with its internal dynamics and the dynamics of its relations with its environment, of competitors, government policies and so on, in addition to the personal 'frame' of an individual personality.

Good and Evil at Work

For its operation the human mind seems to require the making of strong distinctions – good from bad, love from hate. Each pole or opposite functions as a container for its reverse, a protection from excessive love or, conversely, excessive hate. However when the two poles are split too far apart the emotion is unmitigated by its opposite, and the sense of self as containing and managing each component begins to disintegrate. When we join organisations we do so in part to maintain our mental equilibrium: we seem emotionally to need bad and denigrated figures in our lives (whether these are individuals or groups) as well as good and ideal ones. The idea that when we become adult we automatically outgrow the need for fairy stories involving a struggle between simply constructed good and evil parental figures is patently false; hence the content of much TV and film entertainment and of computer games.

These mental mechanisms need to find expression at work as well – the good group or organisation *we* belong to, as opposed to the bad organisation out there or down the corridor. We project the less acceptable parts of ourselves onto others, battle with them there and at the same time lose a significant chunk of ourselves. This can be expressed in splits across whole sectors of society – the good public and the greedy, selfish private sectors, or the lazy, dependent public sector and the efficient, autonomous commercial one. These fantasies are quite independent of realities. They are driven by the human need to create good and bad, to split the world into good and evil, black and white.

The workplace is a setting in which the private world of emotions and meaning and the public world of fact and achievement come together. It is a crucible and container, in which the inner and the outer, the private and the public interact and give meaning to each other. It provides a regular shared setting for mature and realistic experiences and contacts with others, different from the intense intimacies and the biologically determined relationships of the family. Whether it is paid or not, work brings us into contact with goals and purposes wider than ourselves, with consequently broader satisfactions and achievements. It confers a status and identity in the world, a sense of self and personal agency through voluntary associations with others.

Sigmund Freud spoke of the two central achievements that define normality as being the capacity to love another person and the capacity to work. Both require the ability to reach beyond a private, self-centred world and engage with others. Through the evidence of the successes and shortcomings of one's own efforts, work provides the opportunity for a realistic relationship to the external world in both psychological and material terms: to test reality, to destroy (creatively or destructively), to repair and to create.

All work, even the simplest, is based on an objective, something which has yet to be achieved; and it always has a *symbolic* (existing in thought and feeling) component. Even something as simple as 'make another one like that' requires an internal symbolic representation of the purpose that must be achieved. When work goes well it provides reassurance that our destructive impulses are balanced by others, both reparative and creative. A workplace that cannot recognise this human dimension belonging to work is soul-destroying. This is because our minds and hearts are nourished on facts and truths which exist in the psychological as well as the material domain. Work starts with something that is *missing*, an absence that has to be filled, something that is incomplete.

The Emotional Origins of Work

At the deepest unconscious level of our minds, work, and particularly this experience of something missing, also stimulates the 'baby' part of ourselves with its tension between the desires to consume and destroy, and the desires to love, repair and build. Associated with this are a series of common concerns: about aggression and its expression; about confidence or the lack of it; about the capacity to repair and restore; about feelings of depression consequent upon a failure; about the inevitable experiences of uncertainty and confusion; or the fears of success when this is equated with triumphing over and destroying loved ones.

Unless managers recognise that work necessarily stimulates these deep emotions and, where appropriate, provide the avenues for working them through, whether in individual interviews, or often more usefully in the team itself, they will accumulate and periodically explode.

Jim was the director of marketing for a manufacturing company. He came to see the Consultancy Service because he was having a series of conflicts with the sales director which he wanted to understand better and avoid, as they were harming his motivation and career. Over a series of consultation meetings it emerged that the sources of this conflict were twofold – personal and organisational. The first centred on his unresolved feelings towards his father. As a boy he had experienced his father as rather remote. Though Jim recognised that there was no evidence that he did not love him, his father nevertheless seemed to have had difficulty expressing this in a way that would be understandable to a small boy.

This 'small boy' aspect of Jim was still very much present in his working life. He longed for his manager, whom he unconsciously experienced as the father of his childhood, to love him. Of course this is neither a reasonable demand nor advisable in the workplace. Nevertheless such feelings often lie not far below the surface at work.

In meetings of his management team, Jim would often be sarcastic and destructively competitive towards his peers. The managing director felt this was a problem but did not understand Jim's behaviour. During the course of the consultancy it was possible to make sense of this in terms of Jim's wish to be loved above all others in the group. When others were either the centre of attention or did something that Jim regarded as stupid or of poor quality he would put them down, as if to say to his managing director, 'Look at me, at how clever I am; love me more than them'. Unconsciously, Jim equated being clever with being loved by a father figure.

There was also an organisational dimension to this situation, since Jim's approach to marketing was more up-to-date than the culture of the firm generally. Jim worked on the basis that an effective sales strategy depended on a deep understanding of the customer and on maintaining a long-term relationship between the organisation and the customer. However, Terry, the sales director, was of the 'old school'. He believed customers were interested only in the short-term – in price and availability, or in other words, 'pile them high and sell them cheap'. This method no doubt still had virtues but it was clear from the market place that this approach was inadequate, since customers were choosing one firm over another for 'softer' reasons, such as the attitude of the salespeople on the sales floor. The fights between Jim and Terry were therefore also an expression of a strategic conflict within the organisation. The managing director was avoiding this, trying to placate and criticise both sides at the same time, but not prepared to grasp the nettle of deciding that the sales approach needed to be modernised. He in his turn feared being unpopular with Terry.

It was possible to work on these issues both with Jim and with his managing director; to shift the situation both for Jim, through a better understanding of his own behaviour, and for his manager, to whom Jim was able to explain some of his difficult behaviour. Jim was also able to put the organisation's strategic question back to the right place, with the managing director, and on to the agenda of the management group. The discussion of this topic openly, rather than covertly through Jim and Terry, allowed them to make more effective decisions.

This is a story about how a person with a personality, a history and the psychodynamics created by this, interacts with an organisation with its own dynamics. What appeared to be a personal problem was also an organisational one. Although it is not always the case, often what are apparently purely 'personal problems' in organisations are also in reality the symptoms of underlying and unresolved organisational problems. Organisational dynamics tend to push a person with the right sort of problem forward as their 'unconscious spokesperson' to express the issue on behalf of everyone. Thus the wise manager will look at any immediate personnel problem as also potentially providing intelligence about an organisational dilemma.

Jim's choice of marketing as a career was partly driven by the desire to be noticed, to communicate and to be loved, so it is not very surprising that these emotions were a part of the underlying dynamics in this story. For other functions there are other issues: for finance, for example, the issue centres often around control. People are suited to particular careers because there is an unconscious as well as a conscious fit. The significance and depth of such feelings and the deep sources of motivation they provide are rarely wholly conscious in the workplace, though good managers often have an intuitive and unconscious understanding of these human factors and hence an intuitive capacity to motivate their staff effectively.

Rachel sought consultation on her management style because she was regarded as unnecessarily aggressive and brutal in her treatment of her subordinates. She would drive them very hard, making them work long hours, and they complained about her constantly critical judgements of them. Rachel understood that these were indeed deficiencies in her management style and gradually over the course of our meetings she understood how these were based on an excessive focus on the task and a lack of attention to the needs of the people she managed. When she was frustrated with their performance she would criticise but then take over their work, failing to see that she needed to train and develop them.

However, Rachel's case needed to be seen in the context of the firm as a whole, where Rachel had been chosen precisely because of her driving approach and her ability to get things done in what was otherwise a rather laissez-faire environment. The private rhetoric of the board was very aggressive even though their public presentation was apparently understanding and 'nice'. This left the nastier aspects to be expressed by subordinates such as Rachel, who were expected to get things done regardless.

The Changing Organisation

One reason we join organisations is that they provide a setting or 'container' within which the more primitive impulsive aspects of our selves can be expressed in a socially useful form. Aggressive impulses become labour, 'erotic' desires can find expression through the provision of more sophisticated pleasures, through serving others. (Freud termed this process 'sublimation', the turning of primitive desires towards socially useful behaviour.) The particular nature of the work engages and stimulates particular impulses – commerce requires and stimulates more the aggressive and acquisitive impulses, whereas the helping professions draw more on loving and reparative impulses. The structures of organisations and professions should function to provide protection to both the worker and the consumer from being overwhelmed by these impulses.

While we may have chafed at the more bureaucratic organisation structures of the past, these were a source of stability and something that could be variously loved and hated – and they could stand it. With today's organisation, this is less and less the case. The rate of change means that the structures, roles and functions of organisations are changing continuously. Instead of organisations providing a dependable support in people's lives, the situation can be reversed:

Figure 13: Grosz, Ants II. A satirical view of the industrial era.

it is those in work that have to support the organisation – and often when the existing structures are patently out-moded.

Those disappointed expectations of dependability, combined with unpredictable and changing organisational structures which create uncertainty but are no longer able to provide stable psychological containment, lead to stress, disarray and anger in employees. However, most managers have not been trained to cope with understanding how to make sense of the emotional state of their workforce, and to assist employees to manage the emotional impact of their work. Furthermore a career is no longer a matter of finding a dependable employer and committing one's working life to the job. Employing organisations, even if they wished to, cannot these days offer a lifetime's security. The individual is more and more responsible for managing his or her own career.

These changes are producing the need for more sophisticated managers. The need to be able to adapt effectively to a changing world requires a capacity for working in teams. Put simply, it requires the capacity to *hear* the point of view of others rather than the capability of achieving control or adherence to any particular point of view.

The Impact of Work

Different types of work arouse different sorts of emotions. In the public sector, Isabel Menzies Lyth, a psychoanalyst and organisational consultant, has demonstrated that the demands of nursing, with its more or less constant contact with pain and suffering, can deteriorate into defensive distancing from the patient at both the individual level (burn-out) and in the organisation (ignoring the impact of stress, staff are managed by a collective defensive posture such as speaking of the patient as 'the liver in bed No. 9'). It is often the best nurses who leave the profession and they do so because the defensive way in which the hospital organisation is structured stifles their individual initiative and prohibits satisfying sources of contact between nurse and patient – for example, by rotating nurses from ward to ward on a daily basis.

This is the psychological equivalent of dust in a coal-mine, a by-product which, if not dealt with, causes sickness. However, the mental ill-health consequences of the workplace, particularly for those in the most stressful jobs such as nursing and the police, are rarely attended to. This is not intended as a criticism because it is hardest to tackle stress in precisely those jobs that carry the most risk to the worker. To acknowledge stress in these jobs is inevitably experienced as a threat to the omnipotent defences that the individual and the organisation construct as a protection against the recognition of the worker's vulnerability. Nevertheless, some balance has to be struck and fights over pay and conditions are rarely all that is at issue in these professions.

Those in the helping professions are motivated by the wish to make things better for people but can also be partly driven by an unconscious fear and guilt about their own destructiveness. Work which leads to the repair of a patient or client produces reassurance against these fears. Each profession has its dark side.

Doctors can be overcome by their need to repair even where this leads to unnecessary suffering in the patient – as expressed in the old joke, *the operation was successful but the patient died*. Professional codes of conduct help those with the power to do good from being overwhelmed by the opposite, but always present, capacity to do harm. We need our institutions to help us in our conduct with each other; but so much has changed in recent years that they have difficulty in keeping up and are struggling to provide this function.

The Future of Management

The twentieth century has seen dramatic improvements in material working conditions, such as the recognition that coal-dust causes emphysema. The next century is likely to focus on emotional conditions, the symbolic coal-dust present in every work place – not least because only through attention to these factors will organisations be able to remain competitive and retain their employees' motivation. Managers have been trained for a predictable, controllable world – indeed the name itself implies maintenance. However, the excessive use of control as a method of management results in either denial and bullying or in a succession of management fads that promise 'the one best way' of motivating and organising the work-force.

Training for a job entails the internalisation of a *work conscience* that helps prevent the individual exploiting his or her power. However under conditions of dramatic change this conscience is often unsupported and may come into conflict with the anxiety of survival. Realising the psychological realities as well as the material, measurable and objective aspects of the work-place can help us understand better why and how things at work go wrong, whether at the individual, group or organisational level. Organisations need to be viewed more as organisms in environments, with highly permeable boundaries, rather than as hierarchies of relatively autonomous units. Behaviour at work needs to be understood holistically and systemically, as well as in detail – the total situation as well as the particular.

> The ABC Company manufactures microchips. Its market is rapidly moving and highly competitive. The creation of new products is carried out in three stages. The architects come up with a new design, the testers build and test the prototype, and the production team turns the prototype into a market-ready product. The three groups were communicating poorly, however. The architects were lively but arrogant, and viewed the testers as causing undue delays because of problems with the tests they were using. The testers in response asserted that it was impossible to use off-the-shelf tests; each had to be tailor-made and this took time. The testers in turn blamed the production team, who were viewed as clumsy and slow. The dynamics of status in the hierarchy, with the architect on top, were also a response to the state of the organisation in the marketplace.
>
> The success or otherwise of the company's products, which suffered from rapid obsolescence, was essentially dependent on the unpredictable whim of the consumer. In this anxious and stressful world each team blamed the other. However following this analysis it was possible to help the head of the factory not to waste

time on concentrating narrowly on 'improving communication' between the various groups, and instead to re-orientate all three teams to look outwards at the market and to recognise the anxiety it was causing in them. On this basis the three teams together could consider the way they needed to work together to respond to the challenge of external competition. It was possible for each group to see that the 'blame culture' that had grown up was a symptom of uncertainty and anxiety. They needed to draw up more collaborative styles of working, keeping each other informed about problems as they arose, rather than hiding these and then blaming others for the subsequent problems.

Organisations are organisms, extensions of ourselves and to some extent of our biological structure, but this is an element that has received scant attention in the training of managers – who after all have a professional investment in being able to 'manage', in all senses of that word at all times. To recognise the power of psychological, biological and social forces is to acknowledge vulnerability, an experience that managers are generally not comfortable with and have been trained to deny.

Work as a Remedy or as the Illness

Putting our organisations in emotional order is possibly at least as effective a strategy for tackling social problems as are the more conventional political and welfare approaches traditionally used. An organisation whose management is prepared to take account of the more tacit and unconscious aspects of working life, which tries to take account of the emotional consequences of the work on employees and their needs for psychological sustenance as well as for reasonable material conditions, can have a considerable effect on those associated with it. The families of employees and the consumers or clients (the 'stakeholders') will also feel the benefits of the way they are treated.

Most of us have the illusion that somehow the State is a parent and should remedy the ills of society through the education, health and social services. The workplace and how we behave in it has at least as much chance of producing this sort of impact. To further this aim, the manager of a team of people is well advised to provide opportunities for three fundamental needs:

to belong – to feel one is a member, a part of something greater than one's self;
to influence – to feel that one's ideas and actions are noticed and have an effect;
to achieve – to feel some sense of transforming the world.

When these needs are not met we feel stress, itself a mixture of hopelessness, of powerlessness and anger.

Stress at work begins with a feeling of hopelessness. There is an imbalance between the demands of the job and resources, whether personal or organisational, to meet the challenge. Typically, this is followed by a second phase of bodily symptoms, in which stress takes the form of anxieties, tensions and other physical symptoms, sometimes quite serious, which may result in chronic physical illness. Finally there is a phase of burn-out: of negative adaptation, cynicism, apathy and withdrawal from the challenge of meeting the demands of work.

An alternative outcome to stress can be overwork. Overwork is the result of a need to escape, either from a fear of failure and impotence or from intimate family relationships. It is endemic in certain sectors. In City law firms, potency whether physical or mental is at a premium. It is driven by the need to stave off the depression that is associated with being ineffectual or second-best. The power struggles that take place in all organisations at times can often be a reflection of a sense of impotence, which is pushed backwards and forwards between groups which find each other threatening in some way.

It is important to recognise the different types of stress found in both public and private sectors of the economy. There is a fundamental difference between these two fields of work. Broadly speaking, the private sector aims to stimulate demand for its products and is pro-active in its relationship to its environment. It provides avenues for the aggressive expression of competitive feelings. In the public sector, by contrast, the potential demand is generally much greater than the available supply and consequently the tendency is to be reactive to the environment. There are fewer opportunities for the legitimate expression of aggression. It is different in another way too. The private sector is concerned with transforming *material or energy* into products and services which are sold for profit, as objects of consumption, whereas the concern in the public sector is with transforming *people* – by educational, medical or social means. This makes a fundamental difference to the ways these two sorts of organisations are managed, yet each has something to learn from the other. The public sector is better at providing a vehicle for an expression of people's ideals, albeit often flawed. The private sector provides better opportunities for the expression of individual ambitions and desires.

Unemployment: A Form of Grief

To have work of some kind is crucial. Loving and being loved is part of the foundation of our mental health; working and the relationships work provides is the other. Losing your job can be as traumatic an experience as losing a loved partner. The loss is not only loss of the activity or a financial loss, but exists also in the internal world. It deprives the individual of the channels for good acts towards others which provide both reassurance and a way of binding the forces of envy, hatred, and other destructive elements present in every personality.

Thus unemployment deals a double blow. For the unemployed person there is not only the loss of being excluded from the wider world and the freedom that earning one's own living provides, but also of a basic opportunity for reassurance about his or her worth. When the capacity to be effective in the world is removed the results are often catastrophic. The consequence in many cases is depression. The aggression previously channelled outward into society is now turned against the self, a process which can even lead to suicide. It is not uncommon for retirement to be followed quite quickly by serious illness and sometimes death. There is the sense of impotence and depression at the obvious level of losing one's job, but also at the unconscious level of losing a medium for opportunities to create and repair, which help sustain a sense of internal worth and goodness. The loss of this means of psychological reparation can be even more catastrophic than the original external loss of job and colleagues.

The Welfare State has been less than effective in helping with the inevitable emotional consequences of unemployment. When the focus is solely on the material economic impact of unemployment it can be easy to lose sight of the importance of psychological help for individuals to overcome the inevitable depression caused, and the consequent inability to get going again, no matter how much financial and practical assistance is provided.

Intelligence and Knowledge as the New Forms of Capital

Much unemployment has occurred as a result of radical changes in the nature of work during the twentieth century. In the past, successful and wealthy organisations were closely associated with, first, ownership of *land and resources*, and then with accumulations of *capital* (in the form of property and other assets). Now however we are seeing the consequences of a third shift, away from capital, which broadly speaking is plentiful and readily accessible in the form of loans. The move is towards *knowledge* as the key asset which distinguishes the successful organisation; plus the capacity to learn and develop through the application of this knowledge, and the ability to harness and apply it. As Peter Senge, a researcher and writer on organisations, defines it, knowledge is 'the capacity for effective action'. Knowledge is different from earlier forms of capital. It is not a material stuff and hence organisations have difficulty managing it. Knowledge actually increases in value as it is used; to restrict access to it is to hamper an organisation's effectiveness.

Physical labour is a commodity of decreasing value, as machines and other forms of technology can do the work more effectively. Increasingly they are replacing most mundane physical and even intellectual chores. Power now lies in knowledge assets, not in labour. The value of things is largely defined by their scarcity; and it is the scarcity of the knowledge and the experience required for jobs in technical specialities, such as information technology and the finance industry, that have a high value at present.

Evidence for this is the high valuation of information technology companies which are *asset-poor* but *brain-rich*. The new skills required in management no longer involve the maximisation of return on capital so much as the application of knowledge for profit. In the public sector there will need to be a related shift away from the emphasis on the rationing out of resources towards a management style that enables the maximum use to be made of the combined resources of helper and helped.

However, most organisations are structured hierarchically, restricting – sometimes quite deliberately – access to knowledge and resources. The modern organisation has to rethink the very way in which it is organised if it is to make use of this new asset, which may be distributed in quite surprising ways through the hierarchy.

Effective organisations are learning to harness the knowledge of those in contact with the client, promoting learning and development in the workplace. Andy Grove, Chief Executive Officer of Intel, has recalled, 'We were fooled by our strategic rhetoric. But those on the front lines could see that we had to retreat from memory chips … People formulate strategies with their fingertips. Our most significant strategic decision was made not in response to some clear-sighted corporate vision but by the marketing and investment decisions of front-line managers who really knew what was going on.' When the rate of technological change and consequent social and psychological change exceeds the rate at which those leading and managing organisations can learn, then those at the top are often not in the best position to make operational or even strategic decisions.

This chapter has been concerned with some of the less public facts of human nature as expressed in the workplace. It is only when managers and employees are able to acknowledge some of these, not so much to overcome them but to accept the irrational as part of our nature, that they can become a source of creativity. We are each the products of similar biologies effected by complex and diverse experiences, but we are also creatures of our environment more than we care to think. Our ideas and feelings are closely entwined with and interdependent on the feelings and behaviour of others. Recognising this in the workplace is a struggle similar in scale and difficulty to the developmental task faced by the infant in recognising its dependence on the breast.

11

Food for the Mind

The health of our bodies depends on good food and a physical environment which meets our physiological requirements. Modern scientific knowledge is giving us longer lives and better physical health than our predecessors, although these benefits are very unequally distributed in different parts of the world. Better food and housing, a proper balance of work and rest, access to open space and opportunities for healthy exercise, cleaner air and controlling pollution of the land and sea are all consequences of social policies aimed at improving the quality of life. Although all of these benefits continue to be contested, the consistent commitment to public health measures of this sort does indicate the degree of social consent and a shared agreement on their scientific basis.

We should note that sharp disputes still erupt whenever new or awkward facts need to be accommodated. For example, the recent evidence that inequalities of wealth are associated with lower levels of health generally (not only for the poorer classes in society) is likely to remain contentious, since it goes against strong political and economic trends sanctioning greater inequality. Facts never operate in a neutral universe, especially in relation to human questions because we immediately encounter our different values and interests.

Nonetheless, though there is a near-universal agreement that education is a good thing, the question of what sort of education is entirely another matter. Everything from curricula to teaching methods is hotly contested. One person will regard what goes out on television, or appears in the newspapers, as good, informative or mentally nourishing. Yet the same material may be seen as stultifying or evil by another. A perspective informed by a knowledge of the main features of emotional development and by some psychoanalytic ideas can contribute some useful observations about what kind of experience is food for the mind – what distinguishes it from bad or noxious stuff. For these disagreements do share a common, underlying point of view: that the mind has its own needs, just as much as the body. These questions will be approached by describing two very differently situated children.

Darren

The first example is of a baby boy of four months, Darren. His parents have a reasonably good relationship, there is a network of family and friends, and Darren himself is a well-adapted and fortunate little boy.

> Darren has just started going to the swimming pool with his mother. On this occasion, his grandmother, aunt and great aunt have come too and they chat on the short journey to the pool, while Darren listens. On the way in, his mother meets a Sports Centre attendant who says, 'Hello' and admires the baby. He knew her quite well from her regular visits to the pool during her pregnancy. Mother undresses Darren and puts on his brand new water wings. Some little girls in the changing room are fascinated to watch these preparations. He is quiet, but watches everything and everyone, taking it all in – vision, sounds, smells (there are lots of children and adults and sounds of the water). His mother takes him to the pool and one of the attendants holds Darren while she gets in. Darren waits expectantly.
>
> His mother dances Darren around in the water. He enjoys this and continues to be all ears and eyes. After about ten minutes, Darren's grandmother offers to take over so that his mother can have a proper swim. Darren is transferred and the game continues. Suddenly Darren swallows a mouthful of water which goes down the wrong way. He splutters and begins to cry. His grandmother cuddles him but he is not to be comforted, until his mother returns. Once when Grandmother tried to distract him by introducing him to another baby close by in its father's arms, Darren turned his head away and cried bitterly. However, once he is back in his mother's arms, he quietens and sucks her shoulder.
>
> On his trip to the swimming pool Darren was being given some new experiences. He responded with energy and enthusiasm and he could be engaged in all that happened. What is he taking in? Lots of new physical sensations certainly, but he is also working on the meaning of all these events. For instance, what is going on when his mother stops to talk to the attendant? Obviously his mother and the man have something to do with each other. In the course of their conversation he is greeted, referred to, invited to join in but he is essentially a third party, an onlooker. And what of the new water wings? What are they? He watches his mother closely as she blows them up, fits the stoppers, and puts them on. Darren might feel they are good as she's talking to him with a voice imbued with pleasure and she's blowing them up: so far, so good. Going into the water, he keeps his eyes fixed on his mother while he waits to be handed to her. It is clear that she is his point of reference. His sense of security is maintained by his connection with her through their reciprocal looks, touches and sounds.
>
> The combination of events which proved too much for him was his mother's temporary absence and the water going down the wrong way. After that his grandmother's attempts to comfort him seemed only to serve as reminders that his mother hadn't returned to him. Certainly the sight of another baby comfortable in its father's arms provoked greater distress. In the few days before Darren had had a quite demanding range of new experiences including his first solid food, a vegetable puree which he had pushed out of his mouth. Also, he had had his first experience of being in a baby-bouncer. He had loved the freedom to make himself go up and down and to look around in many directions. Perhaps, the feeling of being bounced up and down in the water may have been an echo of the baby bouncer.

For Darren to have been able to respond to these events in the eager and involved way that he did some external conditions had to be satisfied. In particular he needed a parent (on this occasion his mother) close by for him to be able to maintain his sense of security. The feelings evoked may sometimes have been a little too much for his emotional capacity and there may have been too much for him to learn about all at once. For instance, he seemed to have struggled with the experience of his mother doing something else rather than being with him. He had to wait and make do with his grandmother. Perhaps, he had a first taste of the pain of jealousy made completely intolerable when he was proffered the other baby looking quite happy. Or perhaps there was a first awareness of how cross he was with his grandmother for not being his mother, or with his mother for not being with him. As he spluttered tearfully, he was a picture of reproach. 'How could you expect me to swallow all this?' his mournful but determined cries seemed to express.

Yet the whole sequence of experiences and events under these conditions and with these supports was a stimulus to Darren's thought. While his mother was comforting him with her familiar voice she was also commenting, unself-consciously, about all that had happened. While a small baby does not understand words, this sense of feeling emotionally understood by someone else is essential for the growth of the baby's capacity for self-understanding. The mother's natural attitude towards and recognition of her baby being sad, happy, angry, curious, excited, jealous, interested or frightened is fundamental for the baby developing a capacity to tolerate and manage these feelings in later life and to know what these emotions are.

It is for this reason that babies should not be protected from all the pains of ordinary experience; providing these are graded and not excessive they are stimuli for mental growth, grist to the mill. It is important that the baby's real feelings are acknowledged in some way, as this contributes to building up a sense of the self based in reality. If we are not understood or are persistently misunderstood as we encounter life's ordinary difficulties, we are disadvantaged in the acquisition of that language which is essential for our emotional lives and our future mental health.

George

In marked contrast to Darren, George's longer life has been full of adversity. He is 12 years old and spent the first 18 months of his life in an ill-favoured orphanage in a Central European country. After that he was adopted by a middle-class English couple who, unfortunately, quickly became unhappy with each other so that things became very difficult at home. Nevertheless, his adoptive parents were genuinely concerned about George, and in spite of the major problems in their relationship, they tried to make sure that George got as much help as possible. As part of this he has been having therapy three times a week for quite a while.

George has turbulent and unpredictable changes of mood. He gets very panicky and can behave violently when he is frightened or disturbed. On one Monday session he arrived telling his therapist that he would probably be going on a half-term skiing holiday next week, but his mother had said that the trip was not definite yet as there was a forecast of possible avalanches. In the course of the session, George conveyed vividly that he was anxious about this trip, and his therapist was able to link his worry with the many losses in his life (his mother who had abandoned him as a baby, his adoptive father now no longer living at home) and to speak to him about his worry that he was not wanted, and in particular his fear that his difficult behaviour with her might make her want to get rid of him.

While all this was going on, George was holding something in his pocket and eventually he asked her to guess what it was. He brought out a sandwich. He unwrapped it and began to eat it in an exaggerated, almost voluptuous way. Closing his eyes, he murmured 'What a dream of a sandwich.' Then, as if waking up from an ecstatic experience, he said to his therapist, 'Do you want some of it? Just a crumb?' and he put a fragment in her hand, beckoning her to eat it. Suddenly he pushed his other empty hand right in front of her mouth. 'Shit on it. I will eat it. Go on!' he said, inviting her to do so in a seductive tone of voice that made her recoil. Shocked, she was stunned into silence, while trying to recover and to think of how to respond. But suddenly he sat down by her and began to talk in an ordinary voice as if all that he had done a few moments before had not occurred. 'I have a problem...what are avalanches?' he asked, ' I wanted to escape, but it was dark. I started singing to myself going along the road, and I was frightened. But the road was nice, and there was a telephone box. I ran back home.'

The therapist, still shocked, did not know if he was telling her a dream or a story. George silently turned off the light in the playroom, lay down on his tummy, and said 'I want to go to the Alps – shall I bring you a postcard?' Aware that she wasn't really managing to address the avalanche of George's perverse, disturbing invitations, she managed to say that he had two feelings; he wanted to go, but wanted to be with her too, and he was trying to work out how to keep a link between them. A little later George told her he would have to share a bedroom with his mother on the skiing trip. When his therapist spoke about that being difficult for him, he lay down and started to sing as if he were drunk, and to smear spit and mucus over himself and the couch. He came very close to her and began to talk in a completely strange voice. She said to him that he seemed to feel he was now a different person. George confirmed that he was feeling something like that.

In his next session, George played with a bit of plastic cord reminiscent of a telephone wire, pretending that it tasted of 'chocolate' or 'raspberries' as he sucked at it with exaggerated passion. When his therapist said she thought that he was needing to imagine he could make his own special food because he was afraid he might miss her, he spoke in a haunted tone of voice of an avalanche that was coming. He mimed the avalanche sweeping him out of the room and leaving him lying 'dead' in the corridor. But after a while he came back and checked with what seemed like genuine anxiety to see if his therapist was still alive. He then told a 'dream': 'I was in Los Angeles without my parents (George often referred to Los Angeles, drawing on its image from TV and the films he liked to watch). I was swimming in the sea when a huge wave came over me. I tried to swim harder, with all my strength. I struggled, but the wave was too powerful. I woke up ... what a fright!'

The therapist noted to herself how much the imagery of being swept away – huge waves and the avalanche fears – was in George's thinking at this time. She thought these waves might represent George's original powerlessness in the face of all that had happened in his life, but on top of that George was also repeatedly swept away by his own violent rages and waves of eroticised, perverse and empty feeling. She thought that the dream showed what happens when a world of excitement, the Los Angeles of his dream, overwhelms him. Parents and therapist disappear from his mind, he feels the wave of perverse violence will drown him, and no one can help him in his struggle. George listened carefully and whispered to himself: 'You were not there with me.' Then he suddenly switched off the light and started shouting at her that he wanted to sing, and she must say: 'A one ... a two ... a three ... Go!' His strident tone of voice barely concealed the despair which the song seemed intended to hold at bay.

Through the chaotic sequence of these sessions (which are fairly typical of what happens in George's treatment), one can see that George seems to veer between two worlds: a maddening and perverse one, in which shit is offered just when his therapist had been led on to expect food, and a sane one, where he seems to be able to listen to his therapist talk about his feelings; at these calmer moments, George can listen to the meaning being given to his thoughts.

It is clear from the way that George offers the sandwich and his hand to his therapist that he considers that there are two kinds of food. These represent the two types of experience he might have had. When he says that if the therapist shits on his hand he will eat it, is he referring to his view of his early extreme deprivation and the subsequent enraging disappointments of his upbringing including his adoptive father leaving? He seems to be asking what is he supposed to do with this type of experience. Is he supposed to swallow it? He has been enraged and humiliated by his experiences. But, with a perverse air, and as a parody of making a virtue out of a necessity, he says that he will eat it. In fact, he has not really had any option because what happened to him happened without his consent or control. It continues to be an active damaging influence inside him.

When George feels aware of being a child dependent on his parents (who, we should recollect, have their difficulties), or feels he'd like to rely on his therapist, his lack of power to control these adults causes him to become very anxious. He tends to defend against feeling as vulnerable as he is by turning to an alternative system that is based upon a wish-fulfilling denial of his feelings of smallness and helplessness (omnipotence). He also denies that there is anything he does not yet know (omniscience). George's alternative is dressed up as delicious (the imaginary chocolate and raspberry tastes). He frequently immerses himself for long periods in a world of unreal sensual or oral gratification, which is meant to make him forget all the things that upset him.

Thus George is living in his own fairy tale. Hansel and Gretel, the motherless, endangered and abandoned children chance upon the gingerbread house in the forest. Their love of the sweets plastered all over it makes them into the prisoners of the witch. Because of his early deprivation George also fears that he will starve and he has had very little experience of parents taking care of him either in body or in mind; but when he gets immersed in his states of sensuality he is on the way to becoming a prisoner of his own defences. His mind gets full of rubbish – of illusions and beliefs which fly in the face of psychological reality. These states of his are very similar to an addiction to drugs. His fantasies are an internally generated 'bad food' originally designed to combat the 'shit'. But drugs of addiction are also gratifying and so are George's states of perverse sensuality. Furthermore, they prevent him from registering and digesting those painful experiences from which he could learn. Therapy is for him the chance to discover that this is a mistake and that it is dangerous to remain imprisoned in a witch's house.

Good Food and Bad Food

The mental food that therapy offers is a therapeutic relationship in which feelings are named and located. In order to do this a child therapist must appreciate the origins of the child's crippling anxieties which have interfered with ordinary development. Often, very deprived children need a long time to pour out rage, pain and confusion before they can believe that the understanding offered by the therapist is more than just words. Slowly, the therapist and the child find a language in which important issues can be talked about in a way that is adapted to the child's way of seeing things.

This insight is helpful in the discussion of what is good and bad information for children in society. For psychotherapy is made up of concentrated, specialised versions of the sources of mental and emotional nourishment in our everyday lives. The first of these comes from the relationships of our intimate lives. These are the natural arena of growth, where we learn from daily contacts about what is real and meaningful. Lovers, families, friends and working colleagues can all provide us with security to be honest with ourselves about what we feel and think, and to give up self-deceits as a defence against anxiety. When there is an absence of such support we are most thrown onto our inner resources and if these are impoverished, we are in trouble and face the terror of 'anomie', the experience of not feeling recognised by others.

Education, the second source, helps us get the most out of our cultural heritage, the second great resource. Music, art, literature, theatre, dance and cinema can make inroads on our more cut-off (autistic) and self-preoccupied (narcissistic) states of minds. They pull us into a relationship with a world outside ourselves, both through access to the creative imagination of the artist and through joining a wider social community of audience of readers, listeners, and watchers. True works of art, including popular art and great sporting events, offer us a public view of the great issues of all our lives. The third source of renewal is from within us; it is from our own unconscious world expressed in our imaginations and in our dreams. Each of the sources of mental nourishment we have described depend on our capacity to move between the outer world we share with others and the inner world of personal reflection. The fourth, work, is the subject of Chapter 10.

Each source of nourishment can go bad and begin to yield a dangerous harvest. Some kinds of personal relationships are anti-growth, some kinds of art are perverse and sometimes our own imaginations and our dreams can take us in the wrong direction. This is the bad food in the question which started this chapter. The experience of Darren and George and children like them, confirms that human beings do have a certain *innate* ability to make judgements of life experience. It is clear that excessive frustration of basic emotional needs causes disturbed mental development, but also that a certain amount of coming up against limits is essential for normal development, even though it will be resented – either by the person or society as a whole.

In general what is food for the mind needs to be something which reflects the force of this. In a free society one of the reasons why we try to keep the amount we regulate and proscribe to a minimum is because we have realised that there is an inherent value in diversity. We are never sure how things will turn out and it would be dangerous if we began to think that we were entirely sure about what is good for us and what is not. The modesty and generality of this conclusion presents no such 'certainty', but it is nevertheless based upon important clinical facts about human development. It might support useful principles in public debates about the emotional and mental aspects of what we tolerate as a society.

12

Attitudes to Normality and Psychiatric Illness

Mental illnesses are altered by the beliefs and expectations we have about them. In this they are unlike natural phenomena, such as storms or sunspots, which occur unchanged whatever human beings think or do. Although we now know that some physical illnesses can be affected by the sufferers state of mind, the agents which cause infectious diseases, for example, are oblivious to whatever is thought about them. Once an infection with the meningococcus is suspected, it is not sensible for the doctor to sit back and think about the problem. It is critically important for the right antibiotic to be given quickly.

Mental illnesses are different. In most mental illnesses, definite physical causes have not been established. At the level of society, both individuals with mental illnesses and the illnesses themselves are influenced by the attitudes held towards them. This is not to suggest that simple psychological or social factors – habits of mind, prejudices, labelling, stigma and so on – can by themselves cause major mental illnesses, although the malign effect of certain very adverse childhoods can come close to producing mentally sick children and adults. Nor is it the case that drugs do not have an important role in the treatment of mental illnesses. However there is a tendency to rely too exclusively upon drugs, or to place too exclusive a hope in long-awaited pharmaceutical cures. Most of us are uncomfortable about our own emotional balance. It is easier to put one's faith in a cure. But perhaps as a consequence, we as a society, neglect the reluctant benefits which can come from the struggle to recognise, to understand and to modify difficult emotional factors in ourselves as individuals.

In their effects and in the way they feel to the sufferer, mental illnesses can be compared to emotional storms or hurricanes. They cause real and often lasting damage to the mind, the personality and to relationships. Some attitudes or impulses can, for the individual with a mental condition, feel as though they can be both the cause and the consequence of the illness. Although no clearly established structural changes in the brain have been detected, in most of these illnesses the extent of the emotional damage is sometimes so catastrophic that it feels physical. In a modest yet forcible sense, these illnesses are influenced by what is thought about them. A close examination of the attitudes and responses evoked by mental illness can bring about important shifts for sufferers and those who care for them.

For instance, the most devastating of all mental illnesses, schizophrenia, seems to occur at about the same rate in all countries. Yet, for the moment at least, the outcome for the individual seems to be better in less developed, less pressured or competitive societies than in ours, even though they may not have the benefit of modern mental health services. The paragraph below is from a learned article considering this fact. It succinctly puts forward the idea that the effects of schizophrenic illness have been prolonged and made worse because of the industrialisation of modern society.

> In non-industrial cultures, ideas about the nature of mental illness are poorly differentiated from those about physical illness, and the concepts of both usually overlap with or include religious and magical concepts. When a culture becomes industrial there tends to be an overall fading of supporting and explaining magical and religious systems. The accompanying advances of medical technology lead to the separation of the mentally from the physically ill, but yet offer no satisfactory explanation for severe mental illness, thus setting the scene for the rejection and stigmatisation of those affected. [Cooper, J. and Sartorius, N. (1986) 'Cultural and temporal variations in schizophrenia: A speculation on the importance of industrialisation' pp 332-8 in *Contemporary Issues in Schizophrenia* Eds. Kerr, A. & Snaith, P. Gaskell, London.]

Magical and religious belief systems have a special affiliation with mental illness because they all arise, like the imagination, from the area of our thinking which is less conventionally rational. Belief systems usually offer frameworks for understanding particular states of mind, including those we regard as abnormal. In some societies, this framework of understanding explains that the depressed man or hallucinated man may be possessed by evil spirits and therefore needs care or rescue. Demons are regarded as external to the individual. If he or she can be exorcised of these demons, the underlying humanity will be recovered. A belief like this may be helpful both to the individual and to the group. In other societies, the voices may be thought of as bearing important messages for the group about the temper or intentions of the spirit world. The sickness of a particular member of the group may be regarded as a sign that there is some corruption or sickness in the society itself. A soothsayer divines this type of problem and prescribes correctives for society at large and not only for the individual sufferer. This is the reverse of the ancient ritual of scapegoating, where the problems of the group are blamed on an individual. In Western European culture when they were at their most vigorous, Judaism and Christianity offered a comprehensive view of the meaning of the experiences and the adversities of life. This included instructive exemplification of, for instance, depressed outrage at misfortune (as in the story of Job), of destructive rivalry between siblings (Cain and Abel), of powerful insights and self-sacrifice (Christ) and of brave responses to the injured (the Good Samaritan).

However it is important not to become too romantic or nostalgic about these other societies. Quite often they were cruel or terrible, or simply misguided. Witch-hunts at the time of the Inquisition were literally so and folk medicines by and large do not have the potency of modern drugs. Nevertheless, some belief structures in some societies do lend to the ill or troubled a privileged, protected status so that they will be up to a point tolerated or accepted. It is also worth remembering that disordered states of mind resembling mental illness are also actively sought out. Nearly all societies place positive values on intoxicated or trance states of mind, achieved through mushrooms, drugs or rhythmic ritual dancing. That conscience 'which doth make cowards of us all' is temporarily soluble in alcohol, and drunkenness can sometimes offer relief from the restraints of conscience.

Our Sensitivity to Other People's States of Mind

Some of the states of mind connected with mental illness can produce a great deal of anxiety in those around, sometimes as an intuitive response to the perceived intentions of the ill person. They are like an inter-personal radar. A wary or fearful reaction to a person may have a survival value. Non-verbally one may have picked up warnings of a potential for aggression or violence.

> A woman patient who in the past had had violent hostile feelings towards her therapist made the therapist anxious. She often brought a plastic bag with her into the sessions and kept this on her lap. At some point she would take something out of it – usually a book or a letter – but the therapist always feared that it might be a weapon.

In fact, our antennae can put us in touch with a much wider range of information about the ill person's emotions or experiences. For example, a manic patient (euphoric and over-active) may, for a while, induce in others a corresponding elation, but after a while this is replaced in those present by some feeling of futility, depression, irritation or distress. Often these prove to be the very feelings the ill person could not manage and which they are trying to deny with their mania.

However, although this type of inter-personal radar can be accurate, quite often it is too wide of the mark. We all have irrational unrealistic responses to insanity, simply because mental disturbance itself is so disturbing to others. Being sound in mind is as important to us, if not more so, as being sound in limb. Thus the reaction to seeing someone develop a serious mental disturbance is akin to our reaction to witnessing a serious physical injury. There is a profound shock or fear and sometimes excitement. We have to digest in some way the significance to us personally of what we have witnessed.

> A woman in her late fifties had just had a serious depressive breakdown and this dinner was her first social event after coming out of hospital. She was supposed to be recovering but she wore on her face a look of such agony that it was difficult to

> approach her. By her very manner she seemed to be apologising for her very existence, as if she considered herself to be unentitled to be at any table whatsoever.

Again,

> A likeable man in his forties with two young sons, and whose wife had died some months ago, kept making in the course of an ordinary conversation abrupt, jokey references to needing help – he might have a breakdown, this time next term he might be in hospital, he no longer believed in love, and so on. The listener responded by being not quite sure of what he had heard. It was oddly difficult to respond, as no sooner had the thing been said than the moment seemed to have passed. There was an inner reluctance to consider what was being said and what it portended.

To know of these people's pain is awkward and difficult in many ways. What state of mind and what feelings caused the woman at the dinner party to have such a terrible breakdown? What developing state of mind was the newly widowed man sensing, warning or appealing about? What happens within a person when they no longer believe in love? When they are exposed, and unprotected from their more destructive feelings, how can they not slide towards despair? The personal reverberations of seeing and hearing ordinary people in states of distress are considerable. It may stir up troubles in one's own life or personality, such as the death or suicide or mental illness of a relative. Uneasily shelved childhood events can re-surface. Most often however our reaction comes not from some single dramatic event or trauma but out of the day-to-day vulnerability of our childhood.

Our Anxiety about Normality

Resistance in the sufferer to knowing more is almost universal, although in many such situations it is better to grasp than to evade the significance of painful emotions. Often the reality is that they turn out to be less terrible, or terrible in a different way, than we anticipate. Moreover openness does at least allow problems to be addressed. Nonetheless, discretion can have an important function in allowing people to get on with life. There may at times be difficulties within oneself or within others when it is better just to get on with it, to let sleeping dogs lie.

> Winston Churchill, who enabled us to keep together in our 'hour of darkness', himself feared what he called his black dog – depression. He could never stand close to the edge of the railway platform for fear of throwing himself in front of an oncoming train. Yet Churchill always disliked and was suspicious of psychiatrists. Thus during the war his advisers kept it secret from him that psychiatrists (including some from the Tavistock) were playing a part in officer selection and in rehabilitating those who were suffering from battle fatigue. They feared that Churchill would not tolerate the involvement of psychiatrists with improving the

quality of officers selected as well as getting distressed soldiers back into active service. Churchill's avoidance, perhaps, was good for Churchill personally and consequently for the nation, but it would not have been good for the armed forces.

Recently, a prominent and respected broadcaster revealed in a newspaper article that, as a teenager, he had had a kind of breakdown. He had felt that his self, or soul, floated out of his body and looked down upon him from the upper corner of the room. He was convinced that if this entity did not return to his body he would be dead, or worse, he would not exist at all. The propensity for this state and the intense fear of it lasted a long time. Some ten years on from the original episode he was still suffering from panic attacks, during which he was convinced that if he did not concentrate upon every breath he would stop breathing. He felt these states and their consequences had determined his life for thirty years. Following the article he received several hundred letters from readers who had had, they felt, similar experiences. With a few exceptions, however, most considered them to have been liberating and turned a blind eye to the fact that the author's experiences had been terrifying to him.

Some degree of disturbance is almost the norm. Which of us, when honest, feels himself to be entirely normal? A world full of entirely normal people would not be recognisable. Who could speak for us, or embody for us the extremes of the human condition? Our sufferings can have meaning and can connect us with other people. Most people feel that being normal is being able to get by without drawing too much attention to yourself. Given the complexity and strain of what the human mind and personality has to do, this is no mean achievement. Some in fact may value their internal troubles, feeling them to be close to the source of a special capacity or creativity.

More or less normal people have anxieties about being disturbed. These anxieties in turn affect how we orientate ourselves towards other people and their disturbance. Consider the situation in a therapy group made up of six or eight people, men and women who have various sorts of fairly ordinary difficulties. Some are unable to recover from the break-up of a relationship, some feel unable to make relationships, some feel depressed, some will have had experiences in their life that they feel are still with them, distorting their capacity to get on with it. In this particular group most of the members are in work, and some have considerable talents and expertise. Only one, or at most two, have had 'breakdowns' and been in hospital. Only one of the group seems strange to a degree.

The early sessions of the group's weekly gatherings consisted mostly of innocuous small talk. It was to everyone's evident relief when one of the group members volunteered to be the patient and spoke of the problems he was having with his anorexic daughter. A little while afterwards the group focused upon the member who was most obviously shaky. He told how precarious he felt and of his first hospital admission. After a few more weeks he was absent but no one referred to this. The group therapist drew attention to this omission but was ignored. It was only after some repetitions of the interpretation that the group acknowledged his absence and their fear that he had had another breakdown – and this subsequently proved to have been the case. In the course of all this, the members of the group were able to reveal that in the early weeks of the group they had been terrified that if they spoke they would be thought peculiar or mad, as they felt their feelings were not of the 'right' or expected sort. A number reported feeling paralysed by the prospect of speaking of themselves. The very process of self-revelation was experienced as likely to get out of control. They felt that they would fall to the ground or that it would open up beneath them. Each one of them feared he would have become the peculiar one.

Many of us have worries about losing our mental balance. Many people who are to all intents and purposes normal have within their personality areas which function in ways that are felt to be mad and beyond the person's more considered wishes and judgements. The areas stirred up usually involve unruly sexual feelings, pain and unhappiness, but also destructive or aggressive impulses. These feelings may be wild and undomestic and can vary enormously in extent, severity and influence upon the personality. However, they are often what lie behind the odd quirks or neurotic problems which many relatively normal people have and which are the underlying source of the stubbornness of such traits.

Human Nature

Of course, the particular issues will be unique for each person as a result of their individual make-up, character and life experience. However, there are some recurring issues that are more difficult for the personality to handle than others. These are the inherent design problems of the human character. Amongst the great variation and individuality of people's problems and personalities, some psychological hurdles play a regular part.

A patient in once-weekly psychotherapy, a young, successful and normal man, thought of himself in a tenacious way as a special and attractive personality. He had begun to realise that this attitude towards himself had very little to do with his actual talents and achievements which were in fact considerable. It was more that this idealistic view of himself came before any achievement. It remained relatively independent of anything he did. It took, as it were, the credit for his real achievements, which arose out of a steady combination of application and capacity. After realising this with especial clarity, one day he had a dream in which a man was dangerously threatening several others with two blood filled syringes; the blood was infected with AIDS virus. He awoke from the dream sweating with fear.

In the next session he described the dream to his therapist, but then ignored its possible significance, instead spending his time picking up inessential aspects of the therapist's words and casually correcting them. In this way he undermined any point of substance. After a while it was clear that the effect of this was to weaken the insight that he'd been developing in the previous weeks. In behaving in this way he was using his mind to weaken his discovery, and this could be compared to the way the AIDS virus weakens the immune system. Daytime action in the session had succeeded the imagery of dreaming. Many times the realisation that his idealised pleasure in himself was independent of his real work was undone by sequences of this sort.

Gradually it bore in upon the young man that a part of himself was operating over which he had relatively little control. This undid his own and valued insights about himself, even though he knew that these understandings could strengthen his character. He began to sense how hostile the feelings that underlay this behaviour were. If he tried to be more ordinary, he had violent disturbing dreams like the one described above. Sometimes, this vicious hostility emerged more directly. The line of thought seemed to go 'If I am not especially attractive and clever then I seem to experience somebody else as special. I find I cannot bear this. I feel envious and inferior and want to poison the good opinion others have of this person. Quite often it seems to me that I actually poison with my powerful sneers the versions of them I carry with me inside myself. I then seem to believe my sneers so that I again feel special and they become of little real importance. Once this has taken place, the situation again feels better to me. Sometimes my previous awareness of feeling angrily inferior no longer seems at all real to me. I am rather bemused by what all this is about.'

What was discovered through this kind of therapy is that the people who were felt to be special stand for the parents or for the siblings, the parents' other children. The inferiority, which was then felt by the patient, seemed to be as little related to current reality as was the feeling of specialness. One explanation is that it was an undeveloped remnant of infantile feeling. The infant resents the perceived power and creativity of the parents. In this kind of mood, people being together is viewed not as a manifestation of love but as a corrupt, hateful, mutual buttering-up. This kind of resentment was felt to generate enormous power. The internal, spoiling sneer was felt to be as effective as any external action.

Although there are many sources besides envy of unintegrated disturbed feelings in relatively normal people, it is true that envious relationships are particularly difficult for the growing personality. It is such a difficult emotion to remain aware of as it all too easily turns into a spoiling action or a denigrating perception. Frank hostility, violence or criminality are all ways of expressing envy. Transformed into superiority and arrogance, it attributes the inferiority and envy to others. Envy is felt to have so little justification that the self feels it to be unforgivable and the guilt connected with this aspect of the self is often unbearable. However, instead of experiencing guilt the individual may organise him/herself into being victimised, criticised or otherwise got at, often in an envious way. Thus, the ability to experience envy as such can be a sign of progress.

Strange as it seems, powerful feelings can exist within us without our having much insight into their presence. Nevertheless these unconscious feelings and others like them can determine much of our thinking, feelings, beliefs, opinions and actions. As a result of their intrinsic difficulty these issues are often compartmentalised in a hidden (split-off) area of the personality. They can form part of what quite normal people feel to be a mad part of themselves and a source of continuing insecurity. One cause of this feeling of madness is that envy as a force is pitted against the sources of goodness. It sets up false leads which cause confusion, so that the child or adult may not be able to tell the difference between what is good and what is bad. People become disoriented about what and who is desirable and fear they may betray their values. Although envious feelings are an intrinsic part of the human personality, they are greatly increased by any actual, real experiences of deprivation and there is no shortage of these even in quite good upbringings. As we know, many people have to deal with quite extreme deprivations and emotional insults and these can greatly augment the impulse to spoil others' luckier experience.

Personal Boundaries

Fears of catching madness, of being seduced by the lure of mad ideas, of losing one's identity, or of merging with someone disturbed or coming under his or her control, can all contribute to our uneasiness about being with the psychotically ill. Some of these anxieties can be understood on the basis of difficulties experienced in becoming an independent person with a firm sense of identity, an ability to be distinct from other people. These abilities are, for example, tested when people separate from long established relationships.

The term 'attention seeking' is often applied in a derogatory way to the disturbance occasioned by these separation anxieties. Yet, the unconscious wish or need to be in someone's mind is almost universal and is an important matter. To cope with the fact that people are not always present or that one is not always in someone else's mind, we need to be introduced to absence preferably early on, in the proper way, and sustained by the underlying love of parents. Otherwise our personal boundaries may not be very clear or easy. Many infants, not just those unfortunates in the orphanages of Romania, first become aware of separateness through excessive deprivation. This provokes in them very early on fear that they will be left to die. In fact, if as an infant one is not thought about and loved by another person, the chances that one will die at an early age are greatly increased. Rather than succumb to this feared and imagined fate, desperate efforts are made to remain thought about through 'attention seeking'.

In later life even an emotionally sound person will experience separation as a painful absence. For those who are vulnerable, an equivalent event will threaten a potential disaster. To avoid this, people live in and through others, glued to them, mixed-up with them, in bondage to, possessing or being possessed by them. For some people being together with another person but also experiencing themselves as separate is impossible. For others the regulation of personal distance becomes a crucial matter. Being isolated is possible, but being comfortably alone is not. To be too close to is to feel invaded or to feel a wish to invade. To be too distant can mean the abyss. Too much loss in infancy, childhood or adolescence can lead to a kind of emotional cutting-off as the only alternative to overwhelming rage, murderousness or suicidal impulses.

Splitting in Normal People

Unresolved infantile feelings are felt generally as having a power beyond the adult individual's capacity to deal with them. This is another reason why difficulties are often compartmentalised in an area of the personality, and kept outside the main current of life. This splitting of the personality varies enormously in extent. It can range from the most pathological extreme, the fracturing of the personality as it occurs in schizophrenia, through a more coherently and recognisably split personality as in Stevenson's story, 'Dr Jekyll and Mr Hyde', to much more functional and everyday personal situations of ordinary, uneven development where we ignore parts of ourselves that function in a disordered way.

Splitting means that few of us are really all of one piece, but there is still a deep longing for perfection in human beings. Many of us feel that we are supposed to be whole, entire and normal, that this is what is expected of us. For instance, the attractive, somewhat self-absorbed young man above was not only like that as a way of coping with his unconscious envious feelings. Equally important was a strong feeling that his parents had provided him with enough and he was supposed to be all right. For him to recognise that he experienced continuing difficulties with making himself add up as a person was felt to be a betrayal of what he thought the world expected of him. Added to the pressure to disown our fear, stemming from our primitive destructive feelings and our uncertainty as to whether or not we can tolerate separateness, is our longing for the ideal. This is how we think the world should be. These factors colour our perceptions and responses to mental illness. To some degree we all attribute our disturbance to those who are visibly ill and expect them to be cured or feared as proxies for ourselves. The wish to be all right runs directly counter to the truth for both the well and the ill, however unsatisfactory – that psychological development involves a continual and never entirely successful encounter with serious internal difficulties of one sort or another.

As we saw in the example of the therapy group, even when we are in a position where we are licensed to be able to speak of difficult sides of ourselves, what we fear, by and large, are not our own attitudes but those of others. We fear that others will think us the strange one. On the whole, we find others are more forgiving, tolerant and understanding to us than we expect them to be. Sometimes we even realise beyond any reasonable doubt that this or that friend, or the people in the group, are really tolerant and understanding. But we cannot help noticing that this tolerant attitude of theirs does not work in their own cases. They are no more able than we are to reveal their embarrassing thoughts. They fear our judgement just as we fear theirs. Furthermore, we realise that we have to be realistic. People, even the best of them, are not tolerant and understanding all the time. What they say to our faces may not be all that they are really thinking. What might they be saying to each other? Here a realistic sense of what life is actually like becomes inextricably mixed up with our own hypersensitive doubts. In fact, we may respect our friends for not just excusing

"David, you're denying your feelings again, aren't you?"

Figure 14: Our tendency to project our feelings on those who are ill colours our view of them, which can add to their burden.

us in an indulgent way. We appreciate that they may expect from us a genuine engagement, though in truth we do all want to be totally indulged and excused.

Conscience

This discrepancy between our expectations of judgement and the reality of what greets us is accounted for by our conscience. Conscience is but one component of a much larger, more powerful mental structure which psychoanalysts, after Freud, call the superego. The superego is the representation inside our minds of the external world, originally the parental figures who watch over us, guide us, help us, criticise us, and generally help hold the line.

Our conscience and our superego limit what can be acknowledged to others and what we can allow ourselves to acknowledge about our own characters. How severe the superego is correlates quite closely with our personality difficulties. By and large the more mentally healthy one is, the more genuinely straightforward, helpful, decent, kind and clear-sighted is the superego. A benign cycle exists in which potentially guilt-provoking feelings can be tolerated and owned so that they can be modified by other parts of the personality. However, it does not take much for an extreme, demanding, punishing and inconsistent superego to be turned against others and ourselves. This is not just because our own parents may at times have been like that – or more usually themselves had consciences like that – but also because the superego is profoundly affected and coloured by our own primitive feelings.

The effects of this can be seen in deprived personalities, often those who have experienced multiple broken, violent or abusive relationships in the course of their upbringing. They will often have extreme difficulty in protecting what love relationships they have from the emotional chaos or aggression which exists within them. In such cases, characteristically that their children are idealised. When the idealisation breaks down it does so in a big way. They may become persecuted by the normal whinginess of children and fury quickly follows. At this point, the hated child usually stands for the infantile part of the self which received little proper care in their own upbringings.

As part of the effort to protect their loved ones from their own anger this hatred can be deflected on to others who are felt to be vermin – characteristically different racial groups, or those felt to be perverts. There is often a paranoid fear of madness – 'Are you saying I'm mad, or what?' 'Who are you looking at?' One such patient who cared deeply for his children said bluntly he'd kill anyone who exposed his children to drugs. A few sessions later it emerged that some years earlier he had been involved in selling a consignment of hard drugs worth over £100,000.

People like this are not devoid of conscience, as is often thought. Rather, their conscience is so punishing that any experience of guilt cannot be borne. It feels to them like being hated to death. If they were to acknowledge their feelings and impulses it would call forth such violence that they would want to kill themselves. Such feelings are unstable and they are got rid of crudely and violently. In other words, the superego becomes corrupt and inconsistent, like those sixteenth-century cardinals and Popes who offered indulgences when it suited, and who dealt out punishment to the innocent. The tabloid newspapers can give a vivid idea of the inconsistency of this type of superego. Crude moralising is available, unblushing and unconcerned, on either side of the temptations of the Page Three girls in a heady recipe. Although the tabloids serve a raw, vigorous interest, reality is not the strong point of such ways of witnessing our communal life. Simultaneously, in other areas of public life a coercive view of normality can operate. This threatens anyone who shows the ordinary cruddiness of a living person and makes him feel like an outlaw. An excessive niceness or tidiness of manner can imply that if we are not angels then we have fallen. Likewise the idea that human beings function predominantly in a rational way does not really bear examination, yet it remains a strangely potent point of view.

The Reality of Mental Illness

At present, there are contradictory popular positions on mental illness. On the one hand the view exists that the seriously mentally ill are responsible for a rapidly escalating number of violent crimes, including murders. On the other hand the severity, the reality, the chronicity, and the suffering of these illnesses are minimised. The madness of madness, as it were, is denied in an attempt to present it as an illness like any other. Whilst all this is going on, the facts receive relatively little attention.

In England and Wales there are about 600-700 unlawful killings a year. As in most other countries this number has been steadily increasing over the years. In 1957 there were 116 homicides; in 1995 this figure had risen to 522. The seriously mentally ill are not responsible for this increase. People with a diagnosis of schizophrenia are responsible for about 40 killings per year and this mostly, but not exclusively, concerns the murder of relatives or family members rather than strangers. This can be compared with 300 killings, by dangerous, drunken or drugged driving, over and above the overall homicide figure of 600-700.

The proportion of homicides committed by the seriously mentally ill has, in fact, been falling by 3 per cent per year for many years. In 1957 they accounted for 35 per cent of homicides; in 1995 the proportion had fallen to 11.5 per cent. Since 1994 it has been mandatory for an enquiry to be held, often in public, whenever a patient who has had contact with the mental health services commits a murder. There has been no corresponding call for inquiries, public or private, after a member of the general public murders someone, even though it is this category of offence which shows the greatest increase. More drug use, combined with a society-wide resort to violence, is the main cause of the increasing number of murders.

It may be that the relatively small contribution made by the seriously mentally ill to the increasing number of crimes of violence assumes an undue prominence because the crimes committed by the very disturbed occupy a position of especial fear. This is akin to the way that we tend to be scared of spiders or snakes. We find it easier to rationalise dangerous or drunken driving as more normal, although the unconscious motivation behind these apparent accidents may be just as murderous as the crimes committed by the mentally ill. It is probably the madness of the motivation as well as the tragedy of the victim which disturbs us in cases where a schizophrenic kills. We make them carry the burden of our own potential for disturbance as well as their own. Many of the people who commit 'normal' murders are in some way disturbed personalities and in this sense they are not normal, and certainly when someone commits a murder they are not usually in a normal frame of mind. However, these states are closer to 'our' normality than we like to think.

Social trends and political leadership can influence the attitudes adopted in the larger culture. The system can egg on our superegos to the crazy level where we believe that we should really be perfect. Unrealistic expectations like these in turn encourage unrealistic behaviour, so that it becomes less possible to

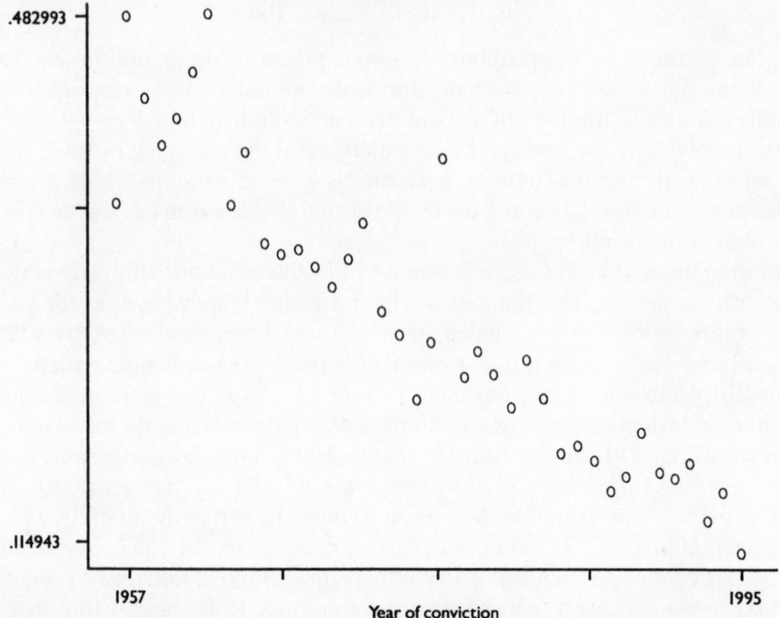

Figure 15: This graph indicates that the number of murders committed by the mentally ill has steadily declined as a proportion of the total number of murders.

tolerate and to put right more ordinary degrees of disturbance. Instead a climate with a terrible fear of blame develops. Alternatively, it is possible for society to endorse the need and value of tolerating a degree of realistic guilt and responsibility without indulging in moral masochism. Through deeds and action based on understanding the meaning of illness, society can take some of the weight off the ill and those who care for them. This absolutely does not entail denying the extent of their abnormality, dangerousness or need. It means acknowledging that probably everyone has a vulnerability to mental illness just in the way that we are all vulnerable to physical ailments.

In this chapter we have tried to look at these things from the inside, as it were, because it is our personal position on these issues which determines our attitude to mental troubles in general. If our attitude – in the sense of an orientation rather than just a surface opinion – allows us to be neither too defended against the meaning and nature of disturbance, nor to go in for too much blaming or scapegoating, then gradually society may be able to organise its mental health services in a better way than it is currently managing to do.

13

Mental Distress and Mental Illness

Then *Sinne* combined with *Death* in a firm band
To raze the building to the very floore:
Which they effected, none could them withstand.
But *Love* and *Grace* took *Glorie* by the hand
And built a braver Palace than before.
From 'The World' by George Herbert (1593-1633).

When, between 1980 and 1982, psychiatrists and psychologists interviewed 18,000 people as a representative sample of the populations of five different places in the USA, 2,700 of them turned out to have a psychiatric disorder. In the UK up to a half of people consulting general practitioners have symptoms which do not have any underlying physical cause. 14 per cent of all people consulting a GP have a psychiatric illness. This is slightly more than those who have diseases of the heart and circulation. Two per cent of the population will see a psychiatrist in any one year and slightly less than one percent will be admitted to a psychiatric unit. A recent report estimated that at any one time 20 per cent of children and adolescents have mental health problems.

'These are the facts, now tell us the truth' applies cogently to our knowledge of mental disease. In this field more than is generally the case, 'the facts' need interpretation. They depend upon the experts' initial beliefs. People take to their doctors a range of human conditions – distress, problems derived from living as well as illness, in other words 'disgust with life in general'. The extremities of the spectrum are relatively easy to identify, but it is much less clear where the precise lines should be drawn between mental health, the ordinary difficulty of living, neurotic suffering, depression and schizophrenia.

In fact, more than one might expect, this is also true of some physical illnesses. There is no problem in diagnosing asthma when a child repeatedly develops the typical severe breathing difficulty, but there is a continuous variation found in any measure of lung function in a sample of children. There is no sharp demarcation between those with normal breathing and those whose breathing is very mildly affected. In spite of this and the fact that there is no doubt that mental illnesses are every bit as real as asthma, there is an ongoing debate as to whether mental disorders are illnesses in quite the same way as physical illnesses.

We think of illnesses as revealing themselves in symptoms. This model of illness implies that illnesses come in episodes afflicting an otherwise normal individual and that symptoms should be treated. This is often the case with mental symptoms too, but *sometimes* they can be part and parcel of a process of mental growth. To remove a symptom of this sort may not be an unequivocally good idea, since if the symptom is more like a problem arising out of the way a person is living their life, it is better *addressed* than suppressed. Coming to terms with these life experiences is necessary if the sufferer wishes to assume his full identity as a person with his own individual history. The poem, 'The World', by George Herbert quoted at the beginning of this chapter is about the universal experience of the destruction of what has been built. Yet men and women also have constructive and loving impulses, and try to rebuild what has been destroyed. Every so often it is possible for sufferers to come through a mental breakdown with a deeper relationship to the world and a stronger personality than they had before.

Although in some ways we know quite a lot about mental illness, little of what we understand is really certain. This insecurity is possibly what leads some experts to become fanatics for one particular line of thought. As one experienced and undogmatic psychiatrist said, 'We are pig ignorant, but we still have to look after people'. Programmes of care are difficult and taxing and there are few effective remedies. There are many ways of classifying mental conditions. Most have their uses but none is entirely satisfactory.

One distinction is between neurosis and psychosis, where the main point of difference is the degree of contact with reality. Crude but clear is the saying that neurotic patients dream of castles in the air, while psychotic patients live in them. *Neuroses* include some lesser types of depression, unreasonable fears, phobias and anxiety, obsessional and hysterical conditions. *Psychotic disorders* are divided into those of mood (the so-called affective illnesses); and those of thought (the schizophrenias). Affective disorders include severe depressions, sometimes with delusions of guilt, or manic disorders where there is elation or excitement. The schizophrenias include severe illness with delusions and hallucinations, and are some of the most devastating illnesses known to man. In between neurotic and psychotic disorders are the so-called *borderline states* with some features of both, and some would consider that severe eating disorders come into this category. Personality disorders are life-long conditions of character. The traits which normally differentiate one person from another can be exaggerated to such an extent that they interfere with proper functioning. As part of his or her character, someone with an obsessional personality disorder will be rigid, controlled, controlling and irrationally organised. Those with anti-social or psychopathic personality disorders may behave as if without conscience. They may be impulsive, touchy and suspicious and prone to commit criminal or violent acts.

As this brief list of mental disorders suggests, a full description would fill an encyclopaedia. This chapter describes the range from ordinary life, through distress to severe depression and schizophrenia.

Ordinary Life

This is an ordinary builder speaking about his life:

> We set up ideals, we then have to live by them. My father was a difficult man, pompous. His ideal was to be treated as important. It was a great strain for him to live up to his image of himself. It was false really. When we were little we'd always walked in fear of my father. We always had the feeling that we'd done something wrong. Guilt's a terrible problem for some people. What happened with my father was that as we grew up we realised that he was a bit of a tinpot tyrant. We ended by not believing in it anymore. He was better once he found he didn't have to do it anymore. He mellowed a bit but he's still very irascible.
>
> I'm like him. It's been difficult. My wife objected to it. She didn't like it. I've had to put a limit on it. That's all you can do, put a limit on it. That's part of learning. You can have too much time to think, though. Me with my work, I need to keep moving, to keep using tools. It's to keep my head in order really.

The builder's description of himself and his life illustrates the personal struggles, the wrestling with his relationships and with himself that makes up such an important part of life and its meaningfulness. He is not in any way a patient but it is clear that some of his worries and feelings have been quite difficult to manage at times. It is his encounter with these issues that make him into an interesting person, someone who has quite a lot to say and who has had a lot of experience, not so much of outward adventure but of inner life.

Grief and Depression

What turns a person like the builder, someone with the ordinary run of troubles, into a patient is that he becomes more concerned about himself and less able to manage. He, or she, goes to someone for help and they too in turn are concerned.

> A widower, Mr Richards, in his sixties, usually never went near a doctor, but did so one evening about two years after his wife's death. In contrast, his wife had been a frequent patient whom the doctor knew well, an incessant talker with a great many complaints. Mr Richards was dressed in dull clothes. It was near Christmas and he came with a 'croaky cold'. His doctor had known the situation over the years and understood the croaky (tearful) cold(ness) as the lack of warmth he had felt since his wife's death. The doctor gave him some treatment for his cold and a few minutes of talk. Mr Richards cried, remembering the unexpectedness of her death and the shock.

Mr Richards is an ordinary man but is he also a patient? Grief, which varies a lot in the way it is expressed from culture to culture, goes on for much longer than the few weeks of intense mourning so often allotted to it in our society. For some years after bereavement, people are much more likely to visit their doctors or to get anxious or become depressed than people who have not lost someone.

Mr Richards has become a worry to himself and his doctor is concerned about him. He has suffered from a normal but painful event, the loss of his wife and he is mourning but this too is a normal psychological reaction. It consists of sadness, longing, preoccupation with the lost one, and often anger and irritability.

Until recently, Mr Richards's doctor's understanding of his patient's croakiness as tearfulness, and of his cold as connected with a feeling of emotional coldness, would have been regarded as fanciful by many scientifically-minded experts. However, it is the doctor who has been proved right and the dismissive experts who were wrong. Those who are bereaved are more likely to become physically ill. Some of this illness is not trivial, for the bereaved are also more likely to die. We know a little more now of how emotional loss affects the body as well as the mind. Amongst other things it profoundly affects the body's capacity to resist disease – the immune system. Researchers in laboratories have shown that volunteers suffering from psychological stress are more likely than others to develop a cold when administered a standard dose of a respiratory virus. People can sense their powerful and distressing feelings of abandonment and emotional coldness flooding into their body leading to a cold, or worse. The doctor helped Mr Richards feel a bit better mentally and physically with some sensitive understanding which restored an experience of human kindness. Mr Richards was on the frontier between normal misery and illness. With a less knowledgeable response he might have still recovered, but he could have become more bitter, depressed, physically ill or some combination of these.

Although depression and grief are different, they often shade together. In grief there is usually some depression and in most depressions some grief is visible. Grief and mourning are clearly responses to loss. Depression, or at least the most understandable forms of it, likewise develop after a loss.

> Mrs Leigh, now an elderly widowed lady, bumped into an old friend whom she had not seen for over a decade. The friend asked her how she was. Mrs Leigh had to confess that she did not feel well. She cried off and on, felt vulnerable and unhappy. Life was not the same since her much stronger husband had died about six years ago. She knew that she complained about life, but knew it did not change the way she felt. She answered her friend's everyday enquiry with a pained creased look on her face, 'Oh you know,' she said, 'I miss my husband'. Mrs Leigh was close to tears. Her friend recognised that Mrs Leigh had always been a bit like this but that she was worse now. The friend felt the familiar old brand of awkward obligation. She wanted to move away, yet felt she should make an effort. She resented the burden that had been so quickly re-established in this brief chance meeting.

This is an example of a prolonged depressive reaction built upon a pre-existing depressive disposition. Almost certainly, this disposition went back a long way. Mrs Leigh had had a dependent relationship with her husband when he was alive. In her childhood her mother was often in hospital with repeated gynaecological problems, during which time her mother's sisters would look after her. This history, with its repeated experiences of 'losing' her mother, feeling both angry with her and also anxious about her, had probably laid the foundations for Mrs Leigh's dependence on others as well as for her tendency to depression.

The name *depression* captures the dispirited, pained, plaintive, low-spirited, constellation of qualities which occur in these conditions. It does not, as a term, describe so well the powerful feelings of anger, rage, irritability and destructiveness that also occur, the aspects of depression that are not so commonly spoken of. The presence of these aggressive feelings, and the difficulty of handling them internally, are factors that lead to depression. These feelings also lead to kinds of personal relationships where feelings of guilt and obligation co-exist with resentment. Often in depression the nature of what has been lost is not so clear-cut. What has been lost may be buried by the depressive reaction, just as an intense inflammation obscures the wound that led to it.

> Mr Allan, a single man in his late thirties, had lost his career as a journalist two years earlier and was now nearing bankruptcy. His life seemed to have fallen apart. These events had been provoked by his developing a moderately severe depressive episode and by the way he had subsequently behaved. He had had lifelong difficulties with male authority figures. As he ceased to argue with external figures in authority, the aggression appeared to persist internally, undermining his capacities so that he seemed to lose his talents and abilities. He had come to dislike himself. At one stage his self-criticism grew out of all proportion and took on an almost exuberant quality. At its worst he had been unable to sleep, had consistently woken at 4.00 in the morning and was liable to sudden but prolonged bouts of sobbing without an easily identifiable reason. He looked gaunt, pale and haggard. He seemed in some way to be contributing to his own misfortunes. He had neglected his affairs and he did not reply to letters. He was angry, difficult and very touchy and often experienced those who tried to offer some help as grossly insensitive and neglectful.

Overall, this is the picture of depression. Attempts had been made at psychotherapy, none of which had taken a hold or succeeded in arresting the downward spiral. Anti-depressant drugs were prescribed, but Mr Allan didn't like them. After his life had been brought to the edge of ruin he had a short period as a patient in a day hospital. Gradually he seemed to be coming out of his depression as he began to make small but constructive beginnings at rebuilding his life. There was a change in mood with moments of lightness and hopefulness.

> At Christmas he went home to stay with his elderly parents and brothers and sisters. As usual, some old family conflicts were revisited during the festive season. But also, for a short while, he had felt looked after in the bosom of the family, particularly by his mother. However, when he returned to his solitary life in the metropolis, he lost that slight liveliness which had previously been such a relief to those around him. His face became immobile and his skin again had a grey quality. He seemed once more to be in an inward-looking state and became neglectful of affairs that should have worried him. When he saw his therapist – he was now in a therapy he was finding helpful – the therapist drew his attention to the unconcerned way Mr Allan had spoken of the letters piling up unopened at home. In particular, there was a debt for which he was being pursued only because he had

not so far bothered to reply. He appeared to be tempting fate. Mr Allan criticised himself for not pulling his weight but said he knew that there would be no serious consequences (and in this he was right). However, he just did not care. This had alarmed the therapist, who recollected only too well the patient's previous dire state. Although he believed that there were not going to be serious financial consequences for Mr Allan, he felt the patient was being destructive of his capacities for being ordinarily responsible. In addition there were hints that Mr Allan was getting some satisfaction out of this state of affairs. To himself, the therapist wondered what had been stirred up by that Christmas visit to the family.

He described to Mr Allan the neglectful, fatalistic but trouble-provoking state. It took some work and effort for Mr Allan to come a little bit out of his dangerously anaesthetised state. It seemed rather like that of climbers in extreme conditions who develop hypothermia or hypoxia out on the mountains. They describe how pleasant it feels to sink down into the snow, to stop struggling, to curl up and let oneself die. To keep on fighting takes an immense effort and is more painful. Similarly, in extreme mental conditions, there are people who develop an almost erotic relationship with death and destruction, who are, as Keats put it, 'half in love with easeful death'.

The therapist's observations enabled Mr Allan to stir himself. As if waking up, he said that he had noticed that he had been more prone to getting locked internally into angry arguments with his former boss and with his father. He was dismayed when he thought how violent these internal rows had become. It then became clear how much Mr Allan had been affected by the interruption in his sessions caused by the holiday break and how the renewed contact with his parents had been very important in reviving his grievances against his father. The therapist said that he thought Mr Allan had been tempted over Christmas by an old susceptibility. This was a grievance against his father, familiar to both the patient and the therapist, for, as he saw it, denying the patient a longed-for idealised understanding with both his father and his mother. He felt his father had prevented this. He felt that his father had made his mother so unhappy that she had been able to look after him without being explosive and bad-tempered. The short-lived comfort after Christmas had been followed by a return to isolation. It had stirred up again some destructive area of motivation within him and he was now engaged in revenge. Gradually, as more work was done he started to feel a little less at the mercy of these feelings and reactions, although a great deal would be needed before he could feel properly secure with this understanding and his need to change.

The more one knew about Mr Allan, the more possible it was to come to some kind of understanding of how a storehouse of destructiveness had accumulated through childhood, adolescence and early adult life. As he had become more disillusioned with himself, as well as with others, it had been unleashed. Without decisive intervention it had proved unstoppable until it had finished and run its course. In one way, over these past two years Mr Allan had been committing partial suicide. He had inflicted damage upon himself and his life. Attacking one's self and destroying one's life as the child of the parents with whom one is angry is one of the most powerful revenges.

For a person like Mr Allan to be able to modify these conflicts, it is essential to clarify with the patient – and for him to grasp the significance of – the roots of the sense of disappointment. It is equally important for the patient to understand how cruel is their anger and rage. Only on the basis of this kind of complex self-knowledge can genuine stability be achieved.

The onset of these self-destructive reactions can be sudden, or they can build up slowly over years. With some new blow or some new loss the reaction can be unleashed with an enormous power. The experience of loss can be felt as a mental pain so intense that it cannot be contained within the mind. Sometimes it is as the emotional storm floods into the brain and then, in turn, affects the mind. There is little doubt that there are brain events connected with these emotional reactions, so that brain chemicals (neurotransmitters) are altered. Here we are at a level where it is very difficult to sort out cause and effect, and it is quite likely that complex interactions occur.

This is particularly obvious in the more severe depressions, where treatment often needs to be both physical and emotional. Thus, both *anti-depressant drugs* and *electro-convulsive therapy* can be essential for recovery from a severe depressive state. At the same time, in many depressions, psychotherapy can lead to important personal understanding which can have a protective role. The individual can become aware in a living way of how the past and present problems in our relationships with our loved ones have led to and are sustaining patterns of conflict. Problems such as these will never go away because they stem from our earliest experiences and from our basic emotional constitutions. Nevertheless the process of emotional understanding through a re-living of these conflicts in psychotherapy can produce important changes, making them less overwhelming for the person and less damaging in their life.

Old people are particularly prone to depression, not only because there will have been much loss in their lives but also because of the biological changes connected with ageing. In the aged when depression is severe it can take the form of physical agitation, moving restlessly from foot to foot, often going nowhere. They become distressed, anxious and/or slowed up, with immobile faces and few movements. They do not eat and consequently lose weight. Although treatment can be effective, severe depressions are dangerous and the life-expectancy of depressed old people is reduced.

> Mr Daniel, a man in his early seventies had suffered a number of losses. His wife had become ill with renal failure and also had had to have a number of distressing abdominal operations. Probably, she was dying. In addition, the patient had a number of illnesses. He was very aware of his declining powers and his position in life. He seemed to be in a rage about these horrible circumstances. Gradually, he became more and more depressed until he was reduced to a figure who had lost several stones in weight. He was prone to stand motionless for 5, 10 or 15 minutes at a time. At these periods he seemed to be like a patient with Parkinson's disease (like Mohammed Ali), taking small steps as if in some way trying to move but not being able to do so. Of course, he did not have Parkinson's Disease but he did have depression. He did not care for himself. He sometimes was incontinent and this too seemed to be an expression of his fury and itself to lead him to still more fury. He seemed to be totally stuck in this state. He received drugs, ECT and attempts at psychotherapy. All of it just seemed to be an irritation to him and again a further source of irritation. Treatments seemed like ventures he was going to defeat. Many

of the nursing staff came to feel that Mr Daniel was in his rage stepping towards death. Eventually, he contracted pneumonia. In this way he became more ill and died.

Depression can be a grave illness, but schizophrenia does tend to be more serious. In spite of many claims to the contrary there is no cure for schizophrenia. There is, however, care and if this is provided in the best way then a lot can be done. Proper care will involve a variety of treatments thoughtfully used. They will include drugs, hospital admission (which may have to be compulsory), sheltered housing, psycho-social therapies – family interventions, efforts to improve the patient's socialisation, occupational therapy, emotional support for the patient, for his relatives and for others, including the professionals involved in his care. Understanding and acceptance of the person and his difficulties – and at the right time expectations too – must all be based upon a deep knowledge of the condition and its psychology, and are important ingredients in the management of these patients' care.

Schizophrenia can be one of the most severe and devastating of illnesses. About one person in a hundred over the course of a lifetime will develop it. Forms of the disorder can occur almost at any age, but most typically it affects young persons as they encounter the physical and emotional turmoil of adolescent and early adult growth. For the majority the outlook is gloomy, although a quarter of those who develop the condition do recover in some way. About a half of these will for most of their lives alternate between phases of acute illness and phases of improvement. The rest will suffer for most of their lives from chronic social, intellectual and emotional impairment. One in twenty of all schizophrenics commits suicide. There is a tendency for the condition to burn out in late life.

A small number of eminent psychiatrists who have devoted their working lives to the care of schizophrenics and their families have been able to build up a picture of the lifetime nature of this condition. Most of these psychiatrists have come to the conclusion that schizophrenia is not so much a disease as the abnormal progress of a whole life. Most serious investigators come to be in awe of the illness. They feel that while much is known, they can be absolutely sure of very little. While they know that some new discovery may revolutionise our understanding of the condition, their experience as it stands strongly suggests that many only partly understood factors have come together to cause the illness. These include complex disharmonies within the personality, special sensitivities to some of the difficulties encountered in relationships, psychological adversities in the course of upbringing in combination with genetic disposition, subtle forms of physical brain damage (at birth, for instance), neurochemical abnormalities, all of which can bear in on a fundamental disposition of the human mind to react in this way. The different proportions in the combination may be unique to each individual yet culminate in schizophrenic breakdown. Once this breakdown has happened, it will have its own damaging consequences at several levels – the neurological, psychological, personal and social.

Quite a number of people who have had schizophrenic illnesses have written about their experiences. One of the most famous of these accounts is that of Daniel Schreber, a senior judge in Germany, who at the comparatively late age of forty two years had his first breakdown in Leipzig in 1884. He recovered and was able to work again, but had a further breakdown seven years later. This time he was in hospital for nine years, suffering from bizarre abnormal experiences. He successfully fought his own legal action for his release. Although his abnormal beliefs continued, they did so in an encapsulated form until some five years later at the age of sixty three he had a final episode of illness from which he never recovered. He died in a Leipzig asylum at the age of sixty nine. Schreber was an exceptional man whose abnormal experiences, whilst uniquely his own, can still give us an idea of the nature of schizophrenic experience. The following description is from the reports of Schreber's psychiatrists, which were published along with his memoirs.

> 'He himself, of this he is convinced, is the only object upon which divine miracles are worked, and thus he is the most remarkable human being who has ever lived upon earth. Every hour and every minute for years he has experienced these miracles in his body, and he has had them confirmed by the voices that have conversed with him. During the first years of his illness his bodily organs suffered such destructive injuries as would have led to the death of any other man: he lived for a long time without a stomach, without intestines, almost without lungs, with a torn oesophagus, without a bladder and with shattered ribs, he used sometimes to swallow part of his own larynx with his food etc. But divine miracles ("rays") always restored what had been destroyed, and therefore, as long as he remains a man he is altogether immortal. These alarming phenomena have ceased long ago, and his "femaleness" has become more prominent instead. He has a feeling that enormous numbers of "female nerves" have already passed into his body, and out of them a new race of men will proceed, through a process of direct impregnation by God. Not until then, it seems, will he be able to die a natural death, and along with the rest of mankind he will be able to regain a state of bliss.'

In his own account Schreber describes voices, which he terms 'Rays of God'. They,

> 'not infrequently thought themselves entitled to mock at me by calling me "Miss Schreber", in allusion to the emasculation I was about to undergo. At other times they would say, "So this sets up to have been a Senatspräsident [a kind of High Court judge], this person who lets himself be fucked!".'

After long acquaintance with God, Schreber was reluctantly forced to the conclusion that God knew nothing of living men and had a complete inability to judge them correctly. God, as was the *Order of Things,* was only used to dealing with corpses. These brief extracts give a flavour of the world inhabited by this cultured and sensitive man. They illustrate the *delusions* (false beliefs) and *hallucinations* (auditory or visual false perceptions), and the experiences of being *influenced by outside agencies*, which characterise the so-called *positive symptoms* of the disorder. Modern psychotropic drugs would calm or suppress the intensity of his abnormal experiences, but more likely than not he would have remained unwell or not fully functioning. More subtle problems, the so-called *negative symptoms*, such as poverty of thought, of emotion and of motivation, would probably have remained. Many of his higher sensibilities and personal capacities in relationships might still have been affected by his illness. In the vast majority of cases, psychotherapy or psychoanalysis cannot cure this condition either.

However, one psychiatrist, Manfred Bleuler, after a lifetime's experience of looking after schizophrenic patients has written, 'the correct therapeutic attitude toward a schizophrenic patient is easier when we accept him as a brother whom we can judge according to our own nature, than if we watch him as a person who has become unintelligible in his thinking and feeling and in principle a creature different from ourselves'. Understanding and responding to some of the schizophrenic patients' ideas and motivations is made easier because some of the contents of schizophrenic thinking and preoccupations are present in all of us.

George Herbert who was not a schizophrenic but a poet, described in the poem quoted at the head of this chapter not only a state of despair because everything has been destroyed, but also the experience of renewal when good things are restored. For Schreber, this feeling was a lived emotional experience which he explained by a delusional belief system. God destroyed his body and the world was to be recreated with a new race of men. People without schizophrenia are also often preoccupied with how to keep their loving relations to the world alive, and can also find it difficult. It is the same set of issues experienced in a very different way. We have seen how people without illness may dream of terrible events or strange alterations to their bodies, or magical solutions to difficult problems. The schizophrenic patient lives in such a world. The fundamental concerns of our human condition operate at depth in every personality, becoming visible in our anxieties, our dreams and our creative endeavours. If we are unfortunate and cannot cope with these anxieties then we may become ill.

Delusions can sometimes be understood helpfully as an attempt to recover from a catastrophic disruption of an individual's emotional relationship with his world. Delusions can be thought of as a way of recreating a renewed link with the outside world. However, the renewed connection with the world is quite unlike a normal solution to these anxieties, where the emotional rebuilding is realistic. In his normal life Schreber and his wife were childless. This was a cause of great unhappiness for him. Many of his subsequent delusions concerned his turning into a woman and having a child by God, thus solving the problem. Other continuities can be traced between his pre-illness problems and thinking, and his post-illness delusions. For instance, one morning in the period between his first and second illnesses he was lying half-asleep in bed when the idea occurred to him, 'that after all it really must be very nice to be a woman submitting to the act of copulation'. Schreber was always very vulnerable to any illness in his wife. His last and final breakdown followed her suffering a stroke. This pre-illness vulnerability can help us understand why Schreber and others like him cannot cope with certain types of life-events.

At the time of the original publication of his memoirs, Schreber's childhood experiences were not widely known nor was their significance fully appreciated. More recently, some of his early history has been given a greater significance than before. His father was the originator of a national movement advocating a system of medical gymnastics for the proper up-bringing of children. This system involved a variety of braces, head and limb restraints and bonds. These, Schreber *père* advocated, should be applied from infancy onwards, to correct supposed bad habits of posture leading to moral weakness and worse. These devices looked like instruments of torture and much of Schreber's childhood was lived within them. It is hard to resist the conclusion that Schreber's later delusional pre-occupation concerning passive submission to a God who has no understanding of living human beings had something to do with these early experiences.

Most people who have schizophrenic illnesses have not been maltreated in this very extreme way, although some small proportion have. As far as is known, children who later in their lives suffer from schizophrenia more commonly come from families where the parents are in states of longstanding conflict at the same time as being emotionally unavailable to the children. It is always possible that

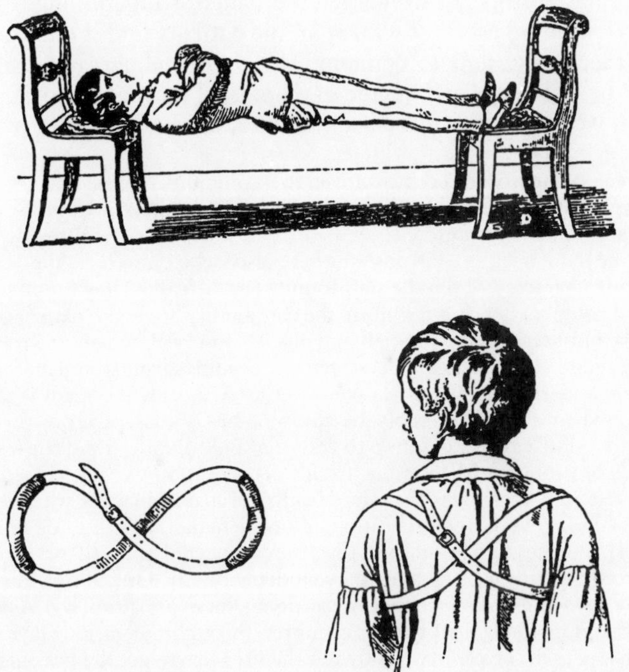

Figure 16: The bridge and shoulderband were just two of the restraints devised for correcting the posture of children. Schreber's father advocated the use of these restraints with all children, including his own.

these abnormal family environments arise to some extent out of genetically-caused disturbance shared by the parents. It may be that it is this common inheritance, rather than the environment *per se*, which is the most important causative factor in the illness. Current evidence indicates that genes do make a difference in schizophrenia, probably accounting for about 50 per cent of the variance. A twin whose identical twin develops schizophrenia is about 50 times more likely to develop the illness than someone within the general population. Such a twin has up to a one in two chance of developing the illness. Partitioning crudely, this suggests that roughly 50 per cent is environmentally determined.

Specialised knowledge gained through the intensive psychotherapeutic treatment of schizophrenia and its related conditions has built upon this fundamental continuity of human experience. Just as in the normal person can be found traces of the schizophrenic imagination, even within the schizophrenic's deepest abnormality some capacity for normal thinking remains. Sometimes after years of illness the normal personality will show itself. The normal and the abnormal ways of functioning have remained in a dynamic tension with each other. Our understanding and human sympathy for the schizophrenic's experiences can help us communicate with him or her. If we understand, it can also be easier to make contact with the normal parts of the patient's personality. A meaningful and helpful relationship can strengthen the patient's functioning. Psychotherapeutic experience suggests that schizophrenic patients find it especially difficult to handle, metabolise and to communicate their feelings and conflicts. This means that the right type and degree of emotional receptivity to their everyday problems, as well as to their deeper difficulties, can be helpful.

A thirty-year-old man had recently moved to a community home from an inpatient ward. Seven years previously he'd become ill, hearing the voices of God and the Devil telling him to kill someone. He had had a few partial remissions since then although he had tried to kill his mother, also schizophrenic. She was also a domineering character whom the staff found very difficult. They found they could never get through to her. For a while in the community home the patient developed good skills and became more socially involved. However, for no apparent reason his mental state deteriorated. He stopped attending groups and became withdrawn, cold and irritable. Once he asked another withdrawn resident what was for lunch and when she didn't reply he threw a heavy glass ashtray through the window. In a staff workshop set up to consider and to understand the meaning of these kinds of problems, the reasons for his deterioration were discussed.

What was important was that the Health Service Managers who funded the community home were operating in a culture demanding 'value for money' and 'clinical effectiveness'. This meant that they expected that all patients should progress to the point of being able to live independently. Only if this 'throughput' was maintained did they feel they were doing their job properly. A feeling of pressure and impatience had been transmitted through the various layers of staff to the patients themselves. Everybody felt the pressure to get the patients to move on. The patients' increasing disturbance coincided with the tense atmosphere in the home, characterised by the question, 'When are you going?' The workshop was able to support the staff to work at creating a more realistic level of expectation for these services and to understand that the patient needed the security of knowing that the staff would not try and move him on prematurely. He needed to feel that there was a safe place there for him. It was then possible to see how the patient had been unable to communicate his discomfort through words. Instead he had probably experienced the staff of the home as being as emotionally impenetrable as his mother. She herself probably needed to be as impenetrably domineering as she was in order to maintain her precarious internal equilibrium. As a result of the discussions the staff began to have more emotional resources of their own. They could see and use the understanding of the way in which the culture they were exposed to was unhelpful, and they could understand how their patients reacted to this type of pressure.

Another characteristic of psychotic thinking is the reliance upon magical or delusional systems as a way of solving problems. Along with this, schizophrenic and other ill patients tend to become dependent upon the decisions of the staff. They endow the staff with the special powers that children feel belong to adults and this can be a way of relating that is therapeutic. However, because it is both easier and also flattering, the staff's tendency to take on the role of giving and administering solutions – advice, surrogate actions, medication for all problems – can go too far. It is sometimes more therapeutic to help patients make contact with their own latent capacities for learning and development.

An eighteen-year-old man from the north-west of England was admitted after becoming withdrawn and isolated. Before he had become really ill, the patient was on a building apprenticeship scheme, but he had been anxious about the possibility of getting injured. When he accidentally bruised his foot he felt very fragile, and he stopped work. His workmates seem to have sensed his vulnerability and had told him it was better for him to go off sick. In the ward he made no eye contact, instead staring disconcertingly into space above one's head while smiling vacuously. Various psychosocial treatments including occupational therapy were offered, but all save some medication were passively rejected as if they were of little interest. A few months after discharge he was re-admitted after banging his head repeatedly on the living room wall. The patient's mother was incurious. She accepted her son's illness dully, as a matter of course. The father was a bit more involved, but still thought his son was merely lazy rather than ill. The hospital staff too tended not to wonder much about what was going on in his mind. It turned out that the patient had written several times to the head of an Arnold Schwarzenegger Body Building course. He wanted the head to teach him how to look like him and offered himself sexually as payment. It looked as if the patient's smiling delusional state involved some belief in a magical route to strength, bypassing any need for the difficulties of working at more realistic ways of becoming emotionally or physically stronger. Perhaps too his parents' passivity had failed to set him a good example of how change might be achieved. On the basis of this understanding the staff felt they had a rationale and a route for trying to help him find his own potential for making a real contact with the world, no matter how limited or restricted this might be at first.

This chapter has described a range of troubles from ordinary distress, through grief and mourning, depression and, finally schizophrenia. It has tried to show how different these conditions are, whilst also showing some of their fundamental commonalities. One of these shared problems is the plain fact that we all have to live with ourselves. We have to cope with what we are and with what our minds throw up at us from their depths. Schizophrenics have more to manage in this way than most of us.

14
Therapy

When mental or emotional difficulties occupy the mind to the detriment of everyday life, treatment may be helpful – or indeed necessary. Just as one might go to a doctor with a bodily pain so one might consult someone experienced in mental disorders when excessively troubled in one's thoughts or feelings. There are five categories of treatment for the emotional and mental problems of life. Each does an essential job but none of them does it perfectly, so that different kinds of treatment are sometimes best used in combination with each other. Although this chapter is primarily concerned with just one of these types of treatment – psychodynamic psychotherapy – we begin by outlining the other main types of treatment (see Plate 13).

On the whole, the major mental illnesses need to be treated with drugs and social interventions. *Chemotherapy* is treatment by drugs, powerful chemicals that have been discovered to have an effect on the body or upon the agents of illness. Those used to treat mental illness include anti-depressants (such as sertraline or prozac), anti-psychotics (such as chlorpromazine or clozapine), sedatives such as diazepam (Valium) or barbiturates, and stimulants (such as Ritalin or amphetamines). *Physical treatment* describes physical interventions such as electro-convulsive treatment or 'shock' treatment (ECT), or, more rarely, brain operations. In ECT, an artificial brain seizure is induced under an anaesthetic and, for reasons that are not fully understood this can sometimes bring about dramatic improvement in some forms of depression. *Social treatment* involves measures to improve the sufferer's social conditions or relationships. It can include protected living arrangements – the old-fashioned meaning of the term asylum – or living in hostels or in special communities. Occupational therapy, protected work settings, or help from a community psychiatric nurse with managing the day-to-day business of life are all forms of social treatment.

For mental and emotional troubles that are disabling, yet less severe than the major mental illnesses described in an earlier chapter, we need to turn to one or another form of *psychotherapy*. The term psychotherapy is, like the term chemotherapy, no more than a general designation given to psychological treatments of the mind. Psychotherapy is often employed in its own right, but it also has an essential role when used together with drug and social treatments;

here it can help patients, relatives and mental health workers understand and cope with some of the difficult feelings and impulses characteristic of the more severe mental illnesses. Psychotherapy is a varied collection: at the latest count there were over 400 different types. Many of these turn out to be interventions that are short-lived, practised by only a few, and after a short while they fade into obscurity. Others are based upon extensive bodies of clinical discovery, experience, and the scholarly development of theory. *Psychoanalysis*, for instance, amounts to nothing less than a general theory of human nature and one which, whether it proves to be wholly true or partly in error, has profoundly influenced world culture for the last one hundred years, since its inception.

Psychotherapies and the Talking Cure

Psychodynamic therapy is a form of treatment founded upon the ideas and aims of psychoanalysis. Its central goal, therefore, as in psychoanalysis, is to clarify and establish the *meaning* of a person's thoughts, feelings and actions seen in the context of the life as a whole – and usually, when a person seeks psychotherapeutic help of this sort it is because of a concern about some aspect of life as a whole. There is often a sense of some unfinished business, or some unease about areas of the past which feel as though they need reconsidering or re-opening.

We know intuitively that the child is father to the man because we are aware of our own histories. We are aware of a continuity between ourselves as children and ourselves as we are now – as partners, husbands, wives, and as parents.

> One thirty-year-old man could remember himself at the age of nine years lying immobile for hours on the sofa, for fear that if he moved the pain in his chest would become a full-blown heart attack. Later in life he always needed the women important to him to be healthy and happy and would become distressed if they were not. He sensed that these matters were connected to the intense but very ambivalent relationship he had with his mother, but he did not know how. He wanted to try and put these things right.

The wish to try to 'put things right' is an important part of the motivation for many seeking psychotherapeutic help. This is a larger aim than merely wanting to be relieved of symptoms or to function better. Often it also involves putting things right with others who are of central importance to one's life. Of course symptoms – anxiety, depression, troubles with eating or sleeping and so on – will be part of the story, yet people do not seek psychotherapy only to be rid of symptoms. Many patients are functioning well in important areas of their lives and yet are still troubled by internal concerns. Others may have considerable difficulty in functioning, and have disabling emotional difficulties they need to improve. Some may feel unable to love. Others may dislike aspects of their character. Psychotherapy may well help with symptoms but most issues of personal concern cannot be regarded as symptoms in the narrowest sense.

There are other important kinds of psychotherapy, taken in its broader sense.

Systemic or family therapies, like psychodynamic psychotherapy, also consider personal and emotional experiences to be important but their emphasis is on approaching family relationships as a system rather than attempting to treat the difficulties within a single individual. This is an approach that can be particularly relevant with couples, children and adolescents, where family structures and relationships are often what people are finding difficult and which may be causing symptoms. Finding different approaches to family stresses and strains, can be very helpful. Re-constituted families, or families where there is marital disharmony, can be greatly relieved by discussing their difficulties with a therapist experienced in these problems

In contrast, behaviour therapy and cognitive behavioural therapy come from a different intellectual tradition. They are widely employed varieties of psychotherapy where the main aim is to relieve or control disabling symptoms, whether excessive anxiety as in phobias or panics, compulsive rituals such as obsessional handwashing, or the so-called dysfunctional negative mind sets of depression. They focus more narrowly upon the outward manifestation of problems In cognitive behavioural therapy, depression is regarded as an irrational state of mind and the product of faulty learning. These more structured therapies do not consider the life history of the person or the emotional meaning of symptoms to be crucial in and of themselves.

The opinion of patients themselves about these various forms of psychotherapeutic treatment is worth taking into account. In 1990, MIND, the mental health charity, interviewed over 500 people who had had experiences as mental health patients in either in-patient or out-patient settings. The respondents voiced considerable opposition to drugs and to ECT, which they tended to regard as coercive or dehumanising. In contrast, the 'talking therapies' were viewed as 'confirming and validating'. The report concluded, 'The message that emerged most powerfully is that people want to be heard, taken account of as valued individuals, rather than as vessels of diseased or badly programmed brains'. Though drugs and, in some limited circumstances, ECT have an essential place in treatment, they need to be part of an overall treatment which treats patients as human beings, with lives and personalities whose significance needs to be taken into serious account. This is the level at which psychotherapeutic need to be integrated into the drug and social treatment more usually offered.

The First Meetings

Most people will have very mixed feelings before a first consultation with a psychotherapist. There is the hope that the therapist will turn out to be an understanding person who can help relieve painful states of mind, and the strain of feeling unable to manage. Perhaps it will be possible to talk about a secret torment sometimes carried for decades. But there will also be doubts and these can get worse as the appointment approaches. The prospect of revealing vulnerable areas of oneself can feel like taking too much of a risk; perhaps it is better just to shut down and carry on doggedly suffering. The feeling uppermost will vary from person to person, but even the most motivated person will have hidden fears. The therapist is trained to be open to the full spectrum of the patient's feelings, because one of the main aims of psychodynamic psychotherapy is to help the person to be emotionally realistic about others as well as about him or herself.

The following is an account of a very needy patient's first encounters with a psychotherapist. Many other people who seek help may not be feeling so much under pressure and their difficulties may be more focused. This patient felt helped and was very appreciative although some of her less obvious feelings of anxiety about the therapist were also discernible.

> Ms Jones was a thirty-eight-year-old single woman who had been referred by her GP because she had become depressed over the previous two years. She had been sent an appointment for this first consultation a fortnight or so before. As she came out of the lift on the fourth floor she was met by the therapist, who introduced himself and showed her to his consulting room down the corridor.
>
> Ms Jones was of medium height with blonde hair from an ordinary working-class family in Kent. Her face was a little pink and her eyes were intense. She had a lively manner and once seated, she began to talk right away with pressure and intensity. She spoke first of her ex-partner and how she had come to realise how possessive he was. Although he would get angry, her basic response was to feel sorry for him. She was very sensitive, she said, and had only to see someone on the bus with a pensive expression to know whether or not they are more deeply troubled. She cannot see a down-and-out or a mentally disturbed person on the streets without feeling involved. Ms Jones also suffers from odd habits. For instance, she cannot throw away old tickets or receipts and she has counting rituals, especially in connection with food.
>
> The dominating facts of her life were that when Ms Jones was seven years old, her mother had had a serious breakdown after her father left home with a younger woman who had been looking after her. Since that time her father hadn't really wanted to acknowledge her and she felt she had lost the most important people in her life, save for her older brother and her grandparents. Her father's leaving had brought on her mother's breakdown, but mother had been vulnerable even before that. Her mother had never really been normal since that first breakdown; she had been in and out of hospital throughout the rest of the patient's childhood and had made several suicide attempts and was emotionally unpredictable, with bouts of screaming, anger and weeping going on throughout Ms Jones's childhood and adolescence.
>
> Ms Jones had left her partner. Shortly after that, her mother took another overdose and was admitted to hospital and it was unclear exactly how serious her mother's physical condition was. After visiting her that night Ms Jones had gone to her own home in the early hours of the morning. The thought passed through her mind that she wouldn't mind if her mother died. She regarded this as a terrible thought – both inexplicable and inexcusable. She began to think she might be going mad and that people were hating her for thinking such things. Then these ideas had seemed to become both cause and effect of her developing depression. The patient's GP had been very helpful and had listened and prescribed antidepressants whereupon Ms Jones began to feel a bit better. However, after a while her improvement had levelled out and

she was still full of distress about the events of her life and troubled by her odd, obsessional ideas.

Speaking rapidly and under pressure, Ms Jones described these circumstances with her mother and her own depression. Now that she herself had been depressed, she could understand her mother much better. But she was bothered by the question of whether her troubles were genetic or whether they had been passed on to her through what she had experienced as a child. In particular, she was worried by her tendency to become preoccupied with thoughts which stuck in her mind in what she felt was an unrealistic way, as used to happen with her mother's obsessions. 'You know some people get good things from their parents and other people get other things, bad things. Did I get bad things or is it in my genes?' There had been times when her mother had thought she was seeing rats. She could remember when she was seven how desperately she would try to make her mother feel better. If she could only stop her mother crying perhaps she wouldn't go away from her again.

Ms Jones said that during schooltime when her mother was first in hospital, she kept going to the classroom window to look for her mother although she knew there was no chance of seeing her. She spoke of this time with great feeling, sometimes interrupting herself with hurried asides about how if 'they' (the school, the authorities) had known then what children were like they would have helped, but they didn't know, though they had done their best. She now wished that she had sought this kind of help sooner; she did not know why she had not. She implied that perhaps it had become possible for her to do so now because she felt she was past childbearing age; and she was terrified that if she had come sooner she might have been expected to have children, when she felt herself to be quite incapable of looking after them.[1]

At this point the therapist intervened because he was struck by the hectic, anxious way the patient was talking. He said he thought that some of her hectic rush was because she was now unsure about whether she could take the risk of allowing these issues to emerge fully. Being less rushed would lead to more time with these issues. Then she returned to the subject of her death wish about her mother. A few months earlier she'd been referred for cognitive therapy to a psychologist who had told her in a reassuring way that she didn't really want her mother dead; rather the true purpose of the patient's thoughts was to wish for her mother's depression to go away. Ms Jones had felt worse afterwards, because that had not felt right to her and the thoughts had not gone away.

At this point the therapist said that she had probably spent so much of her mental life desperately trying to keep her mother going, when she herself still felt so much like a petrified grief-stricken seven year old, that she couldn't bear to know that she was indeed very fed up with her mother (later she told him that this had made a great impact upon her).

The patient's emotional engagement was now intense. She began to pour out how she had felt at school and what had been going on in her mind. She had been unable to learn because she was in such a state. She had stopped eating and the school had tried to help by literally spoon-feeding her. The patient didn't really know why she couldn't eat, but what she did know she couldn't explain to anyone. She thought that food had its own name written on it, so that, for instance, chocolate was inscribed with the word 'chocolate'. She actually wasn't sure if she was eating food or words and she became so frightened at the strangeness of this feeling that she couldn't eat. She would constantly spit onto her sleeve so that it became wet and disgusting.

As he continued to listen to her, the therapist sensed a kind of mute desperation spilling out all over the place both in the present, and, from what she was saying, in the past. He said to her that she must have been filled with frightening words and thoughts which she couldn't spit out, because she had no one to speak them to. She must have been in a state of great grief about her mother's illness and her father's going. She might not have felt like eating. Food, or indeed anything outside her own mind, was probably felt to be bad until known to be otherwise.

Ms Jones seemed interested. She told the therapist how as a gawky teenager she used to take a little boy in a pram for walks on a Saturday afternoon. The boy's father eventually wouldn't let her do this. In a not unkindly way the father had told her, 'You always bring him back crying'. He had not apparently disliked her but he seemed to have noticed something was happening. She thought she must have had an irritating quality. She noticed too that she sometimes squeezed the little boy's hand too hard. She thought she was a terrible person, how was it she was like this? The therapist made the point that perhaps the little boy was getting something she hadn't had very much of for herself. He suggested she might have been passing on something of this to the little boy. Ms Jones went on to speak of her deceased grandmother who is still a living figure for her. She prays to her. She knew it was silly, she said, but she thinks that it was her grandmother who got her to the Tavistock. She felt so pleased, she was really glad that she had come.

In this consultation session, the therapist worked hard to understand the totality of Ms Jones's predicament. He did this by trying to identify and to take in Ms Jones's main anxiety at any given moment. This not only involved the therapist in careful listening but also in trying to pick up those emotional situations which, while being less explicit, were powerfully affecting the way the patient was feeling, particularly during the session. When the therapist spoke of the patient's difficulty with eating when she was seven years old, it was used as a way of alluding to the way in which, for instance, she needed to gulp down everything that was being said.

Transference

Although Ms Jones's attitude towards the therapist was overwhelmingly appreciative, there were moments when less positive feelings surfaced. The therapist arranged to see Ms Jones for a second consultation a month after the first. This gap (which was perhaps a week longer than ideally it should have been) was to enable the patient to react to the first consultation, to digest something of it and to regain a new equilibrium.

Ms Jones began by saying she had had lots of dreams after the first session, including one in which her mother was dead. She had written some things down, and seemed just about to say that she had brought them with her, when she changed her mind and said instead that she hoped the therapist would realise that

> the previous consultation had been very important to her. She felt better. 'You know, not completely or anything like that but somehow, I can't find the words, better'. Then she confessed to a strange thought the day before – what if she came to see the therapist and wasn't able to talk, and just stayed silent? This thought had got a grip on her and stuck in her mind. As if to override the imminent possibility of falling silent, she talked under pressure. So whilst she was desperately attesting how much she had felt understood and how much she had to talk about, she was not at her ease.

The therapist pointed this out to her and then connected it with her fear that she wouldn't be able to say anything. Barely able to let the therapist finish, she interrupted him and said she had just been thinking 'what if Dr X just sits there and says nothing?' The therapist said that as well as its being important that he realise how valuable that first session was to her, it was also important to notice that he could be a frightening or disturbing figure, someone she feared might go silent or withdraw. She seemed to appreciate being spoken to in this way and she became more relaxed.

When the therapist described to Ms Jones her two views of him – the one appreciative and the other fearing he might withdraw and go silent – his comments were based on an understanding of transference. Transference consists of the way in which we relate to the world on the basis of crucial past relationships, usually those with our parents and siblings or other family members. These early experiences are a mixture of both actual happenings and what the individual originally made of those experiences. These early feelings, fantasies, and ways of perceiving and relating to the world form powerful templates, which influence or even determine the way all subsequent experience is viewed and understood.

The transference is addressed for very particular reasons. When the therapist commented to the patient on her view of the world at that moment – in particular her view of the therapist – he was not simply (as patients sometimes feel therapists to be doing), pulling everything back to himself, wanting to put himself at the centre of her thoughts. Instead, by showing her what she is making of what is going on at the moment, he is illustrating for her in the here-and-now something of what she experiences in her relationships in general. If this can be grasped by the patient it can be something of a relief. In consultations, and later in regular therapy, interpretations of the transference – of what is going on in the session between patient and therapist – spell out the kinds of processes that in everyday life we instinctively note, judge and appraise as we relate to each other, often without consciously attending to what we are doing.

Transference is an ever-present feature of the human mind. It is in all our relationships, to a greater or lesser degree, all of the time. What is unique about the therapeutic relationship is that it provides a setting in which the transference can be observed, identified, recognised and spelled out. Amongst much else, it allowed this particular patient to begin to make sense of her own feelings and behaviour, and so gave her back the possibility of a renewed sense of meaning in her life. The question, 'Why am I like this?' was very distressing for her, not just because she felt some of her thoughts to be shameful, but also because she had no sense of her own emotional biography. In other words, it was a real question in her case, not just a cry of complaint. What is arrived at through an understanding of transference is not a formula routinely applied. It is a point of view advanced to the patient as a living possibility, an account of one of the many influences, internal and external, which bear in on all human beings.

Yet no matter how much insight one has, one's own transference state is never entirely knowable. Transference is an influence whose activity will always escape us in some way, since we are unable to see how our very manner of seeing is influenced. The cartoon showing the man so engulfed in the dinosaur's footprint that he is not actually aware of its immense presence makes this point (Figure 17). It is salutary to realise that we are constitutionally incapable of being purely objective or of being, even at our maddest, purely subjective. All the time in the session the therapist is making judgements about what to take up and how. In doing this he is using his clinical skills developed upon his previous clinical experiences and his theoretical knowledge of how the human personality is put together. At the same time every patient is unique, and the particular mix of this patient with this therapist is also unique.

Figure 17: 'Well I don't see any point in looking any further. It was probably just one of those wild rumours.' Transference is like a dinosaur footprint. It belongs to the past and because we live within it we can never fully achieve an objective vantage point from which to see ourselves.

From the patient's point of view, there can be two faces to psychotherapy. When the therapist is felt to be receptive to the patient's emotional predicament, the experience of feeling understood can be valuable and gratifying. The other aspect is that the therapist is felt to be watching, scrutinising and sometimes critical, and this is much more disturbing and unpleasant. This feeling of being scrutinised has a clear basis in reality because in order to do his or her job properly the therapist is trying to achieve a diagnostic insight into the patient and the problems brought. The aim is to give some relief through a psychotherapeutic attitude towards the patient's internal workings, but the process of getting access to them can be felt to be a persecution.

Defences

By and large Ms Jones did not feel too persecuted, because she felt under so much internal pressure that having her anxieties registered and understood was for her the over-riding issue. For other people, those who may feel more settled in themselves, the disturbance stirred up by psychotherapy is considerable. Others, more precarious, may be touchy or sensitive and in these circumstances the dominant feeling can be a prickly, 'Are you just going to sit there staring at me?' This means that the first minutes of a psychotherapy session can be tense, disturbing and uncertain and the first consultation can be remembered ruefully for a long time. The following exchange comes from the first few minutes of an initial interview immediately after the therapist has introduced herself. Here the patient found it very difficult to put her own words to some of her feelings.

> Patient: What are we going to say then? Therapist: Are you wanting me to say something? (Short pause) Patient: This is silly! (She burst into tears and sobbed and there was a long pause during which she tried to stop crying.) Therapist: Can you tell me what is making you cry? Patient: I'm just fed up today, that's all. Therapist: In what way? Patient: I don't know in what way. (The patient was still crying quietly.) Therapist: You can't tell me what you mean when you say you're fed up? Patient: No, I don't know what I mean. Just a bit depressed, I suppose. Did you ask a question then? I wasn't listening. Therapist: Can you say what thoughts you have, because you now have a little smile on your face … and you're looking up for the first time. Patient: I thought how funny this was! What are we going to talk about then? Therapist: What do you think we should talk about? Patient: I don't know. You've got your list of questions, like they all ask. Therapist: Like what? Patient: I don't know, they've all usually got some sort of list of questions. Are you just going to sit here staring at me all the time? Therapist: Are you going to wait for me to ask you a list of questions like they all do?

In fact, this patient went on to get a lot of help from this session, but at first she found that the unstructured space of a psychotherapy session tipped her into feelings whose nature she did not know, with a person whose role she claimed to have little sense of. At first, the therapist's open receptivity led to a bout of sobbing containing some of the feelings which were most central in making her life a struggle. Yet she was unable or unwilling to put her own words to her feelings. Instead at first she tried to recover by treating the situation as comic, although this didn't feel very convincing to the therapist. Then she wanted the therapist to fit in and follow the pattern of becoming one of 'them' who usually have a list of questions to go through. Her attitude conveyed clearly that she felt these questions would be pointless because she has already seen so many of 'them' without its doing her much good. However the list of questions she was seeking would have provided a temporary relief because it would have been a known structure protecting her from these difficult feelings. This kind of process is what is known as a defence.

Unconsciously and spontaneously, all of us use defences like this throughout the day to protect ourselves from too much anxiety. But in the special setting of psychotherapy the aim is to understand the underlying problem which makes the defence necessary. Although this patient went on to have a helpful three-times weekly therapy, she hung on to this defensive feature of breaking off suddenly from her own difficult feelings. Becoming gradually able to face this way of defending herself proved to be crucially important in helping her to understand it. If the therapist had given way immediately to the pressure to ask questions the problem would have been bypassed rather than clarified.

The therapist tries not to ask questions when he or she feels that questions will place a wrong hypothesis into the dialogue with the patient. Instead, he wants to know what is going on in the mind of the patient, and in particular about the anxieties driving the behaviour of the moment. The young woman above was upset about something unknown and wanted the therapist to fill this void with her own questions and preoccupations – which would not have helped the patient in the long run.

Sometimes this situation is felt to be an unfair balance of power which some people try to redress it by asking the therapist direct questions.

> A man who had lost his only son in a car crash was very distressed in a session. He asked the therapist if she had children of her own, and became fretful when she did not answer the question, as though she were holding his distress at arm's length. Instead, she picked up on and articulated the anxiety that was prompting his question: was she able to comprehend his deep sense of loss and upset? Was she capable of understanding what it was like to be him? He was calmed and settled by her understanding of this way of expressing his fear that she wouldn't be able to appreciate the extent of his loss.

The best way to reassure is to be able to relieve the anxiety through interpretation of its sources. Reassurance needs to be based upon the principle set out in Dr Johnson's letter to Bennet Langton: 'Whether to see life as it is will give us much consolation, I know not; but the consolation which is drawn from truth, if any there be, is solid and durable; that which may be derived from error must be, like its original, fallacious and fugitive.' No one really likes being emotionally examined. Most of us do not want to seek out too much personal knowledge. Aeschylus spoke of how 'wisdom comes to men but against their will'. Getting 'wisdom' can sometimes feel like the emotional equivalent of going to the dentist without an anaesthetic. Indeed our minds spontaneously seek to cover up the difficulties and seal over their traces.

Why Put Yourself through Psychotherapy?

Since this probing aspect of psychotherapy is so often disliked, why should anyone want to put themselves through encounters of this sort?

One of the reasons is that it is a dull sort of relief indeed to be shut off from one's inner life, which is what is achieved by the excessive use of defences. It is a greater relief to be able to open up even though doing so is not easy. That is why Aeschylus also spoke of the 'discipline of suffering' as a 'mercy of the gods'. Psychotherapy at its best can help enlarge the mind, and illuminate its contents. Nor does it all have to be trial by suffering. It is not always recognised that psychoanalysis and psychotherapy aim to increase common sense and a grasp of reality, as well as opening one up to the nuances of emotional and imaginative life. There is an intrinsic pleasure in coming to know what is going on inside oneself and in others, and to grasp more fully many aspects of life, both the practical and the emotional. Moreover it can also be a revelation to recognise the impact of our inner worlds, our psychic reality, upon our thinking, attitudes and perceptions of ourselves, since it is as influential, or even more influential, than the effects of actual childhood events.

Thus in all psychotherapy, although we need to take fully into account historical facts, or the facts of an individual's day-to-day circumstances, it is important to recognise that we have a world within us which powerfully affects how we operate and how we perceive things. The nature of this world is not caused in some simple manner by previous events or external traumas.

> One young woman came to seek help to decide whether or not she had been ill-treated by her mother whom she thought was very disturbed. The vagueness of the details she gave of this ill-treatment led those who had seen her to ask clarifying questions, in an attempt to work out if these things had happened or not. It was possible for the therapist to understand something of great importance when the patient herself began to say that she didn't know why she was so concerned to establish the truth because she knew she wouldn't feel any better whatever the truth turned out to be. She realised that this very strained young woman experienced little receptiveness from others towards her general state of mind. Instead, everybody joined in to ask probing, intrusive questions.
>
> This understanding enabled the therapist to step back and adopt a more open stance, trying to take in the patient's state of mind. This was met with a flood of relief, as she could get some understanding of the many, much more everyday, tensions which had before only been held in with great tension. Almost certainly, her mother had emotionally ill-treated her in some way, but what was important in helping her was not this issue but understanding how her inner world was completely dominated by questioning, searching figures who were of no use at all in understanding the difficulties of her life or what was really going on inside her.

Even the most carefully brought up, or the most carefully protected and untraumatised individual will never turn out to be an angel, or entirely free of neurosis. Human beings have the best and the worst of potential already within them. Psychotherapy offers an arena for examining in a setting of genuine tolerance some of these inherent potentialities – including one's negative potentialities, such as a pleasure in destructiveness, through which we are the agents of our own and sometimes other people's misfortunes. Confronting these matters is never going to be easy or straightforward.

Most people who have psychodynamic psychotherapy benefit, but not all. In the real world many things can go wrong and they sometimes do; one is dealing with difficult issues and difficult relationships. Much formal research into the effectiveness of psychotherapy in all its various forms has established that most forms of treatment are effective to some degree. And by contrast, the vaunted effectiveness of new wonder drugs is usually much more of an index of the marketing drive of drug companies than it is of real cure. Moreover, as we have seen, transference phenomena powerfully affect how people perceive situations. Psychoanalysts, psychotherapists, doctors and scientists are no more immune to the effects of these distortions than anyone else is. It is a contradiction in terms to talk about pure objectivity applied to human relationships. Certainly no method of research in the human sciences guarantees against the distorting effects of wish-fulfilling belief systems and unless we struggle continually to address the reality with honesty, imagination and openness there is no guarantee either that we will become more knowledgeable about benefits or about the limitations of psychotherapy – or indeed of any form of treatment for mental and emotional problems.

Note

1. This consultation took place several years ago before the more recent advances in obstetrics which have made it commonplace for mothers to bear children well into their forties, and beyond.

15

Registering Time

Typically, a young child is supposed to be innocent and curious before he grows into a bold and optimistic young adult who then proceeds to become a sagacious and serene old person. Of course, this is a gross idealisation of the reality, for there are many trials and troubles that lie upon this path of development. Not least, new and alarming experiences generally make us feel as small and vulnerable as a baby and it is difficult to tolerate this as an inevitable emotional accompaniment to change and maturation. This chapter is about man's lifespan development. It offers no recipes or solutions and seeks only to describe some of the problems.

> 'I want to grow down', one six year old said. Birthdays to her were not markers of moving on, but demands for going forwards which she dreaded. She wanted to go backwards. She was afraid of not being able to manage becoming more independent from her mother and of the growing expectations that she should be able to share people and possessions with other children.

For us to be able to mature over the course of a lifetime it is necessary for us to notice the passage of time and ultimately to allow the sands of time to run out. Difficulties with this can start surprisingly early.

Birthdays and other anniversaries come round every year, but years move along in one direction only. In order to function well through day and night, spring, summer, autumn and winter, all forms of life have had to develop biological clocks, to remain in tune with these regular cycles. Our cycles of wakefulness and sleep and of metabolic activity are switched on and off by these clocks which take their setting from environmental cues such as day-length. Other cycles, such as the female menstrual cycle, are monthly whilst still others are seasonal.

However not all the biological changes taking place within us are repeated over and over again. Many are in linear time. They happen only once as part of a single developmental sequence. The individual has a non-renewable life-cycle which moves from infancy, through childhood, adolescence, adulthood and finally a planned senescence ending in death. There are *biological* tasks and roles characteristic of each phase. There is a position for each individual in the generational cycle of child, adult and parent, and grandparenthood. Although we locate ourselves in this cycle according to our age and development we are also positioned in relation to others. A female child will become a grown-up woman and perhaps a mother, but will always remain her mother's daughter (see Plate 14).

As a *social* animal, man has group rites which signal the whereabouts of individuals within the group generational structure. In our society, starting school, leaving school, getting the vote, passing the driving test, becoming sexually active, becoming a parent, getting a bus pass and so on, all have connotations for where and what one is. As man now creates so much of his own environment, this man-made environment is producing shifts in the timing of phase-appropriate activities. For instance, the tasks of learning and growth traditionally associated with childhood and adolescence are being extended far into young adulthood and recently even further into one's life.

'Time' in all of these domains – personal, generational, social, biological and developmental – can be perceived differently. But each domain provides its own characteristic cues to mark the passage of time. Loss of body hair is just one of the many signs of ageing but it may suggest to the individual concerned a return to a pre-pubertal hairlessness. A twenty-five-year-old mother with two children of eight and five will think of herself very differently from a newly married thirty-four-year-old woman who has not yet had children.

Our Perception of Time

People are expected to be able to reconcile this out-of-step procession of individual, family and social history. Along the way our personality is meant to mature and is supposed to correspond to our years. We, nonetheless, say of some young people that they have always been middle-aged. Many people feel they have within them some place that never alters in which, for instance, they feel like a child, a boy rather than a man, or a girl rather than a woman. They find that this inner feeling doesn't correspond with their body. The number of such variations and contradictions is enormous. All these many alterations with their different dimensions of meaning can be thought of as being like clocks measuring where we are. A bewildering number of internal clocks are registering time within us.

'Midway through this way of life we're bound upon, I woke to find myself in a dark wood, Where the road was wholly lost and gone.' This was how Dante began his allegory of his descent into Hell. At times of more rapid change we automatically go through periods of review and reflection. The mid-life crisis is but one of the best known of these periods of re-adjustment, but any time of transition at any time of life will need to be followed by some kind of personal re-organisation and re-adjustment. If we don't do this, in a way, we avoid maturing.

A young student came to the Clinic for help at the point when he was about to enter his adult life. He had an unusual way of visualising the passage of time. In his

> mind he replaced the hours on the round dial of the clock with the months of the year and created for himself the impression that each year was a repetition of previous ones. He found the sense of time passing very difficult.

This student tended to become confused about how long he had been coming to see his therapist. Once he was startled when he found himself asking his mother was he twenty or twenty one? He wanted or needed to obscure the passage of non-renewable time.

Some people can look as if they are perfectly well able to be aware of time passing. They may appear to have lives packed full of incident and event but closer scrutiny reveals only restless motion, which obscures stasis at the level where development is necessary.

> A seventeen-year-old girl came to the Clinic dressed in skimpy, fashionable clothes with a cigarette between her fingers. She looked ultra-cool and obviously didn't want to think of herself as someone asking for help. She had walked out of her foster home where she had been abused, she said. Subsequently, she had been surviving on the streets around Kings Cross. She was waiting for the social services to find her a flat. Chewing bubble gum somewhat anxiously, she agreed to come in to the therapist's room and explained that she always had to have something in her mouth. Suddenly she asked, 'Are there any jobs here?' and backing this up she continued, 'I am a good worker. I could start straight away'. The therapist was struck by the immediacy of this wish to move in. In stark contrast to the reality of her wait for housing to offer her a flat, she was immediately imagining she would find a place inside the Clinic.
>
> Later in the session it came out that she was pre-occupied with finding the teenage mother who had abandoned her at birth, whom she thought was Swedish. She had a fantasy of going to Sweden and knocking on her mother's door. She would be recognised and invited in. 'She wouldn't say no to me, not again, not this time', the girl said. The therapist could see that this hope was so very similar to the unrealistic, naïve and precipitate facility of her request to move into the Clinic.

For this girl there were many events in her life, moves from place to place, relationships or new ventures, but the underlying situation was being repeated each time. In truth, she was barely holding herself together with a fantasy of a relationship with her mother which had no foundation in external reality, nor any basis whatsoever in her own experience of life. With a complete lack of realism or common sense, this outwardly streetwise girl had repeatedly sought people who would provide the solution and who would 'take her in', or, 'wouldn't say no to her, not this time'. Repeatedly and predictably the outcome would be likely to be the same – disappointment, cynicism, carelessness and personal risk.

There was almost no way that she could on her own escape this cycle of repetition. The facile, self-destructive fantasy of meeting her mother was the lid on a cauldron of dissatisfaction. She was really profoundly (and understandably) disappointed with her actual experiences of being mothered or, more accurately, not mothered. She needed some especially fortunate life-experience or a therapist to provide a different kind of home than the one she was currently seeking. The therapist would try to help her gain some awareness of the true extent and origins of her disappointment with her life so far. Through gradually achieving a degree of insight she might begin to be able to stop endlessly living out the old pattern and develop into a person with a life of her own.

Repeating and Standing Still

This girl's deprivation was extreme, yet most of us repeat basic problems in our personalities or in our relationships over and over again. As we do so, we are living out a version of cyclical time whose periods can vary from a few hours or days to almost a lifetime. Like the student with the 'year clock' we fail to notice our error (other than momentarily). There are several reasons why our attachment to our earliest loves, hopes, desires and wishes can have an almost incorrigible durability. A traumatic disappointment or difficulty may push one to seek an unrealistically ideal solution. In some ways, the cool girl was like this. On other occasions, it is our loyalty to our earliest loved ones which creates the indissoluble bond. It can feel unfaithful to move on, especially if this bond is connected to a parent, brother or sister who was needy or in trouble. In reality there is never a single reason or explanation for a process as complicated as the evolution of someone's life.

Some of these issues were well illustrated by J.M. Barrie in *Peter Pan*. Peter Pan never grows any older in Never-Never land; he is the boy who refused to grow up.

> Wendy, who always liked to do the correcting, asked Peter how old he was … 'I don't know', he replied uneasily, 'but I am quite young … I ran away the day I was born … it was because I heard my father and mother', he explained in a low voice, 'talking about what I was to be when I became a man.' He was extremely agitated. 'I don't ever want to be a man' he said with passion. 'I want always to be a little boy and to have fun.'

Wendy who is genuinely sympathetic to Peter's distress but a little smug about her superior knowledge of the world, has sewed on his lost shadow, which he had failed to reattach. Peter begins to 'jump about in the wildest glee'. He claims he has re-attached the shadow. 'How clever I am!' he crows, 'oh, the cleverness of me!' He has already forgotten that he owed his bliss to Wendy.

> It is humiliating to have to confess that this conceit of Peter's was one of his most fascinating qualities … but for the moment Wendy was shocked 'What conceit!' she exclaimed, with frightful sarcasm. 'Of course I did nothing!' 'You did a little', Peter said carelessly and continued to dance.

Peter's problem with recognising that he depends on other people lies at the heart of his character. Wendy comforts him when he cries in his sleep from nightmares but he doesn't acknowledge this. He does not know what a kiss is and he rears away from Mrs Darling when she offers comfort, unlike the lost boys who are eager for it. As with the shadow this freedom from needing others is a way of triumphing over the loss of something important. Wendy waits for Peter to return to see her and is sad to feel forgotten. He, in contrast, has no knowledge of the passing years, and no idea what such sadness is. Later in the story Peter is shocked to see that Wendy has grown older.

There is a link between this absence of a sense of time passing, the inability to mature, and the intolerance of dependence. Recognising that there is goodness in others and not just in oneself involves accepting the intrinsic separateness of other people's existence. This is not easy. It means that there is a limit on what we can do for ourselves and therefore what we need from others. This may be especially difficult when early relationships are very painful or involve too much loss, as was the case for the young girl above.

They were very painful for the author of *Peter Pan* as well. Barrie's mother, who was very dominant in the family and never recovered from her grief when one of his brothers died when Barrie was six years old. Barrie seemed to have longed to restore his world to a pre-catastrophe state, but in fact never seems to have felt that things could be put right in a real way. His *Peter Pan* stories were originally written for the sons of two close friends to whom he gave a home on their parents' death. Two of these five boys died in the Great War. Tragic events like these often lie behind man's problems with maturing.

Eternal Youth

We all have a tendency to deny the reality of time passing. Often we go on maintaining that we can avoid the true state of affairs. Eternal youth and beauty offer a timeless solution to these difficult problems of growth. We may feel that we own the world and can do with it what we want. Today more than ever before. When we dream the same dream repeatedly we can glimpse that place or area within us which cannot, or will not, alter or evolve. In our dreams we can be creatures in a timeless world. But on the other side of this impasse is the reality: life existed before we were around and it will go on without us; there will be future generations of children.

In waking life, efforts to repeat ourselves exactly are always partial failures. As Heraclitus noted, we cannot step into the same river twice, because the flow of water – time and life – has moved on between any two attempts. Yet the degree to which repetition is shown can be stunning. Change is something we can resist unconsciously at the very same moment we believe we are embracing it.

16

Age

Many old people continue until the end of their lives to make a personal contribution that is deeply missed when they are gone. In these old people whose zest for living is undiminished the capacity to remain open to new experience is a fantastic quality. Their generosity to those who are mature but who still need occasionally the comfort of a parent is deeply reassuring. Many of these loved old people are quite able to accept that their life will have a limit and can welcome death as an event coming like a good friend, at the right time. The sculptured and lined attributes of the aged are an antidote to our modern tendency to make being forever youthful our only goal.

> One much loved woman, Miss Tait, a lifelong spinster in her eighties, began to lose something of her usual vigour. She was nauseous and lost weight. After a short while a malignant, inoperable tumour was diagnosed. Over the succeeding months she gradually weakened but the inroads made by the tumour were gentle rather than nasty. Often she seemed to be denying that there was anything wrong. 'I'll be better next week, don't you think?' On other occasions her conversation seemed to indicate that she was perfectly aware of what was going on. 'It's been not a bad life. I've had my life. I'm ready now. I'm tired', were asides which were scattered through her conversation. She said that her only worry was her younger brother whom she'd always looked after. She hoped to be re-united with her mother.
>
> She began to sleep a lot and spoke of having very vivid dreams. 'Such dreams', she would say, 'I've never had such dreams before'. One dream seemed to have made an especially vivid impression upon her. 'There was this cock pheasant and he came up to the window, that window there [her bedroom window]. He was very bold. He gave me such a look with his one bright eye and his cocked head. He was cheeky but I shooed him off. He didn't go easily but I made him go.' Miss Tait was nursed devotedly by her relatives and was well looked after by the GP, the Macmillan nurse and for the last few days by the local hospice. She died peacefully.

Miss Tait had her death as well as having had her life. The pheasant – insistent, cocky, bold – seemed like a benign image of death as well as perhaps representing the man she had never married. Senescence, the process of ageing and eventually dying, is not an illness. It is the normal, final part of the lifespan.

It is a part of life which is generally not welcomed. Swift's 'Every man desires to live long; but no man would be old' sums up the general vote. Clearly later

Figure 18: Rembrandt etchings. The first etching shows an old woman looking confident. The second one shows his mother afflicted by emotional and physical vulnerability.

life brings a train of losses and indignities to be coped with. Physical vigour is lost, illness is frequent, disabilities mount. The ability to enjoy using our talents in work and leisure is reduced or lost. We are no longer at the centre of it all.

The Challenges of Old Age

To maintain an evolving sense of identity in old age we have to accommodate large changes in our relationship to ourselves and these have to be achieved with declining mental and physical powers of adaptation. The tasks required during the potentially long years of old age concern five main issues: loss itself; our increasing dependence; the fear of death; the experience of loneliness; and our generational position. How we cope with loss depends upon how we were able to negotiate earlier developmental hurdles where loss is also a central issue, such as weaning or separation anxiety which takes place as we go to nursery or to school. The significance belonging to such earlier phases of development is revived by any loss later in life and has to be worked over anew.

It is in this way that insecure early relationships and traumatic losses in childhood and adolescence make the individual permanently more vulnerable but especially in old age when resilience is reduced. For the toddler, learning to walk, the new pleasure of mobility is a recompense for no longer being carried around by mother. But compensation or consolation like this are harder to come by in old age and this makes recovering more difficult. It is easier for disappointment and sourness to settle in. The second phase of dependency in the human lifespan can revive all the unresolved conflicts and anxieties connected with the first, when we were infants and children totally dependent upon our parents.

Needing care when one has lived an adult life takes some getting used to. Being unable to look after oneself or becoming incontinent are dreaded by many old people. We then need other people to look after us and consequently, in old age, our attitude to receiving help comes under the microscope. The balance between being able to appreciate what is being done and being persecuted by it fluctuates for most people. When we feel too angry or humiliated by our neediness to appreciate being looked after or feel any gratitude, we blame the messenger; he or she is the person who reminds us of our hateful neediness.

> One old lady described her experience of the day before: 'My bathing lady was there, and Jenny [another helper with general cleaning up tasks] arrived early, so in my little bathroom there were two short, large, round ladies – the helpers – and me, all thin and bony. It did look ridiculous!'
>
> On other days, however, this lady experienced being bathed very differently. The helper arrives at the 'wrong' time and provokes testy irritation. The bath is spoilt and the day is dominated by 'getting off to a bad start' and 'everything is in a muddle' and so on.

For both the doer and the receiver, being dressed, washed, fed, cleaned or tended is directly reminiscent of a mother's care for her baby. A parent has to tolerate becoming a child to his son or his daughter. Consciously, the old man or woman does not want to be dependent but they have no choice. When tired, ill or out of sorts we all want to be picked up, literally or metaphorically. There is a desire towards being small and dependent hidden in most of us which the physical needs of old age bring out. We regress and re-experience old versions of infantile feelings: love and gratitude towards the carer along with intense dependence, but possessiveness, resentment and clinging like a child when the son or daughter or nurse wants to go out or talk to someone else.

Conflicts for Those Looking after the Old

Those who care for elderly people often feel grateful for having been given the chance to look after their parents, or the residents in old people's homes, in a physical way. It is a child able to return the favour. It is an opportunity to put things right. But it can be hard for relatives, sons and daughters, nephews and nieces, or nurses to perform these services with as much love as they may wish. It is hard work. It is understandable that relatives can become impatient, resentful and angry. They resent that they have lost the parent who cared for them and that now they must do the providing. Any original ambivalence in the relationship can be magnified. While it may be very hard for a previously haughty woman to accept that she needs help, it is equally hard for the daughter to provide her now with that love which she felt her mother had denied her. Long hidden conflicts of rivalry can be resurrected. Some children feel triumphant over their fallen foe and others feel hatred, sadism and cruelty. Where there is physical abuse of old people, the emotional dynamics are similar in many respects to those of child abuse.

The Fear of Death

Death anxieties are common in old age and may be stirred up just by the realisation of daily advancing infirmity and its inevitable end. These anxieties are often denied and turn into a hidden fear of death. Religious beliefs and superstition can play an important part in determining individual attitudes to death. Death can be thought of as a merciful friend (pneumonia used to be called 'the old man's friend') or as the beginning of eternal damnation. Nonetheless, a man or a woman's attitude to death is primarily dependent upon his or her inner world; whether in our guts we feel we should be loved or deserve to be hated.

> Mr Wardour, a normally healthy old man, tended to think he could recover his former strength and deny that old age was upon him. Over the course of a few days he became agitated and mathering. Many of his concerns focused around his being constipated. His relatives tried to help him with this and the nurse gave him some laxatives which worked. But unusually for him there was something querulous and insistently irritating about his agitation. His daughter ended up losing her temper and the old man became upset, saying how he didn't like being old anymore than she liked having to look after him. In their heart to heart talk something was freed up for him and he could tell her that he didn't like the idea of dying. His fear that he might die was palpable. After he'd put this into words the air was cleared and he could be more like his old self.

Mr Wardour's agitation was his denied fear of death. When he could experience his fear of death rather than push it down he could regain his mental balance.

Loneliness and the Generations

Because partners, brothers, sisters and friends become infirm or die, loneliness is bound to accompany age. But the elderly are also prone to a particularly painful state of mind with the loss of internal companions. Our internal world is, by definition, experienced alone but normally we feel it to be inhabited by friendly and familiar presences – the friends and loved ones of our generation, our mothers and fathers from the previous generation, and the children as the next. For some old people this internal world can begin to feel uninhabited or depopulated, reviving infantile anxieties about one's dependency on the central caregiver.

Problems with accepting our generational position can be connected with difficulties in accepting the fact of ageing. This affects the stability of our adjustment in old age. Later in life, we regret the ever-swifter passing of the years and we may be genuinely muddled about how old we are. Our inner reluctance to live with the reality of ageing processes is one of the causes of this confusion. Many old people do feel a pride in their longevity, but this is built on a firm foundation of earlier years when the painful feelings of loss connected with bodily changes caused by ageing were faced. For women, recognising the loss of their sexual fertility and beauty, and for men, the loss of physical strength and vigour, can be a very painful process. As a result we make many attempts to deny the reality of what is happening.

Handing over to the next generation and making way for them is not always easy. This is why many old people become critical of younger people in general ('the young people of today') whatever they feel about named individuals. The young people represent the baby of the family arriving and taking over our place with mother and father. In the last part of life our hope for the future depends on our having sympathy with the generations younger than ourselves. They are inheriting the world. If we identify with those following us we can be relieved by the lessening of self-imposed demands that we should do everything. If resentment is too strong we are not able to sustain our link with the world which will go on being without us.

Adapting when Older – Therapy in Later Life

It used to be thought people over the age of forty had very little capacity to change psychologically but this is no longer a view we can accept. Understanding the psychological tasks of old age allows the anxieties and difficulties of the old to be understood. Through this understanding the old can feel better and clearer in much the same way as can the young. Although the basic elements of personality are not going to change, you can teach an old dog some new tricks. Recent research studies have shown that psychotherapy is an effective treatment for the depressions which are so common in late life.

However people over the age of sixty are not referred for psychotherapeutic help in the same way as are younger adults, although public expectations of what social and health care can or should be provided for the elderly are changing. Many psychological treatment services come to an end for the over 60/65 age group. This 'gerontophobia' – the fear and dislike of ageing by younger generations – calls a halt to understanding being available as a help whilst getting older.

> Mrs Colvin, a seventy-one-year-old woman, was seen for once-weekly psychotherapy for one year. The therapy seemed to get off to a good start as Mrs Colvin talked about interesting areas in her past life. She had been independent and energetic before becoming depressed after her second marriage had broken down when she had retired in her late sixties. Each week brought a new story of her life in London before the War.
>
> She wanted to write and complete her autobiography but found this very difficult. She had started writing twenty five years before when her eldest son, then aged twenty three, was dying of a sarcoma. She was unable to take her autobiography beyond her own teenage years. After the death of her son Mrs Colvin had continued with her own professional life. Her first marriage then broke down and she remarried a man half her age. She lived in continual fear of cancer and was always having investigations to exclude the possibility of a malignant growth.
>
> The therapist, a younger woman, was enthralled and found herself keeping

> longer and longer notes following each session. A pleasant atmosphere pervaded the time of the sessions. But nothing was changing. 'No change' was also apparent in Mrs Colvin's appearance; her face bore no lines and she had an ageless quality about her.
>
> In one session Mrs Colvin said that she would like to take a photo of the therapist, in order to frame it and hang it on the wall (she was a very good photographer). Naming the date and time some sixty years ago, she went on to say that she would like to spend the rest of the session discussing an episode of her autobiography and gave a precise page reference.

As the therapist wrote up her notes, she arranged to see a supervisor to discuss the therapy, as she felt so controlled by Mrs Colvin and at a loss as to know how to intervene. After some discussion with the supervisor it was possible to understand how the patient's central difficulties had repeated themselves in the treatment relationship. The therapist had written down the patient's biography after each session, but actually got nowhere – just like the patient. She had found herself captivated by her history but unable to address her depression. It is sometimes only through repetitions in therapy such as these that these life-patterns can be appreciated.

> Mrs Colvin had had a truly tragic history. She had lost several members of her own family during the Blitz. She dealt with this by putting her life 'on hold'. This was the impasse in her autobiography. She had managed the next awful loss of losing her son by marrying a man similar in age to him. She and the therapist were gradually able to see that she had held on to the illusion of eternal youth through this marriage. Mrs Colvin had kept her son alive in the limbo of her never getting on with her biography. The therapist, constantly taking notes (which had ended up almost the length of a novel), had been employed in the therapy as a secretary, or as a constant companion.

When the therapist could understand how inhibited she felt by her being young enough to be Mrs Colvin's granddaughter, she was able to recover her therapeutic expertise. The therapist was now able to help her mourn the loss of her son rather than become a replacement child who would see the patient until she died.

Mrs Colvin was then able to address the effects of losing her parents. Gradually she was able to think more realistically about what she needed as she became older. It seemed that at the beginning of treatment her solution had been that she needed the therapist for life. The therapist and Mrs Colvin began to understand that any change of home reminded her of the loss of her home and family in the Blitz. So long as the therapist had felt inhibited about mentioning the end of treatment to Mrs Colvin, it had remained impossible to disentangle the occurrences during the Blitz from her more manageable fears of the inevitability of old age and death.

The Need for Care

As part of the normal progress of ageing, the different systems of the body – lungs, heart, kidney, muscles and brain – decline steadily and in step with each other. Just as muscle power wanes from early middle age onwards so also there is a loss of mental powers. Brain functions such as memory, concentration, reaction time and learning all deteriorate in gradual and predictable ways. Our nerve cells die because they do not replicate so there is a loss of brain tissue. And those cells that remain do not function so well. These innumerable small deteriorations slowly add up to a significant reduction of functional capacity. As a result old people are not able to adapt physically or mentally to the range of circumstances they once could manage easily. Although the rate of ageing varies from person to person, it occurs in every one of us.

The underlying loss of adaptive power increases with the years and the organism becomes vulnerable to the smallest physical or mental stress. Therefore, as ageing progresses we all begin to need increasing levels of emotional, mental and physical support from other people in order to keep functioning. The physical dependence of the old has a parallel at the mental level and there is a need for mental support when we are old. The ideal milieu when we are old provides some receptivity to the deeper anxieties connected with ageing combined with a careful mixture of predictability and stimulation.

Thinking about old people's needs for day-to-day care is as important as providing the practicalities. They are the two faces of one task: care needs to look after emotions as well as physical requirements. The more integrated the two aspects, the better. This has implications for individual caring relationships and for the social organisation of supporting services for the elderly.

> Recently an old man was moved into sheltered housing. The local authority had assessed his needs. The statutory provision was impressive. Help was arranged for a wide range of domestic tasks in order to meet his needs. Washing, shopping, cleaning, bathing, help to get up in the morning and to go to bed at night were all set up. But each of these items of assistance was done by different people. Each of his helpers had stand-ins at weekends and holidays. Moreover, there were administrators and supervisors from the several organisations involved. The number of people this anxious old man had to keep in mind was ridiculous.
>
> At first he complained angrily that it did not make sense that he could never ask any one of his carers for any help which crossed the carefully defined boundaries. Why couldn't he have one flexible helper for an hour or two a day, he asked. He fluctuated between periods of persecution, whenever uncertainties in the arrangements emerged, or when his state of mind was less buoyant, and better times when his capacity to manage the complexity of his care happened to be greater. The human capacity to subvert a mad system should not be underestimated. In due course some of the helpers did get to know the old man as a person, even though their visits were so brief.

The small army of people who appeared at this man's door because of the 'contracting out' policy of the local authority had been driven there by central government's views about the most ruthlessly efficient way of providing 'care'. The mismatch between what was provided and the old man's need for familiarity was stark. The fragmented organisation made the carers more alienated because it prevented any of them from being in a position to respond effectively to the old man's emotional needs. They could not form a complete picture of the old man's distress – of his dependence (so unwelcome to an independent character), his failing faculties (he can hide these rather successfully and manage a bit of a performance for his many visitors), his loneliness (the prevailing efforts at jollity by both parties in these transactions avoid this), his anxieties about his life.

In later years there is a lot of time for mulling over the past. What has one done with one's gifts and opportunities? What does the state (good, hopefully) of one's relationships with family and friends mean? There are anticipations of the future. Will one be the last surviving member of a generation? Will children and grandchildren forget? There is one's own disengagement. But why do we devise social care arrangements that tend to deprive people of someone to give them a little bit of company with these kinds of thoughts – not too much and not too little? These divided up systems of care can be understood as social defences against recognising dependence and need. They are expressions of gerontophobia. And none of us relish a farewell, especially when it is final.

Similar dynamics of denying or hating need and incurability have been behind those sudden ill-prepared transfers of vulnerable old people from long stay hospitals to nursing homes, without proper consultation and safeguards. Of 24 mentally infirm old people transferred to nursing homes from Park Prewett Hospital in 1994, 5 died within 22 days of the move. In 1995, three elderly women with learning disability died within eight months of being moved from Davenby Hall in Cumbria. They had lived there in the previous forty years. The physical care provided in the nursing home was more than adequate but staff was not allowed to accompany the women from the stable environment where they had lived for many years to the new homes.

Familiar staff provide a continuity of care which is extremely important for old people with dementia, for example. Each staff member carries a store of knowledge of each resident's life, character, habits, preferences and needs which the demented person is no longer able to manage for him or herself. Loss of this mental containment can be life-threatening for people with dementia.

Dementia is a generic term denoting the loss of psychological functions such as memory, personality and the ability to orientate oneself in time and space. It is caused by physical damage to the 'hardware' of the brain. *Senile dementia* – Alzheimer's disease – is the most common form of dementia in late life. It is not a normal part of ageing but an illness which happens to occur in the elderly. It is categorically different, more malignant in its erosion of psychological functions, than the normal forgetfulness we all experience as we age. Its cause is unknown but it is a physical disorder of the brain rather than a psychiatric illness with an emotional component. The loss of brain tissue is very marked compared to the normally ageing brain.

Its progression is very variable, but typically it is a slowly deteriorating condition lasting some years and ending in death, usually from some concurrent illness; people suffering from dementia are much more vulnerable to physical illnesses. At first its effects may be very mild, but in the later stages of dementia a physical regression takes place with the loss of all adaptive capacity, the ability to remember from moment to moment, the ability to clean or care for oneself as urinary and faecal incontinence develop. Although there may be lucid moments there is a total dependence upon others – relatives, nurses or carers – to provide what one can no longer provide for oneself. Any disruption in the narrow, predictable limits of a stable environment usually causes decompensation with a worsening of mental confusion. That is why the maintenance of a consistent rhythm of routine by well-supported carers is so important.

Observations have been made in old people's residential establishments of the effects of regular time spent with an old person by someone who just quietly tries to notice and listen. Previously confused remarks can come together in less of a jumble. The residents can regain the experience of being able to make themselves understood. The carers can feel that their work is less mechanical and meaningless. A comforting personal relationship, however temporary, fragmented and confused, becomes possible. These are difficult illnesses which can be very painful for relatives who witness their loved one becoming a shell of their former selves.

Questions for Society

As individuals there are difficult challenges for us as we age. There are difficult questions for society too. Sociality, locality and family are much less likely to be closely linked throughout life. We move around; infirm old people are not very often cared for principally by their adult sons and daughters; there are huge numbers of professional carers now contributing to the total picture. A highly mobile society is not well adapted to the needs of the old, whose preferences are likely to be for a more settled and simplified way of living. We tend to think largely in terms of the financial costs of our old age. Our main public concern is that state pension funds will have to be replenished by a smaller and smaller proportion of working young. But as we have seen, to meet the needs of the elderly properly has a real emotional price that we discuss less often. To meet these needs can be deeply satisfying because it is a real engagement with life and all its frustrations.

There are still other tendencies at work, including wiping out and denying the need that currently exists and the need that will operate in the future. Life expectancy is increasing rapidly and the proportion of people over 80 is rising. In three or four decades many of us may be able to live for well over a century. These issues are new as practical options and we will have to decide. The burial practices of the ancient Egyptians were justified by their cosmology. But what motivates the refrigeration of the deep-frozen corpses of the present, whose owners imagined themselves waking to new lives in future centuries?

17

The Future

Science and technology have given us tools that have changed the world and that would make ancient man marvel. The advances in the humanities and the arts, though no less significant, have been less spectacular. Our knowledge of the human character has changed as the humanities and the arts have changed: slowly and subtly. As a result the scientific ideas of the ancient world tend to be of historical interest only whereas the ideas of ancient literature, the Bible and Shakespeare are as relevant to man today as they were the day they were written. In science even the rate of its advance is accelerating. In marked contrast the cause – man – of this exponential growth is not. Late (very late) twentieth-century man or woman is recognisably the same as Biblical man or woman. The 400 years since Shakespeare's time have not made his view of the human drama out of date. This contradiction of a man-made abundance of scientific and technological developments with man himself unchanging in his fundamental nature, creates some important but familiar tensions. While men and women bend the environment with their technology, they can also struggle to adapt themselves sufficiently to these discoveries.

Human Destructiveness and Creativeness

> If Aristides were asked to diagnose the present malady of the world he would tell us that the scientific and technical advances made in the West in the past few decades had completely outdistanced man's capacity to make use of it.

This is from a public lecture given by Lord Soulbury[1] in Manchester in April 1949, a little over fifty years ago. The scientific and technical advances the speaker referred to were the recent discoveries about the nature of matter, of nuclear fission and the building and using of the Atom bomb. For the first time in history, peoples and their political leaders had to learn how to keep the human species alive when it possessed a capacity to destroy itself. In the decades of the Cold War, with Mutual Assured Destruction (MAD, for short), the Cuban Missile Crisis and the eventual collapse of the Soviet empire, the possibility of a global nuclear holocaust was a daily preoccupation. For the moment the immediate danger posed by human destructiveness on this total scale has receded somewhat. Many species have to be on constant guard against aggression and destruction from others, but man has to watch himself as well.

Adding to the problem of human destructiveness, the current rapid advances in genetic biotechnology and in medical science combined with those in computing are now presenting to the species a new problem – human creativeness. If the species continues over the next two hundred years, the understanding of vital processes – of immortality, the creation of new life and new life-forms will be achievements which will have come from man's knowledge and work (see Plate 15). These are the powers that we used to attribute to the Gods.

This encounter between relatively unchanging human beings and the state of permanent change created by science and technology across innumerable advances will be represented, in this final chapter, by reports from two areas of medical advance – heart transplantation and prenatal medicine. These examples were selected from work by two young psychologists who study how patients and medical staff deal with the problems and opportunities presented by major medical advances.

Heart Transplantation

The first heart transplant was carried out in 1967. It is a rationalisation to regard a transplant as an operation like any other, in which a faulty organ is simply replaced with one that works – 'spare part' surgery. Heart transplants have a profound impact on the patient's and doctor's mind. At the moment it is still a life or death treatment. The recipient knows that without it the chances of survival are very limited. At the same time, patients have to trust their doctors enough to allow them to remove their hearts from their bodies. The 'business' of heart transplantation gets into the lives of every member of the medical team too. The members of the medical and surgical team need to be dedicated and highly trained and they are working at the edge of their knowledge – more often than not under great pressure. They have to take difficult decisions, which include rejecting some candidates for the operation because their physical condition makes them unsuitable. It demands continuous availability. They have to be ready to perform the transplant at any time as there is no way of knowing when a suitable organ will become available.

Those patients who do get on the waiting list face an uncertain time. They too do not know when they will be called. They are on a treatment regime with strict dietary restrictions. The amount of fluid they may drink is very limited. Patients who cannot or do not comply run the risk of the operation's being cancelled once called for the transplant because their physical condition is not good enough for them to survive the operation. This may involve wasting a donor's heart, as sometimes the team is not able to call in another patient in time.

Heart surgeons, therefore, are under considerable pressure to find ways to motivate the patients to comply with the restrictive preparatory treatment regime during a long and uncertain period. The stakes are so high that the doctor-patient relationship will necessarily have its very intense aspects. Doctor and patient need to be able to negotiate with each other in this very dependent relationship in a way that manages the many strains involved. Sometimes clear, fixed roles are the best way of doing this. The doctor has the role of being an omnipotently providing authority and the patient that of patiently accepting everything. But, more often than not, this pattern is not adequate and ends up with both the doctor and the patient being placed under enormous pressure, without there being any means of release. No one can be constructive all the time any more than good and patient all the time; yet the success of this venture often seems to require just these qualities.

> Mr Hardie was a very intelligent young man, waiting for a heart transplant. He had once been active but now found it difficult to move around. Often he was confined to his bed at home. The effort he made to attend his weekly psychotherapy sessions was visible. He was very aware of his situation. He would talk about the uncertainty of the waiting list, about death, about his family's support and also about practical aspects of life after a transplant. Not long after his sessions started, he began to bring with him into the consulting room a bottle of mineral water, putting it on the low table between his chair and the therapist's. He would drink from it freely during the sessions. The therapist found it quite hard to continue to listen to what he was saying because she was aware that he was drinking far more water than the permitted amount, which was making his heart failure worse.
>
> The therapist felt she wanted to stop being a psychotherapist and start acting like a doctor, telling him that he shouldn't be drinking all this water under any circumstances. She felt that his self-destructive water drinking in front of her was a powerful communication. His illness was controlling him to such an extent that he felt he had no control over his own life. He was clearly taking back some control by drinking at his own pleasure during the session. But more than this, the therapist realised that he had put her into a similar out-of-control position by drinking the water in front of her. Because she was a psychotherapist she was supposed to take in and understand his feelings, not to make medical remarks about controlling his fluid intake – but she still had to witness his non-compliance. By behaving in this way he was making her operate with one arm tied behind her back if she wished to maintain her psychotherapeutic function and exposing her to something over which she had no control. She pointed this out to him (rather than either just ignoring his actions or telling him not to drink). With some relief he said that now perhaps she could better understand what he was going through. He spoke of his frustration and anger with his illness and with the doctors, as if he had to find someone to blame for his state other than his ever-present sickness which was so cruelly mastering him.

The members of the transplant team are human beings too. They are vulnerable to the same anxieties and it can be hard for them not to become controlling or angry with recalcitrant patients because they feel so intensely that they are expected to make the treatment work. Yet from a psychological point of view, it was quite understandable that Mr Hardie should need to exert some control over his life, or over the timing of his death, because he had to live in a way that was almost totally dependent on the treatment regime. Moreover, even if he obeyed every rule and restriction to the absolute letter his survival was still uncertain. Some patients in these circumstances choose not to accept the offer of the waiting list, but to take their chances and die at home. When a patient takes a decision like this, it can divide and disturb the medical team.

It is always hard to cope with the immediate reality of death. In Mr Hardie's case, occasionally making others do the worrying kept at bay his fear of death and his sickness at his own powerlessness.

> Mr Stewart had severe heart failure symptoms when the transplant team first saw him. He had been incapacitated for many years. He had had to give up his work and stay at home. Although this is not an unusual story for a transplant patient, Mr Stewart's capacity to adapt and to accept his limitations was quite striking. He had been a postman and when his heart first started to fail he changed jobs so that he worked only in the office. As his incapacity became even worse he resourcefully arranged to work from home using the telephone. He kept himself busy without in any way neglecting his medical needs. Life was not easy for him. His medical state meant that he had to be admitted many times during his assessment and waiting period.
>
> After almost ten months on the waiting list he had the transplant operation. He made a good recovery and was soon engaged in physiotherapy to strengthen his weakened limbs, to be able to keep up with his new cardiovascular capacity. After a few months he was fit enough to go back to work. Instead, to everybody's surprise he became depressed and withdrawn. Almost eighteen months later he was still off work. The medical team was puzzled by what could cause someone to fail to make use of such a successful operation. Mr Stewart had made a good physical recovery and was still a model patient, complying very well with the treatment. But he could not return to work.

When the psychotherapist first saw him, Mr Stewart was very withdrawn but he attended the sessions regularly. On one occasion, after a few months, he arrived a little late. He had clearly rushed to get to the hospital on time. As he sat down, he told the therapist that he had had to run two blocks to be on time.

The therapist pointed out that he seemed very conscious of this ability to run. He replied that he had never really understood this. He had had the operation and as soon as he had woken up from the anaesthetic his breathing was better (rapid recovery is common after a transplant). Only two weeks later and for the first time in years, he was walking around with no need of assistance. He looked at the therapist seriously and said that because of all this he was convinced that the donor had been an athlete. There could be no other explanation for his new physical strength. He was living on someone else's life, he said, because it was no longer his own heart within him. He added that he knew that the heart is really only a muscle, and his had been replaced by another muscle, but that he still felt very confused.

Mr Stewart had a reasonable understanding of the practical aspects of the transplant: the defective organ had been exchanged for a good one. But he was struggling to be able to experience his new capacity as being part of his own identity. He was struggling to allow the new heart to be experienced as his own in a way that was wider than the merely physical, although he had managed to let himself borrow it when he ran to get to his session on time. He had sessions regularly for a long time but in the end it was still unclear how much he had been able to integrate having his heart, the seat of his soul as he saw it, replaced by a very useful but ultimately foreign part. He did eventually return to work but in a different job altogether, one that was quite unrelated to his previous employment.

The way a person perceives the new heart and relates to its presence varies considerably. It depends on his or her personality and characteristic points of anxiety. Many adapt very well, but for some the new heart can come to represent the return of some repressed, or previously buried aspect of the person's personality that now for the first time has to be more fully integrated. Mr Stewart did not know anything about the donor. His fantasy that the donor was an athlete and his earlier over-ready adaptation to his increasing invalidity, as if he had somewhat too easily given up his active life, suggested some hidden conflicts about physical vigour.

For other heart transplant patients these fantasies can be more negative or paranoid. In these circumstances, instead of the thought that the donor was an athlete the fantasy might be that he or she could have been a bad person.

> Being in control was fundamental to Mr Abbott. His relationship with his family was based on keeping track of what everybody was doing all the time. His approach to the transplant was to know everything about what might happen and to deny having any major worry about it. The general impression was that he would cope with the operation, as he knew so well all that could happen, including the side effects of the drugs.
>
> After the transplant, he started having side effects from the medication in the form of severe diarrhoea. He became convinced that there was a sinister reason for this. He knew himself well, he was not eating anything that could cause it, and he was taking all the medications properly. Therefore 'he', the donor was causing the diarrhoea; it was this outsider, his heart. He felt the donor was out to get him.

After a major operation such as a transplant, patients sometimes become mentally confused and disorientated because of the toxic effects of metabolic alterations upon the brain. The treatment of these states of mind must therefore include very careful attention to the patient's physical condition. The patient also needs constant and reliable people around them to allow a gradual recovery from this disorientation. But the problem for Mr Abbott was also psychological. He had a long psychotherapy starting in the immediate post-operative period, when he was still very disturbed. This gradually helped him recover from his suspicious and frightened condition. However he continued to feel the new heart was a foreign and bad thing inside him causing all his unpleasant symptoms. After quite some while this began to give way to an acknowledgement that this very same heart was also improving his health.

He was then able to acknowledge the presence of previously warded-off feelings about himself and about those close to him, which were very new and emotionally painful to him. These included anxiety, fear and jealous insecurity which had in the past been avoided by his controlling attitude to his family. He came to believe that these feelings had always been in him but that it had needed his chest to be opened up and his heart to be taken out and exchanged for another before they forced their way into his mind. From the moment of this realisation (two years after the transplant) Mr Abbott began to benefit from the transplant in a more wholesome way, both mentally and physically.

The speed at which the transplant improves the patients' physical capacity is a startling example of what medical knowledge and technology can do. It is extremely rewarding to see a transplant patient recovering lost physical abilities, often after having suffered years of weakness and incapacity. Yet the psychological impact of the heart transplant, as the patient struggles to make sense of the experience, can take a long time to unravel. In some people it is permanently deferred and may never become conscious or more integrated. What we may not have sufficiently realised is that as far as the human recipient is concerned, the surgical team is transplanting the metaphysical heart as a container of someone else's personal identity at the same time as transplanting the heart as a pump. One way of thinking about the emotional reactions which ensue is that they are the mental equivalent of an immune or inflammatory reaction, because the mind as well as the body has to accept the new heart.

If it were not that under normal conditions the baby in the womb is safely protected from the mother's immune defence system, it would be rejected quickly in just the way that without immunosuppressive drugs the body rejects a foreign heart. The embryo and the foetus are a privileged antigen inside the mother's body and in this way are given time in the protective, oxygen- and nutrition-providing intra-uterine environment to develop and grow into a baby. At the psychological level there is time for the mother to get used to the baby as a part of her (and vice versa) but she also experiences the baby inside her as having a separate growing identity. As we have seen, the processes of pulling apart the original near-identity of mother/father and embryo, of becoming physically and psychologically separate and independent, overlap but are different; psychological birth and separation occupy much of post-natal life and are never entirely complete.

For reasons that are obvious without being fully understood, reproduction, pregnancy, the embryo and the foetus inside a mother, and the baby which is eventually born, are all of the deepest and most intense emotional and behavioural significance for everyone. Experiences connected with human fertility and procreation go straight to the centre of the human psyche. Finding out and seeing what is going on inside a mother, and being able to see the babies inside her is of especial significance. It is an actualisation of some of the deepest wishes of childhood. It evokes awe and anxiety as if one has penetrated into a secret, perhaps sacred place.

Man, in order to be inventive, needs to be inquisitive and sometimes is meddlesome. Gaining knowledge is essential if problems are to be identified and enough new solutions to them found. But knowledge of any sort always has emotional as well as practical significance. The feelings connected with acquiring knowledge can be associated with a sense of possessing the thing that is known or with gaining power over it; and one of the infantile prototypes of enquiry or investigation is the infant's curiosity about what kind of creature mother is and about what is inside her. If one knows her, one has possession of her and what may be inside her. If one knows her, one may be able to help, if needed. But as well as the infant's love of the mother's body there is also fear and hatred of it, for the rivals it potentially contains.

Knowing about the Baby inside the Womb

Like other branches of medicine, reproductive and foetal medicine is pushing beyond the limits of what has ever been thought possible. Only forty years ago we had few ways of knowing what was going on inside the womb, let alone of being able to intervene, except in the crudest way. The obstetrician or the midwife could palpate the pregnant mother's abdomen, could perform a vaginal examination and sometimes sort out how the baby was lying, could diagnose twins or auscultate with a trumpet-like foetal stethoscope to listen to the baby's heartbeat. The only way of seeing inside was to take a potentially dangerous X-ray. Now, however, ultra-sound scanning with computer-enhancement give moving images of the living foetus on the monitor screen, visible to all. These, along with a variety of metabolic tests, can provide information on its growth, normality or malformation, and the location and functioning of the placenta.

Because of the significance of procreation the anxiety about having bad feelings is very strong. If therefore the mother's inside and the foetus prove to be healthy and growing, the reassurance will be great; but if things are going wrong or the baby is malformed, or it dies as a result of an intervention, the feelings of concern, responsibility and guilt will be correspondingly intense. It is very easy for a potentially helpful diagnostic intervention to end up feeling like a trespass. The intra-uterine operation planned as a rescue goes wrong, and suddenly is felt to be a crime. As we know, many people do actually regard abortion as murder and a few of them have exacted a terrible revenge. For those of us who are more thoughtful the emotional significance of some of these situations present us with personal dilemmas of the most searching and difficult sort which leave a permanent mark on those parents and professionals who have experienced them.

Our increasing ability to know whether or not a foetus is abnormal enables us to have the choice of intervening, when before the issue just didn't arise. Therapeutic abortions carried out on the basis of information gained through pre-natal testing have saved many parents and their unborn children an enormous amount of pain. But knowledge of this sort, and the actions we undertake as a consequence, touch unfailingly on our deepest anxieties. Because of the power of the meaning of the baby inside the mother we often struggle even to take in and to digest the facts.

In recent years older women have routinely been offered tests for the detection of foetal chromosomal abnormalities. These have been particularly useful in identifying foetuses with Down's syndrome. When the chromosomes are abnormal, the parents must then decide whether to go ahead with the pregnancy, or instead to abort the foetus. The two main tests available each carry a 1 per cent risk of miscarriage. Amniocentesis, one of the tests, involves inserting a needle through first the abdominal and then the uterine wall to draw off a sample of amniotic fluid (see plate 16). *Chorionic villus* sampling is the second and more recent test.

Recently, a new risk-free method of estimating the risk of Down's syndrome has been introduced. An ultrasound examination at 11-14 weeks, known as a nuchal translucency scan, measures the depth of the fluid in the back of the baby's neck. Aided by a computer programme, doctors can calculate the probability of the baby's having Down's syndrome. The test can inform parents of the level of risk and therefore help them to decide whether or not to proceed to an invasive test, which will give a definite yes or no answer. The aim of this screening test is to reduce the number of unnecessary invasive tests and therefore the number of miscarriages of normal foetuses.

When the majority of parents hear that their chances of having an abnormal baby is significantly lower than the average for their age, they decide to leave it at that and do not proceed with the risk-bearing test. However, 10 per cent do opt for testing – even when the chance of a miscarriage caused by the procedure may commonly be up to eight times higher than their chances of having an abnormal baby.

As part of a study of the factors involved in making these decisions, a group of mothers was asked about their thoughts, feelings and fantasies about the unborn baby as well as about their own past and current life experiences.

> When the test showed that the chance of having an abnormal baby was significantly lower than the average, the women who subsequently decided against having an invasive test were hugely relieved. At the same time, seeing the ultrasound image of the baby relieved many other anxieties about the pregnancy. These mothers all regarded their first ultrasound scan as being an examination of their baby's normality. Women in this group felt that, given the odds, it was unnecessary and even unwise to undergo a procedure which carried a much higher risk of losing the baby than the risk of having an abnormal baby. They were able to recognise that their anxieties did not necessarily reflect the baby's real condition and they could use the sources of objective knowledge to assuage the fears that almost every mother has about her baby.
>
> These mothers could tolerate that the doctor's findings were probabilities, and could go on to use the doctors to help them reach their own assessment of the risks. They didn't like the idea of subjecting the baby to a potentially injurious test. In the mother's mind her baby was most probably normal but also helpless and a creature who should be protected from possible hurt or disturbance. Mothers in this group felt that the baby was healthy until proved otherwise rather than, as in the other group, that the baby was damaged until proved otherwise.
>
> The group of women who went on to have the invasive test could not tolerate any degree of uncertainty about the baby. Their expectations about the baby's normality or otherwise were virtually unaffected by the evidence provided by the

> scan showing that the baby had a significantly lower risk than average of being abnormal. No amount of uncertainty about the baby's normality, however small, could be tolerated, because for these mothers any uncertainty seemed to spell a bad outcome. They had all decided to have the invasive test, which could give definite answers, even before the results of the nuchal scan were known. They overrode their awareness of the risks of amniocentesis or CVS. This possibility was pushed to one side by the greater fear that the baby was abnormal.

What these women *believed* about the baby's physical well being was more important than the doctors' objective probabilities. They were unable to recognise that their ideas were just ideas. It was difficult for all these mothers to recognise that however powerful was the picture of the baby they subjectively had, it was moulded by what they feared or what they hadn't been able to resolve within themselves and consequently it was not the best guide as to what they should do. However small their chance of having an abnormal baby, they believed that it would happen unless it could be proved otherwise. The clinical findings suggested that the baby represented what they already felt to be damaged within them or their relationships. In some others the belief seemed to reflect an identification of the baby with a baby in their mind who was never meant to be conceived. Some of these mothers were anxious and pessimistic about the baby's future. They seemed to feel that the baby, even if normal when born, would continue to be a source of worry or trouble to them.

These two groups of mothers also differed in their understanding of other events and experiences in their lives. On the whole, the ones who could decide against the invasive test had been able to process their early traumatic, painful or disappointing experiences in a more successful way. Although the distribution of good and bad life experiences was not dramatically different between the two groups, the ability to process uncertainty about the baby appeared to be linked to the meaning the mothers had been able to forge out of their experiences.

Medical and Scientific Objectivity Means Knowing about Emotions

True scientific objectivity in deciding the right course of action must now aim to include our awareness of the deeper anxieties about pregnancy and babies which so affect human thinking, if for no other reason than that they cannot be excluded. We either take them into account or deny them. Yet denying the existence of these emotions no more means that they do not exist than can the ostrich's sticking its head in the sand make it invisible.

Some other parents find it very difficult to accept the evidence that their as yet unborn child is terribly malformed: that it has severe *spina bifida*, no eyes or a maldeveloped forebrain (anencephaly). It may help those who have the difficult job of helping parents in this kind of situation to know that one anxiety which is felt, in some way by all of us, is that the development of a monstrous child can be felt as a confirmation of what parents most fear in their own deepest nature. Thus they feel that they are to blame for the baby's predicament. In contrast, a healthy, sound baby reassures them that they are not bad and that the damage they have done in their minds is not going to be visited upon them. The existence of the next generation is a reprieve; we are not going to be punished by having our futures destroyed.

No Time

A growing range of diagnostic and surgical intra-uterine interventions is now possible. As things stand many of them are dangerous, but in the circumstances in which they are used the benefits outweigh the medical risks. Some intra-uterine operative procedures are interventions of the last resort and are only done when the foetus is dangerously ill. Speed is often necessary to deal with emergencies during pregnancy and childbirth, when a delay of a few hours can lead to foetal death. The decision has to be made now, the consent has to be given now, and tomorrow or next week is too late. The choices made under these conditions cannot be coolly considered. This means that both the patients and the doctors are exposed with little warning to raw powerful feelings. The process of dealing psychologically with these sudden, intense experiences has to be put off until later and it proceeds much more slowly. 'I did not know what I agreed to' is a common feeling for women who have had to decide there and then whether to consent to a potentially life-threatening intra-uterine operation. This does not mean that the woman feels misled or misinformed, indeed every effort is made to explain. It is because everything happens so quickly.

> One mother whose baby needed an intra-uterine operation in order to stand a chance of surviving said, 'I did not know whether it was right to go ahead with the surgery or not. I did not know whether what they were going to do to her would have made her suffer more or whether she was already suffering inside me. I wanted her to stay alive but I could not bear the idea of her dying because of the operation. I remember myself thinking: what if she was to die from what she has or what if she was to die from what I do to her? Everybody thinks that I should have been over this by now but I am not.' This mother also knew that her baby's heart had stopped on three occasions whilst the physician was trying to complete the operation. The baby had had to be resuscitated and her heart restarted with an electric charge inside the uterus. Unfortunately, on the third such occasion it became clear that further attempts were futile.

Many parents have living healthy children they would not have had were it not for the new techniques for operating upon the foetus or the placenta inside the uterus. At the same time that scientific advances are leading them into uncharted waters, the professionals and the patients are having to face experiences beyond the reach of any psychological preparation. Sometimes however there is a little more time for people to look at how they feel about what is happening to them and to decide what to do.

Perfection and Imperfection

Mr and Mrs Vernon's baby was discovered to have a serious inherited metabolic abnormality, but after a lot of soul-searching the couple decided to have the baby. Both parents seemed to be able to feel that what was damaged inside them at a psychological level did not require automatic rejection. But tolerating their baby's abnormality was by no means easy. A few years later the couple wanted to have a second child and Mrs Vernon decided that although she didn't like the idea she wanted prenatal screening and, if necessary, would have a termination this time.

However, her husband did not really want her to have the tests. At first, it was because he couldn't reconcile himself to the possibility of terminating the pregnancy. Nevertheless, he eventually agreed, saying that one thing he had learnt from the experience with James (their first-born) was to respect human nature. He explained what he meant: 'to respect how I feel and how you feel and the way we both feel about each other and the way we had felt and we now feel about James. But human nature is also our physical nature. It is not possible to respect peoples' feelings and not respect the way they are born. The way they look, whether they are intelligent or not, and as with James whether they are mentally backwards or not. Can I respect the way you feel and think without also respecting the way you look? [Referring to his wife.] I still have the same dilemma about the baby but there is also the reality. And the reality is that you could not manage to look after two abnormal children and nor do I want to be the parent of only abnormal children.'

Mr Vernon's views convey many parents' painful conflicts when they discover that their baby is abnormal. As in the other chapters in this book, our aim here has been to describe the facts as we see them rather than to prescribe solutions. The solutions, if such there are, can only come out of our understanding of the many different factors involved, including the human psychological factor. We have to tolerate that we are not able to get it entirely right.

The Uncrossed Divide

Human beings use their knowledge, skills and creativity endlessly to make tools, machines, artefacts, weapons and discoveries. This creativity – the productions of the human mind – co-exists alongside the biological creativity of mother and father making babies (see Plate 17). In many ways our reactions to man-made inventions are similar to the reactions of parents and children as the pregnancy comes to light. Our reactions are comparable to those of the mothers who now have to decide whether to have the test or not and how to proceed when the result is available. They are influenced by the same basic emotional conflicts that are evoked by procreation.

Until recently, there was an uncrossable divide between the creations of the human mind and that procreation which happened because of life processes over which we had little control. Now the 'facts of life', which have held since the beginning of pre-history are being changed by man, and changed quite quickly. Immortality, the creation of new life forms, chimeras, combinations of the animate with the inanimate computer will all be happening in the laboratory rather than in our bodies or in the bedroom of Zeus. In the years to come there will be as yet unimagined, man-made inventions for us to respond to, obliging us to decide if we can whether to nurture and bring them into being or to stop them. Prometheus and the Mother-Goddess of Fertility have got into each other.

Note

1. Lord Soulbury's lecture was on the relevance of classical literature to the modern world. Today, fifty years on, we tend to be less well-educated about the classical world: Aristides, according to the Encyclopaedia Britannica (the entire contents of which are in the c.d. drive of the laptop computer with which this chapter is being written), was a general and statesman of Athens best known for founding the Delian League, the forerunner of the Athenian empire.

Useful Information

On the Contributors

Robin Anderson (Chapters 2, 4) is a Consultant Child and Adolescent Psychiatrist and chairman of the Adolescent Department of the Tavistock Clinic, who has written extensively on adolescence and psychoanalytic topics. He is also a training analyst at the British Psycho-Analytical Society.

Jenny Altschuler (Chapter 8) is a Consultant Clinical Psychologist and Systemic Psychotherapist in the Child and Family Department of the Tavistock Clinic where she also teaches family therapy. Much of her writing deals with the psychological impact of physical illness on the family and with gender.

Sara Barratt (Chapter 8) is a Senior Clinical Lecturer in Social Work in the Child and Family Department of the Tavistock Clinic specialising in Systemic Psychotherapy. She teaches at the Institute of Family Therapy, runs courses in Bulgaria and has written about collaborative work in adult mental health and general practice.

Shirley Borghetti-Hiscock (Chapter 17) is a psychologist in the Adult Department at the Tavistock Clinic. She has much experience with helping patients and their partners cope with the emotional impact of physical illness and in consultancy to medical teams. Most of her work has been with transplant patients and pain management.

Rachael Davenhill (Chapter 16) is a Consultant Clinical Psychologist in Psychotherapy in the Adult Department of the Tavistock Clinic where she teaches on working with people in later life. She is also a psychoanalyst in private practice.

Caroline Garland (Chapters 6, 7, 9, 14) had a background first in English literature and then the study of play in chimpanzees before becoming a Consultant Clinical Psychologist and Psychoanalyst. She works in the Adult Department of the Tavistock Clinic, where she heads the Unit for the Study of Trauma and Its Aftermath.

Mando Meleagrou-Dixon (Chapter 17) is a psychologist and child psychotherapist. She is Psychotherapist and Research Fellow at the Harris Birthright Research Centre, King's College Hospital and at The Women's Therapy Centre in London.

Margaret Rustin (Chapters 1, 3, 11, 15, 16) is a Consultant Child Psychotherapist, Organising Tutor of the Tavistock Child Psychotherapy training and Dean at the Tavistock Clinic. She has co-edited *Closely Observed Infants*, a book about the child observation the Tavistock Clinic pioneered, and *Psychotic States in Children*.

Jon Stokes (Chapter 10) is the Director of the Tavistock Consultancy Service. He is a Consultant Clinical Psychologist and an Adult Psychotherapist. He was chairman of the Adult Department of the Tavistock Clinic from 1987 to 1992. He consults on organisational psychology to the management of commercial, public and voluntary organisations.

David Taylor (Chapters 5, 12, 13, 14, 15, 16, 17) is a Consultant Psychiatrist and Psychotherapist and was chairman of the Adult Department of the Tavistock from 1992 to 1999. He has also been chair of one of the Department's clinical units. He is a member of the British Psycho-Analytic Society and is a practising psychoanalyst.

Often Used Terms

Anxiety: can be a disabling symptom but as a normal condition it is one of the mainsprings of human endeavour. Many anxieties are reactions to actual dangers but others arise entirely from within us. We can be anxious because in our imaginations we fear that our aggressive impulses may have got out of control and harmed those we love. Often, therefore, we need to behave constructively in order to reassure ourselves that we have not done harm. Other major anxieties are threats to our survival. These too can come from within because we can fear our own self-destructiveness.

Death Instinct: Freud's final theory of the motivational drives of life divided them into the life instincts and the death instincts. Life instincts are motives operating in the service of love, growth and reproduction. They tend to combine the biological elements of life into unities and to creatively connect people and thoughts. Survival, sex and social tendencies are all manifestations of life instincts. The death drive is seen at work in tendencies towards self-destructiveness. The aims are death, nothingness and stasis. Our life is the outcome of the dynamic tension between these two opposing drives. For example, mountaineering is a particularly obvious expression of life vs. death. While it puts its practitioners more keenly in touch with a sense of the value of life, it results in many deaths, not all of which are inevitable. The life vs. death conflict runs throughout the life cycle.

Defence Mechanisms: these include repression, regression, reaction formation, isolation, undoing, projection, introjection, turning against the self, reversal, splitting and many others. Repression, for example, refers to the putting out of awareness of mental contents. In certain conditions, however, the repressed may return. A degree of all of these mechanisms is normal and is to be found in all of us. Defences are adaptive ways of lessening psychological strain, pain or disturbance and allow everyday functioning. However, in neurotic or psychotic conditions they may be greatly increased and contribute to a loss of mental efficiency.

The Ego: Freud used the term *das Ich* which is the German for 'the I'. His translators coined the Latin term 'the Ego'. It is the part of the mind which functions as a mediator between the power of the primordial instincts (the id), the super-ego and reality. The ego is the organiser of defences and the designer of actions and plans. It also means 'the self'. Because we can be very self-regarding and take ourselves as love objects (which is called narcissism) the term ego is sometimes used colloquially as in 'He's got a big ego' or 'He's got lots of ego'. If it's really big then it becomes a form of megalomania.

Fantasy: is often used as a technical term in psychoanalysis when it is spelt phantasy. It refers to the unconscious mental representations of our powerful, instinctual feelings and wishes. As such it is a much wider concept than the everyday usage of fantasy as a conscious daydream or imagining.

Identification: Attributes of others can be copied so that we transform ourselves according to the model the other provides. Much of this process takes place outside our awareness. Modelling oneself upon admired or loved figures is an important process in the making of character. It is not uncommon for those close to someone with a serious physical illness to feel themselves to be ill. This can happen for many reasons – guilt, or deep sympathy and connection, competition or superstitiously averting suffering from the other.

Narcissism: Narcissism takes its name from the legend of Narcissus who, without realising it was himself, fell in love with his reflection in a stream, leaning so close that he fell in and drowned. A narcissistic person tends to be fascinated by himself or what he does. A narcissistic object choice refers to choosing someone (unconsciously) on the basis of his or her similarity to our self-admiring estimation of his or her self. We are all like this to some degree, although there are many differences between individuals. Narcissism is usually a defence against deep anxieties connected with loss or about our inner self.

Object: This term is used frequently in psychoanalysis to describe people in their role as 'the object' of an individual's interest. It has a wide range of reference which includes images, representations, structures and organisations 'in' people's minds.

Oedipus Complex/Situation: The loving, the hostile and the rivalrous feelings of the child towards its parents occur in a specific and limited number of ways. In the 'positive' form there is a wish to take the place of the same-sex parent, a desire for their death, and a wish to sexually posses the parent of the opposite sex. However, because of the fundamental bisexuality of human beings there is also a 'negative' form with possessive love for the same-sex parent and a jealous hatred of the opposite sex. Furthermore, the three-sided nature of many relationships presents to each human being conflicts which are difficult hurdles in our development. Taboos upon incest are almost universal but our inner surrender of Oedipal wishes is often incomplete.

Omnipotence: Although many people consciously experience themselves as weak or inadequate, there is often a contrary belief which is held unconsciously that one's impulses are all powerful. At this level these feelings may be both admired and feared.

Projection: We attribute to other people some of our own emotions and thoughts. Empathy, for example, depends upon our thinking that other people have the same kind of feelings as we have. Sometimes, as a defence mechanism, projection involves getting rid of bad feelings or unwanted parts of the self. This leads us to perceive others unrealistically, as bad, dangerous or inferior, when they are not.

Splitting: To avoid the conflicts which can come with having to come down on one side or the other we use splitting where contradictory views of the same issue or person exist side by side without awareness. For instance, having a need to have friends and enemies is sometimes based upon a need to keep good, loving feelings split off from bad, hostile feelings.

Super-ego: This is the part of the mind which lays down social standards, produces judgements, guilt and feelings of worthlessness or self-regard. It is responsible for the voice of conscience but also has very primitive unconscious aspects. The idea is that it arises from the parents 'within' the child's mind who are often distorted by the nature of the child's imagination. The super-ego can be helpful and supportive or severe and inconsistent. Freud, who was often wrongly associated with advocating a view of human beings as lacking higher values, in fact considered that whilst mankind was more primitive than he or she knew it was also much more moral.

Transference: Emotions from the past are re-experienced in the present along the lines of the original situation. Unnoticed, transference provides much of the significance of our everyday lives. Certain relationships evoke intense transference feelings more obviously: being nursed revives some of the dependency we originally felt towards our mothers. People with power such as bosses and politicians stimulate many of the child-like feelings we first felt towards our parents. In order to understand the patient's emotional life, character and life-experience the therapist uses transference. In this special context re-opening the feelings of our early lives provides a chance to know oneself better.

Unconscious: most of our mental life is not accessible to our consciousness. This is one of the most important of Freud's contributions to our modern view of the human mind. It is difficult to accept that many of our most important steps in life are unconsciously motivated. For a long time many asserted that the mind could only be conscious. Though neuroscientists may still argue about the details, all have realised that most mental processing takes place unconsciously. Even feelings, like guilt, may be unconscious.

Working-through: this is psychological work where a particular emotional event is gone-over, often many, many times before that person can gradually come to change the way he or she reacts or perceives. Although it occurs in psychotherapeutic treatments it also occurs in life. For example, mourning involves painfully working over all the different aspects of the lost person before the person can move on. Although repetition and compulsion are powerful tendencies in the human psyche working through permits a degree of modification.

Other Reading

Introductory Lectures on Psychoanalysis: Freud library: 1 by Sigmund Freud, Penguin Books, 560pp. (1991). The founder of psychoanalysis still has much to teach us. In these public lectures delivered during World War 1 Freud set down for the general public the full range of his theories and observations.

Bereavement: Studies of Grief in Adult Life by Colin Murray-Parkes. Penguin Books, 288pp. (1998). A classic study of bereavement and the stages of grief which has not been improved upon by more recent accounts.

The Child, the Family and the Outside World by D.M. Winnicott. Penguin Book (1991). Winnicott's writing is always accessible, clear and evocative and in this classic volume he succeeds in giving a vivid impression of the child's world.

Inside Lives: Psychoanalysis and the Growth of the Mind by Margot Waddell, Duckworth (1998). Follows the inside story of the major developmental phases from infancy to old age. Has many examples from everyday life and literature as well as clinical accounts.

Multiple Voices: Narrative in systemic family psychotherapy Renos Papadopoulos & John Byng-Hall (Eds.) 242 pp. Duckworth. A collection of interesting accounts of different applications of family therapy by a group of expert practitioners.

Understanding Trauma: A Psychoanalytical Approach by Caroline Garland. Duckworth 226pp. (1998). An original, yet accessible description of the psychological effects of adverse life events and traumas with good case illustrations from a specialist unit.

The Anorexic Experience by Marilyn Lawrence, edited by Kate Mosse. The Women's Press, 160 pp. (1995). Eating disorders of all sorts are common and cause a great deal of suffering and disability, especially amongst the young but sometimes going on through life. This straightforward book provides a sympathetic approach to the feelings underlying these syndromes and is invaluable for those who wish to understand more.

The Unconscious at Work, Anton Obholzer and P. Vega Roberts, Routledge (1994). A collection of recent work by members of the Tavistock Consultancy Service giving and in-depth idea of psychodynamic issues in the work place.

Index